THE ENGLISH PRESS IN POLITICS
1760 – 1774

The English Press in Politics
1760–1774

by

Robert R. Rea

UNIVERSITY OF NEBRASKA PRESS · LINCOLN

Publishers on the Plains
UNP

Copyright © 1963 by the University of Nebraska Press

Library of Congress catalog card number: 62–15969

All Rights Reserved

MANUFACTURED IN THE UNITED STATES OF AMERICA

PREFACE

THE REIGN of George III has always been a subject of interest to Americans, but national and political prejudices, inherited from that formative period, have long combined to restrict our vision and limit our interpretation. Only in recent years have we begun to recognize the realities and subtleties of eighteenth-century politics, and the work of revision, though a generation old, has yet to make itself felt in many areas of scholarship tangential to political and constitutional history.

While much has been written concerning the press and its leading figures, little effort has been made to incorporate the swarm of hacks and scribblers into the historical narrative. This book attempts to bring them all upon the stage of politics, to introduce the chorus, and to describe the methods used to create that public opinion which made John Wilkes and Junius important. It is a study, not of public opinion per se, but of the political press which produced that ephemeral force— and was a power unto itself. In dealing with the press, the broadest use of the term has been employed. Newspapers, periodicals, pamphlets, broadsides, and satirical prints represent its physical aspect; the "authors, printers and publishers" sought by general warrant and information ex officio provide the human element. In undertaking a synthesis of the history of journalism, the tattered fringes of literature, the complexities of politics, and the niceties of law, one is made acutely aware of many shortcomings whose elimination time and circumstance will not allow. The present state of historical studies seems, however, to justify the attempt which periodicals and pamphlets support. Much remains to be gleaned from newspapers, but until further monographs like Robert L. Haig's *The Gazetteer* and Lucyle Werkmeister's studies in *The London Daily Press, 1772–1792* are available, little more can be derived from that source. This book will have served its purpose if it refurbishes the stage settings, introduces a company who have long awaited their turn before the curtain, and delineates the several parts they play. Others are invited to write their lines.

An author's debts are manifold and cannot all be paid. It is pleasant to be able to recognize the tangible and intangible encouragement provided over the years by John J. Murray, Fredrick S. Siebert, Jack M. Sosin, a host of friendly librarians, and the Graduate School of Auburn University.

As this began with Phyl and Pam, it is proper that theirs should be the last word.

v

CONTENTS

CONTENTS

LIST OF ILLUSTRATIONS

(Following page 86)

INTRODUCTION

The Mirror of Politics

THE CONSTITUTION of eighteenth-century England was her glory and her pride. Established by the Revolution of 1688, refined in the fires of war and turbulent political experience, it stood at mid-century an edifice of liberty no less admired in foreign lands than it was at home. This advantage it held over any form of government then known or imagined: it was alive in the hearts of Englishmen and capable of transformation as the nation itself might change.

The structure of politics seemed, however, to allow little immediate scope for political growth. Early in the century the generation of Sir Robert Walpole, having firmly established the Hanoverian succession against the Jacobite supporters of the deposed house of Stuart, and having reduced the German Georges to grudging acceptance of parliamentary supremacy, set itself against further innovations. Indeed, the whole system erected upon the pedestal of the Glorious Revolution was conservative. Parliament, victorious in its struggle with the crown, exercised an authority surpassing that of any king. Rooted in the soil of England by a system of representation based upon landed property, and nurtured by a trade that moved across the seven seas, the House of Lords and the House of Commons represented the political nation in all of its higher social and economic aspects. Hence the significant truth of Henry Seymour Conway's bold assertion that parliament

> constitutes the good people of England; . . . the people of England till our legal dissolution can possibly have no existence but within these walls; . . . the voice which denies our authority without doors, hurls a treason against the majesty of the British people. The nation has chosen us as its agents for a term of years: during that term therefore we are virtually the nation.[1]

Constitutionally, and of necessity, such a sweeping claim incorporated in its generalities the additional factor of the crown. Stripped of his arbitrary power, the King of England still graced the scene of politics and, through his friends and influence, might wield a decisive force. Neither George I (1714–1727) nor George II (1727–1760) were

1

political nonentities; where honors, places, or foreign policy were concerned, they demonstrated most clearly that royal favor was requisite
to political success. None were more ready to identify themselves as the
king's friends than those proud men who bore the label Whig and
claimed the credit for binding monarchy in the silken chains of law
and bringing the blessings of constitutionalism to a prosperous nation.
Tories there might still be, but every officeholder was a Whig.

The close relationship between a crown dependent upon the constitution and a parliament that was a microcosm of the nation explains
the atrophy of party politics in the eighteenth century. When there
was no thought of government without the king, and no significant
issue between the crown and parliament, there could be no basis for a
constitutional opposition.[2] All men agreed upon the basic truths of
English politics, and opposition to ministers in office—the king's servants—could only rest upon the sands of personal rivalry and jealousy.
About the "reversionary resource" of a Prince of Wales who might
oppose his father without challenging the system, an opposition party
might be formed, but that possibility disappeared in 1760, with the
accession of the young King George III. Yet the most broad-bottomed
ministry could not contain all the office-seekers; there were always
"ins" and "outs," and their struggles to gain or maintain a place in
government produced the personal and factional fights that characterized Hanoverian politics.

Englishmen were nonetheless interested in politics because it revolved about men rather than measures. "It is our meat, drink, and
clothing," wrote Horace Walpole, "—meat to our printers, drink to our
ministers, who settle all over a bottle, and is intended clothing to our
Patriots. We have always talked of the goodness of our constitution.
It must be a very tough one, if it can stand all its distempers and all
its physicians."[3]

Increasing public interest and the heightened tempo of political
change during the reign of George III brought to many observers a
realization that the lights and shadows which had appeared constant
since 1714 were slowly shifting. The Jacobite threat was dead, or no
more than an undergraduate toast at Oxford; the king, no longer
German born, gloried in the name of Britain; popery might raise a
drunken mob, but sober minds turned more oft to Methodism; the
Good Old Cause of Whiggery had triumphed and was a cause no
longer. Yet in this golden age when victory followed British arms from

Quebec to Pondichery, a subtle change was working in the hearts and minds of Britons. William Strahan, printer, posed the question to Benjamin Franklin in 1763: "Has not our Constitution undergone some unperceived Alteration, when a Minister cannot keep his ground even with a Majority of three to one, in the House of Commons? Does this arise from the great Increase of Power & Property without Doors, or from what other Cause?"[4] The Earl of Chatham dramatically proclaimed that "Whoever understands the theory of the English Constitution, and will compare it with the fact, must see at once how widely they differ. We must reconcile them to each other."[5] Some years later, the Earl of Shelburne summed up with brilliant aftersight:

> Government and people are perpetually changing, without either being aware of it, which of itself must produce confusion. Government becomes weaker and the people stronger insensibly. . . . The House of Commons under its present institution, has had its day, and Parliament itself is no longer considered as Omnipotent as Lord Mansfield used to call it. As Knowledge has spread and the representatives have become corrupted, it has ceased to impose, and has no longer the same confidence with the people. It may still do a little good or prevent a little harm of itself, but it is the public opinion which decides, which the House of Commons must obey, as every part of Government must. . . .[6]

The English constitution was in the process of reinterpretation before the bar of public opinion; the jury was made up of freeborn Englishmen—

> Canaille, forlorn grubs and gazetteers, desperate gamblers, tradesmen thrice bankrupt, prentices to journeymen, understrappers to porters, hungry pettifoggers, bailiffs followers, discarded draymen, hostlers out of place, and felons returned from transportation. These are the people who proclaim themselves free born Englishmen, and transported by a laudable spirit of patriotism, insist upon having a spoke in the wheel of government.[7]

"What time do we not live in," wrote George III, "when a parcell of low shopkeepers pretend to direct the whole Legislature."[8] An unenfranchised populace could not in fact control a government based in all its forms upon private property, but "a wicked mob and a foolish ministry may produce strange events." Many must have agreed that "it was better in old times, when the Ministry was wicked and the mob

foolish. Ministers however wicked, do not pull down houses, nor ignorant mobs pull down Governments. A mob that can read, and a
Ministry that cannot think, are sadly matched."9

No man did more to rouse in the people a sense of their importance
than William Pitt, of whom George II once remarked, "Sir, *you* have
taught me to look for the sense of my subjects in another place than
in the House of Commons."10 Yet, paradoxically, few men had less
appreciation of the means by which to raise the public voice against
a faltering, fumbling ministry than Pitt. As Horace Walpole pointedly
observed, "Though an Administration ought to be composed of virtuous men, it is by no means desirable that an Opposition should be
so."11 Into the position of primacy in molding public opinion stepped
one who, lacking the purity of Pitt, knew how to stir the caldron of
popularity—John Wilkes. Junius, himself a master of propaganda,
aptly weighed the importance of this man to the development of public
opinion when he wrote:

> You will not suspect me of setting up *Wilkes* for a perfect character.
> The question to the public is, where shall we find a man, who, with
> purer principles, will go the lengths and run the hazards that he has
> done? The season calls for such a man, and he ought to be sup-
> ported.12

It is this inherent capacity to form and direct popular emotion
that makes the name of Wilkes as prominent as that of Pitt, that justi-
fies a study of hack writers and bankrupt tradesmen in the golden age
of parliamentary orators and placemen. "One good Writer was of
more Importance to the Government, than twenty placemen in the
House of Commons"13 when that body came into conflict with the mob,
which Horace Walpole saluted as "the third House of Parliament."14

The press was the key to the portals of public opinion, the last recourse of politicians bereft of royal favor or electoral expectations. It
could force a public man "to choose between his duty & his reputation.
A dilemma of this kind . . . will not indeed work a miracle upon his
heart, but it will assuredly operate, in some degree upon his conduct."15
Edmund Burke, while decrying "the abstract value of the voice of
the people," stoutly maintained that "as long as reputation, the most
precious possession of every individual, & as long as opinion, the great
support of the State, depend entirely upon that voice, it can never be
considered as a thing of little consequence."16 A free and untrammeled

press was, therefore, of primary importance in political life, and the ever-present possibility that those in office might some day go out served as a check upon ministers tempted to engage in restrictive measures. To every opposition, a free press was the very breath of life.

The liberty of the English press had, in a sense, been secured by the cessation of licensing in 1695. "The press was emancipated from the censorship . . . and the Government immediately fell under the censorship of the press."[17] Liberty, however, was sharply qualified by the stringency of the libel laws, which held that "the direct tendency of . . . libels is the breach of the public peace." Truth or falsehood being immaterial, the law considered only this tendency, and if the publication of a libel could be proved, the offense against the public was considered complete. The liberty of the press was found to consist of "laying no previous restraints upon publications. . . . But to punish . . . any dangerous or offensive writings, which . . . shall on a fair and impartial trial be adjudged of a pernicious tendency, is necessary for the preservation of peace and good order, of government and religion, the only solid foundations of civil liberty." Thus Blackstone. The obvious corollary was that "to censure the licentiousness, is to maintain the liberty, of the press."[18] The political implication of this doctrine was stated by Chief Justice Holt early in the century: "It is very necessary for all governments that the people should have a good opinion of it."[19] Manifestly, no opposition, dependent upon public opinion, could support such an interpretation, which must automatically restrict discussion of public measures and criticism of public men. This difficulty was the source of much of the rhetoric concerning the liberty of the press among popular lawyers who realized the legal weakness of their position.

Lord Chancellor Hardwicke, to whom censure of superiors was "a freedom unknown to our constitution," spoke more pointedly than was his intent when, in defending the part played by the press in the Glorious Revolution, he said of the writers on the side of liberty, "They were warranted by law for what they wrote, *and they had the sense of the nation on their side.*"[20] By 1760 the sense of the nation and the law were rapidly drawing apart, and the conflict between law and opinion occupies a large part of the history of the press and politics during the early years of the new reign.

The critics of a truly free press concentrated their attention upon the "spirit of defamation . . . a kind of heresy that thrives under persecution. The *liberty of the press*," wrote Tobias Smollett, "is a term of great efficacy, and like that of the *Protestant religion,* has often served the purposes of sedition."[21] Lord North declared that "the first thing we lay our hands on in the morning is a libel; the last thing we lay out of our hands in the evening is a libel."[22] And while submitting that "the liberty of the press is a blessing when we are inclined to write against others, and a calamity when we find ourselves overborne by a multitude of our assailants," Dr. Samuel Johnson bewailed the lack of subordination which characterized his age. "It seems not more reasonable to leave the right of printing unrestrained, because writers may be afterwards restrained, than it would be to sleep with doors unbolted, because by our laws we can hang a thief."[23]

The claim that "the wicked industry of some libellers, joined to the intrigues of a few disappointed politicians have . . . been able to produce this unnatural ferment in the nation" was readily destroyed by Burke: "If a few puny libellers, acting under a knot of factious politicians . . . are sufficient to excite this disturbance, very perverse must be the disposition of that people amongst whom such a disturbance can be excited by such means."[24] He, and others, saw that the unrest of their epoch lay deeper. They saw, but were unable to say, that "free expression is destined not to repress social conflict, but to liberate it."[25] The eighteenth-century struggle was fought in the courts of law, where passions were discounted, and within the halls of parliament, where they were subject to control. Both Camden and Mansfield, representing the extremes of legal and political opinion, set their faces against a spirit of disobedience "which might . . . provoke and excite the passions of the people against their rulers."[26] The most violent exertions of the popular party were aimed not at liberating the press for its own sake, but rather at protecting or extending the right of a jury to return a general verdict in cases in which the press was interested. John Wilkes very nearly exhausted the eighteenth-century potential when he stated, "The *liberty of the press* is the birthright of a BRITON, and is justly esteemed the firmest bulwark of the liberties of this country."[27] The time for definition had not been reached. Dr. Johnson might safely maintain that "political liberty is good only so far as it produces private liberty," and ask, "Suppose you and I and two hundred more were restrained from printing our thoughts: what then? What proportion would that restraint upon us bear to the private happiness of the nation?"[28]

Had he wished to do so, Johnson might have supplied his own answer, for as an author he was familiar with many of those men—printers, publishers, and booksellers—whose cumulate interest was the measure of the relationship between private and public liberty. In 1758 he had recognized the fact that "not many years ago the nation was content with one gazette, but now we have not only in the metropolis papers for every morning and every evening, but almost every large town has its weekly historian."[29] The reading public was rapidly expanding, and the eager perusal of newspapers and pamphlets in every coffeehouse extended reader contact far beyond the rising circulation figures. The public demand for information was met by presses kept busy night and day. When the reign of George III began, London was served by at least eighty-six newspapers, and pamphlet presses were legion. The factor which Johnson failed to recognize was that the press had become a force in itself, a vested interest representing increasingly great financial investments and possessed of control over the most effective avenue of mass communication—the printed word.[30] Thanks to a miscalculation in the drafting of the stamp tax of 1757, an error not corrected until 1773, there was no significant economic restriction upon newspapers, and a host of new publications appeared, many of them, like the *London Chronicle, Public Ledger, St. James's Chronicle,* and *Public Advertiser,* destined to play prominent roles in the political journalism of the years 1760-1774.[31]

The publishers of this period were "tradesmen interested in profits, not only by purveying information but by serving it up 'seasoned with opinions and prejudices in the interest of a political cause.' "[32] As the political life of England was largely lived within the walls of parliament, access to the debates in both houses was of great importance to the trade. Although reports of debates had been published for many years prior to 1760, both houses of parliament remained jealous of their privilege of free and unreported speech. Originally designed to protect members from royal persecution, this right now served to isolate them from the great body of the nation and popular opinion. In breaking through this shield of parliamentary prerogative, the press played a notable part in the reinterpretation of the constitution.

The motives which spurred publishers to defy the sovereign power of parliament were as much economic as political; constitutional theory was fitted to the ultimate goal of profit. Dr. Johnson's dictum that no one but a blockhead would write except for money had its corollary in Walpole's observation that "they who print for profit print only for profit."[33] Henry Sampson Woodfall, who published Junius' letters, numbered his friends among the court circle and had little sympathy for the radical tendencies of his famous author. Government interference might be described as destructive to the liberty of the press, but it was more particularly disruptive to the profitable publication of a newspaper.[34] Antagonism to government interference clearly reflects the increasingly prevalent concepts of laissez faire economics.

The effect of the profit motive upon a publisher is demonstrated in the career of John Almon, one of the most radical of contemporary publishers; as his wealth increased he grew more and more conservative, until he was ready to accept a subsidy from the ministry whose overthrow his paper was attempting to accomplish.[35] On the other hand, the possibility of economic success without ministerial assistance tended to eliminate the government from the newspaper business. While every ministry of George III influenced the press, none controlled it.

Common opposition to governmental interference, petty and ineffective though it might be, bound publishers to the critics of their persecutors. That the political opposition might be led by the greatest landowners of the nation did not seem incongruous to the middle-class citizenry: it was the natural structure of politics, and it provided a safeguard against arbitrary governmental action. After the delirium of the Wilkes case, no minister cared to risk implicating a prominent political opponent in the press attack against him.

The publisher also sought and to some extent found protection in granting anonymity to his correspondents, the writers who provided the bulk of his political material. Anonymity was a double-edged sword, however. A correspondent as popular as Junius might cause circulation and profits to soar, but if his prose was as prickly as that of Junius, his publisher might face lengthy and expensive legal proceedings. The rising tradesman took his chances willingly, and the established businessman grew cautious.

The economic and social respectability of the press is amply illustrated from the lives of its representatives. John Newbery, who died in 1767, left to his widow shares in four London newspapers as well as a thriving trade in children's literature and patent medicine.[36] William Strahan's interest in the *London Chronicle* and the *Monthly Review* enabled him to expend £5,000 for a third part of the reversion of the patent of King's Printer in 1766, and in 1767 to build a new printing establishment at a cost of nearly £2,000. In 1774 he entered the House of Commons for the same borough that returned Charles James Fox. Upon his death, Strahan's estate was valued at £95,000.[37]

Neither the laurels of political liberty nor the more tangible benefits of economic independence quite guaranteed to the press its freedom from governmental intervention. Throughout the reign of George III, ministers maintained their managers and supervisors of the press. Usually under-secretaries of state or the treasury, these men watched the press for unfavorable comment, advised their superiors on legal questions, and, according to their abilities, wrote in support of government. Upon occasion it was the under-secretary who arranged the details of pension or subsidy between ministers and publishers and authors, for "there were Gatton and Old Sarum newspapers as well as Gatton and Old Sarum boroughs."[38]

Below these men, some of whom, like Charles Jenkinson, rose to great prominence, swarmed a shadowy host of clerks, spies, and coffee-house runners who were generally known as "messengers of the press." Their position and duties were ill-defined; their names appeared only in courts of law. William Bibbins was employed by the Treasury to secure all political pamphlets, magazines, and other publications. So also was Nathaniel Crowder.[39] These men, despised as informers in their day, were a direct link between government and the press. They probably worked in league with the king's messengers-in-ordinary, Nathaniel Carrington, Robert Blackmore, James Watson, and John Money, who executed the resulting warrants.[40]

The London *Gazette,* in which the government published proclamations, state papers, and some news, was of little service in forming public opinion. The position of writer, long held by Edward Weston, brought with it a salary of £300, out of which £30 was paid to a deputy writer, who also garnered various fees totaling about £70. Its official nature made the *Gazette* a significant factor in the communication of information, but lacking the economic stimulus of a private venture, it was at best a rather stolid purveyor of stale news.[41]

Two further media of mass communication played major roles in the late eighteenth century: the satirical print and the pamphlet. Contemporary history and literature were pointedly illustrated by satirical prints. No line of critical approach was overlooked, and like books and pamphlets, prints were advertised in the papers before they were offered to the public. Their significance is suggested by Wilkes's attention to William Hogarth's relatively innocuous print *The Times* and Hogarth's rejoinder, that famous portrait of John Wilkes which immortalized his ugly physiognomy. In the ten years following the accession of George III, the production of satirical prints and drawings far surpassed that of the preceding quarter-century in quantity, vigor of expression, and a freedom of criticism which splashed the throne itself.[42]

Between the ephemeral print and the self-perpetuating newspaper stood the pamphlet, the classic form of eighteenth-century political expression and the primary medium by which conflicting interests wooed popular support. Anticipating the conclusion of the Seven Years' War, Arthur Murphy wrote, "I tremble to think what will be the fate of our Newspapers and factious writers. Robberies on *Finchley-common,* deaths and burials of men in very good health, &c. will afford the former but scanty subsistence; and as to the latter, I hear their landlords begin to dun them already for their quarter's rent."[43] Murphy's doleful prognostication (backed by government funds) proved quite wrong. The "factious writers" found ample material for their pens in the next decade. The newspaper column was as yet too short for statistical comparisons or legal arguments, and the propagandists of all factions fired their heaviest barrages in pamphlet form. The shilling pamphlet was the hallmark of a political lecture,[44] and the publisher's name below an anonymous author's title was the trademark of faction. The *Critical Review* aptly observed that

> whenever any contest arises that has the good fortune to engage the public attention, there are always a set of puny witlings, who, from the love of fame, or want of a dinner, enter as volunteers on either side, sometimes on both, in consequence of which out come a heap of catch-penny pamphlets, to amuse and divert this our pamphlet-loving age.[45]

Whether a tirade of a few sheets or a thoroughly digested statement of policy drafted by Burke or supervised by Grenville, the pamphlet remained an important path to public attention; pirated by rival printers, summarized in newspapers and magazines, it was read by high and low alike.

These were the tools with which great men sought to create public opinion and small men sought to express it. In a reign which witnessed the creative culmination and subsequent disruption of an empire, in which the very roots of politics and society were threatened by new and revolutionary ideas, the press was the mirror of English politics—a mirror possessing a life and a light of its own.

CHAPTER I

Political Reconstruction and the Organization
of the Press, 1760–1762

THE ACCESSION of the third Hanoverian to the throne of England came at a moment of national greatness. Never before had English arms gained such widespread victories; on both land and sea the old enemy, France, was being pushed from her precarious imperial holdings and tormented by the sight of British troops on her very doorstep. Victory was attributable to the guidance of William Pitt, his Majesty's secretary of state, but the effectiveness of Pitt's genius depended upon his co-operation with the first lord of the treasury, the Duke of Newcastle, who kept the minor cogs of political life well lubricated with place, pension, and honors, so that higher policy might advance smoothly. The union of Pitt and Newcastle drew together under one banner nearly all the elements that formed the ill-defined body sometimes called the Whig party.

For half a century the great Whig families had been able to retain control of British political life by representing fairly accurately the aims and desires of the English people and by casting upon their Tory opponents the odious epithet of Jacobite. By mid-century, however, the underlying political unanimity of the nation had robbed the old labels of all meaning. There were no parties but rather many small factions clustering about one or another political leader. Long tenure in office made that group surrounding the Duke of Newcastle the most numerous; alliance with Pitt brought to its support the unrivaled master of the House of Commons, the darling of the common people. Their union appeared firm. Newcastle left higher policy in Pitt's hands in return for freedom to manipulate the controls of his political machine. Unfortunately, Pitt had less sympathy and understanding for the duke's problems than his Grace had for those of Mr. Pitt. Inner friction might prove disastrous to the ministry if increased by external pressures, and such forces were ready to assert themselves in the first days of the new reign.

13

George III, who ascended the British throne October 25, 1760, at the age of twenty-three, entered into a heritage subtly different from that of either of his two Hanoverian predecessors. For him there was no threat of a Stuart pretender, nor was there an heir impatiently waiting to come into his own. George III had no rival; neither had he a close friend among the leading English politicians. Raised within the confines of Leicester House under the supervision of his mother, the Princess Dowager Augusta, George had learned to appreciate the grace and affability of the Earl of Bute, the Scot who had become mentor, father confessor, and political adviser to the serious young prince. Under Bute's tutelage George had been "nurtured on constitutional platitudes . . . [and] the current verbiage about virtue and liberty" and instilled with the idea of removing from the political scene the "proud, ambitious, and deceitful men" who had so long dominated politics. There were no seeds of tyranny in either George or Bute, but once able to set their plans in action, there was material aplenty for a violent upheaval in English politics—for as the aging Granville had once remarked, " 'Give any man the Crown on his side, and he can defy everything.' "[1]

The program which the new court undertook aimed at separating Pitt from Newcastle by inserting Bute as a responsible partner in their coalition. It mattered little whether Pitt or Newcastle acceded to the new design. Pitt was first approached but spurned a union with Bute at Newcastle's expense. The old duke was less firm and by February, 1761, had yielded to Bute's intrigues. On March 25, the earl became secretary of state for the northern department.[2] Bute was now in position to strike at both Pitt and Newcastle, for his alliance with the latter was no more than a temporary expedient.*

*The attitude of the court is well illustrated by this contemporary squib:

> Quoth Newcastle to Pitt, 'tis in vain to dispute;
> If we'd quarrel in private, we must make room for Bute.
> Quoth Pitt to his Grace, to bring that about,
> I fear, my dear Lord, you or I must turn out.
> Not at all, quoth the Duke, I meant no such thing,
> To make room for us all, we must turn out the King.
> If that's all your scheme, quoth the Earl, by my troth,
> I shall stick by my master, and turn ye out Both.

Historical Manuscripts Commission, *Report on Manuscripts in Various Collections*, VI, 47.

Against the duke, Bute prepared to turn that very weapon upon which Newcastle's significance rested—control of the House of Commons. It was not a difficult task, for the nucleus of power lay ready to Bute's hand: a body of members loyal to the interests of the court and ready to listen to whosoever spoke for the court. The immediate prospects of a general election assured an open field, and Bute, who realized in advance that "the new Parliament would be the King's"[3] was not disappointed. The parliament of 1761 brought to an end the supremacy of the Duke of Newcastle. A greater borough-monger than he had appeared upon the scene—the King of England.[4]

Having secured himself against Newcastle, Bute was free to devote his attention to Pitt, whose chief defense, beyond his own brilliant tongue, was the popularity of his policy. Words spoken and programs defended in the House of Commons were of little avail, however, if they failed to reach the street; no government in the eighteenth century dared lose contact with public opinion.

Newcastle certainly had little concept of the latent power of the press, but he had for years continued the payment of secret service pensions to a handful of potential propagandists. Along with the secret agents, spies, and other functionaries, these men formed an unsavory but necessary adjunct to smoothly running government. William Guthrie, James Ralph, and David Mallet formed Newcastle's propaganda department and cost him about £4,000. Guthrie received £200 a year, Ralph £300, and Mallet, while not regularly paid, had been given £300 for penning an attack on the unfortunate Admiral Byng.[5] In addition there were occasional writers who looked to those near government for their sustenance. Arthur Murphy and Dr. Philip Francis might be so classified, as both were under the influence of Henry Fox at this time.[6]

If Newcastle was behind-hand in using available talent, Pitt erred even further. He boasted of having early "contracted an indifference to party-papers,"[7] and his stanchest supporters who were fully cognizant of the magnitude of this weakness admitted that he "trusted as little to the press for the applause due his conduct, as he did to parliament for the approbation of it."[8] Yet such an attitude was much in keeping with Pitt's character. Despite the appellation "Great Commoner," he never descended to the level of those who adored him. Pitt moved above the world of practical politics in a sphere in which popular opinion was but an abstraction represented by gold boxes and Lord Mayors of London. It may also have been that Pitt recognized in the press a rival influence which reached far beyond the hallowed walls of parliament—a rival which he chose to shun.

The early days of the new reign were peculiarly adapted to an active policy of molding opinion. Many of the papers which drew inspiration from the flood of war news might, with proper direction, be channeled to fit the needs of faction. Among the newcomers was the *Public Ledger,* a daily paper edited for Francis Newbery by Griffith Jones. Its career began January 12, 1760, and enjoying the contributions of Oliver Goldsmith, the *Public Ledger* rapidly rose to prominence.[9] Not only were there papers, there were also scores of writers in search of employment and prepared to adopt any view that might be profitable. As one of these men observed, their number led them to seek popularity by "vying with each other, which shall say most. . . . And as at least ninety-nine hundredth parts of the people take their opinions from the papers, everything is hereby run to excess. Wise men repeat what weaker men write."[10] Even those who were later to adopt the most radical cause were, for the moment, undecided and ready to accept any lead provided by the masters of politics.

The new court party headed by the Earl of Bute was aware of the possibilities inherent in the situation. As early as December 20, 1760, Bute and his adviser George Bubb Dodington discussed the desirability of establishing a paper which would directly reflect their aims and ideas. Early in January, 1761, the means of influencing public opinion was once more the subject of a conference. "We wished to have some coffee-house spies," wrote Dodington, "but I do not know how to contrive it."[11] Bute was already moving in another direction. His position in the country, and his wealth, made him a natural light toward which writers directed their dedications, and his native pride made him welcome and reward their flattery. " 'Most of our best authors are devoted to me,' " he declared in February, 1761; the remainder he would pension.[12]

Such were the preliminary steps which had been taken by the time Bute entered the cabinet. Working in the full confidence of the king, he had broken Newcastle's power and was developing the tools with which to attack Pitt. Bute deserves credit for at least supporting, if he did not plan, the press attack upon Pitt and his war policy, which swelled the political literature of the summer of 1761. Knowing that Pitt was isolated in the council chamber, Bute set out to wrest from him that popularity which the Great Commoner at once needed and disdained.[13]

The court effort to secure popular support centered upon two topics: condemnation of "Mr. Pitt's war," and a plea for political union and "the extinction of party." The second line was the more significant, for by decrying party and national differences, by attempting to rally public enthusiasm around the person of the young king, the groundwork was laid for a revolution in politics. Certainly no British monarch within the memory of men had enjoyed such instantaneous popularity. The plea for party extinction was welcome in the ears of the king and Bute, as well as those of the numerous country gentlemen who represented a dormant Toryism. Wartime unanimity made the goal seem very near, but there were a few old Whigs who maintained that "this has always been the Tory method of getting into influence. . . . But what they really mean is to lull the Whigs into repose, whilst they . . . extinguish them."[14] Horace Walpole looked gloomily to future disturbances, saying, "I have a maxim, that *the extinction of party is the origin of faction.*"[15]

It was the attack upon Pitt's war policy, however, that produced the most numerous pamphlets and articles. Throughout his administration, Pitt had been remarkably free from public censure. Only when a new spirit appeared to guide and direct criticism was his policy seriously questioned.[16] The first effective blow fell in November, 1760, with the publication of Israel Mauduit's *Considerations on the Present German War.* Walpole believed that Mauduit wrote under the countenance of the Earl of Hardwicke, Newcastle's friend and adviser. Hardwicke was quite capable of outlining the arguments which Mauduit used, and few contemporaries gave much credit to their "squeaking acquaintance" who had once been "a wholesale woolen-draper." The style of the pamphlet, however, is not Hardwicke's, and while far removed from Pitt's point of view, it is unlikely that the great lawyer would have favored such strong arguments against "the old system."[17]

Mauduit's *Considerations* was an appeal to the financial interest of the country against the costly nature of Pitt's diversionary activities and German subsidies. The arguments were old but were "handled in a manner not unlikely to raise a flame among the vulgar, and abet the prejudices of many."[18] An immediate success, the pamphlet was so often used by members of the House of Commons as a guide against Pitt's policy that he declared it "had made a great many orators in that

House."[19] A successful war was still popular, however, and a host of replies appeared before the year was out. The best of these was *A Vindication of the Conduct of the Present War*. None destroyed the impression made by Mauduit's pamphlet, however. His arguments grew in stature as each new edition of the work appeared, and they remained unanswered by ministers on the floor of the House of Commons.[20] For his work Mauduit was rewarded with a good place by Bute and perhaps a pension of several hundred pounds.[21] His was but the first blow to strike Pitt; others were preparing, both political and literary, which would tell even more effectively against him.

The attempt to regroup politics about a new center was notably advanced in March, 1761, with the appearance of the pamphlet *Seasonable Hints from an Honest Man on the Present Crisis*. Inspired if not written by Lord Bath, its source attracted much attention to it, and it came to be recognized as the rallying cry of the new court party. Bath praised the political purity of the young monarch and called on him to break off all factious connections, to make ministers once more dependent on the crown, and to accept the proffered support of loyal Tories. Having "all the appearance of a manifesto preparatory to some considerable enterprize,"[22] Bath's pamphlet was as significant in its field as Mauduit's had been in that of foreign policy. Throughout the summer a quiet reformation of political alignment began to take place as Englishmen turned their faces toward the court.

An increasing number of pamphlets began to reflect a growing desire for peace. The merits of various conquered territories were published so freely that Pitt was led to exclaim, " 'Some are for keeping Canada, some Guadeloup; who will tell me which I shall be hanged for not keeping?' "[23] And keep some he must, for negotiations were under way with France to bring the war to an end. If British pamphleteers were of little service to Pitt, the French agent, François de Bussy, was actively encouraging the propagandist torrent which demonstrated the indeterminate nature of England's war aims.[24] Such efforts supplemented the system which Bute, aided by the brilliant young Scots lawyer Alexander Wedderburn, was erecting to control the expression of public opinion and rob Pitt of popular support when the final break should come.

The course of negotiations with France sped on that day. No supple diplomat, Pitt sought recognition of defeat from his enemy only to learn that her final effort had not yet been made. Within the cabinet,

Newcastle, aware that financial and commercial interests were desirous of peace and balking at war-heightened taxation, spoke for peace. Bute, who had supported the war throughout the summer of 1761, dared not let Pitt triumph at the council table. In August he made his pacific inclinations known to Newcastle's friends; Pitt was brought to agree to terms acceptable to France, but at that very moment France bound Spain to her cause, and hopes of peace were shattered. Despite certain intimations of the Spanish action, the English ministry would not listen to Pitt's warning plea for a preventive attack upon Spain. Supported only by his brother-in-law Earl Temple, Pitt declared he would not follow where he could not lead, and after a bitter cabinet meeting on October 2, both Pitt and Temple gave up their seals of office.

Pitt was gone, but the war remained, and Bute must now guide the nation's destinies. When Dodington wished him "joy of being delivered of a most impractical colleague, his Majesty of a most imperious servant, and the country of a most dangerous minister," Bute replied: "My situation, at all times perilous, is become much more so; for I am no stranger to the language held in this great city: 'Our darling's resignation is owing to Lord Bute, and he must answer for all the consequences'; —which is, in other words, for the miscarriages of another system, that Pitt himself could not have prevented."[25] To his aid he called George Grenville and Henry Fox, to whom he entrusted the House of Commons, and Pitt's seals were delivered to the Earl of Egremont.[26]

The test of Bute's ability to shape public opinion had come. If Pitt could draw upon the numerical and vocal weight of his following in the country and in the City, he might push the ministers hard; he was never more popular and shared his laurels only with Earl Temple. The nation owed much to Pitt, and the ministers prepared to reward those years of service, the termination of which had not as yet been formally announced. Refusing greater honors, Pitt accepted a peerage for his wife, and a £3,000 annuity for himself. This form of remuneration was suggested by Hardwicke, and on October 9, Bute informed both Hardwicke and Newcastle of the use he meant to make of it. The news of the pension and Lady Hester's title, Countess of Chatham, was to accompany the announcement of Pitt's resignation in the *Gazette* of October 10: "which surely must have an effect upon the cry of his disinterested popularity," observed Newcastle.[27] The announcement appeared as scheduled, and as an added touch, a soothing declaration of Spain's peaceful intentions was printed in close proximity.[28]

The result was all Bute hoped for. A rumor concerning Pitt's honors had circulated on Friday the ninth, but had been widely contradicted by Saturday's papers as "a design to tarnish the lustre of a certain great character." Then about ten o'clock Saturday evening, the *Gazette* was published. An observer in Dick's Coffee House noted that "it was really diverting to see the effect it had upon most people's countenances . . . ; it occasioned a dead silence, and I think every body went away without giving their opinions of the matter."[29]

The shock of seeing Pitt's name attached to a pension and a peerage overthrew his popularity among the commonalty with startling rapidity. "What! to sneak out of the scrape, prevent peace, and avoid the war! blast one's character, and all for the comfort of a paltry annuity, a long-necked peeress, and a couple of Grenvilles!" wrote Walpole. "The City looks mighty foolish."[30] "The City and the people," reported another, "are outrageous about Lady Cheat'em . . . and her husband's pension."[31]

As the popular revulsion swept to a peak, Pitt was branded with "every term of reproach that malice could apply." Hired writers in government service filled the columns of newspapers and ground out pamphlet after pamphlet. The effort was admittedly successful; Pitt's glory was dimmed and his great work forgotten.[32] The giant, as Walpole vividly remarked, who was "stalking to seize the Tower of London . . . stumbled over a silver penny,"[33] and the public was bitterly amused that

> No letters more full or expressive can be,
> Than once so respectable W. P.
> The first stands for Wisdom, War, Wonder, Wit,
> The last points out Peerage, and Pension, and Pit.[34]

It was not the Great Commoner who first reacted to the attack but his brother-in-law Earl Temple. Recognizing the danger of losing popular support, Temple announced that "he meant to appeal to the public for his justification" and was active in urging Pitt to the same step.[35] On October 15, Pitt wrote to his friend and ally in the City, Alderman William Beckford, declaring straightly that he had resigned because of "a difference of opinion with regard to measures to be taken against Spain," and the "gracious public marks of his Majesty's approbation" were "unmerited and unsolicited."[36]

Beckford, who had disbelieved the rumor of Pitt's resignation until he heard it from Pitt himself, had sedulously endeavored to protect Pitt's honor with the public by denying that he had accepted anything from the government.[37] The official announcement of the pension had been a crippling blow—enough, as Walpole suggested, to make even Beckford blush,[38] and the hot-blooded alderman wasted little time in rushing Pitt's letter to the press. A copy was given to William Bristow of the *Public Ledger,* and he was advised that it should be published with the writer's consent. So readily did the public accept its erstwhile hero's defense that 3,000 copies of the *Public Ledger* were sold before noon—by which time the *Gazetteer* and other papers were reprinting it, and the *Ledger* was selling at five guineas a copy.[39]

The ministers now found the City all "fire and flame." Newcastle felt that "nothing can be more offensive to a King, more insolent in itself, more treacherous to council, or show more marks of a disappointed heart." He shuddered at the "certain proof of malice, revenge, and opposition," and was ready to cast all blame on Bute. Such an appeal to the public, said the Duke, was "extraordinary and unwarrantable," but it had brought back to Pitt "his mad noisy city friends."[40] These friends promptly presented their thanks to "the Right Honourable *William Pitt,* for the many great and eminent services rendered this Nation" and lamented the loss of "so able, so faithful a Minister."[41]

The cause of the ministerial failure to maintain its advantage over Pitt was belatedly pointed out to Newcastle by Chesterfield: "For God's sake, why was not Mr. Pitt's pension tacked inseparably to a peerage for himself. For if . . . he must have both or neither, I dare say he would have accepted both together."[42] Hardwicke, however, felt that this was no affair of theirs. "In truth ministers should retain persons who can write well," he advised his son, ". . . but if they neglect that, it is not to be expected that their friends . . . should expose themselves." Hardwicke's chief regret was that now "everybody, however great, will think fit to appeal to the mob in this way."[43]

In spite of a very recent warning from Dodington (now Lord Melcombe),[44] Bute had not yet gained effective control of the means of mass communication. Beckford, acting in behalf of Pitt, regained the initiative, and the press warfare rose to new heights. "Pamphlets on Mr. Pitt are the whole conversation," wrote Walpole, and he was none too flattered by the accusation of having written some of them.[45] Fox's chaplain, Philip Francis, came to the fore as the author of *Mr. Pitt's*

Letter Versified, to which Walpole gave credit for halting a laudatory address to Pitt being drawn up at Leicester. Arthur Murphy, also closely associated with Fox, produced the bitterly satirical *Letter from a Right Honourable Person and the Answer to it, Translated into Verse* about the same time.[46]

Charles Jenkinson, Bute's private secretary, began his active career as a government press manager during the literary strife following Pitt's resignation. Jenkinson, who had entered politics as a "useful typographical *commis,*" worked his way into higher politics with little regard for faction or party. He had written in support of the Pitt-Newcastle ministry, and at George Grenville's instance had received a £200 pension from the duke. As early as November, 1761, Ralph Griffiths, publisher of the *Monthly Review,* felt it worth his while to suggest to Jenkinson his readiness to undertake any printing tasks government might find for him.[47]

While Bute was already unpopular because of his Scottish origin, he had not, prior to the end of 1761, had to face any severe criticism in the English press. National resentment against a foreigner had been expressed early in the reign by placards calling for "no Scotch minister,"[48] but as yet no master had appeared to whip up English resentment to the boiling point. John Wilkes, to whom this task would be entrusted, may have contributed a few political essays to the *St. James's Chronicle,* and a young journalist named John Almon wrote in the *Gazetteer* as an "Independent Whig" and "Lucius," in defense of Pitt, but such efforts were voluntary and poorly organized.[49] Pitt would do nothing in his own cause, and Temple, though righteously indignant, had not yet been stirred to independent action. Edmund Burke, a young Irish author as yet unfledged in politics, shrewdly observed at the end of the year that Bute's tactics had answered his ends perfectly; the torrent of Pitt's popularity had returned after having been beaten back, but "it was no longer that impetuous and irresistible tide, which in the year 1757 had borne down everything before it; it was weakened, divided, and ineffective."[50]

The immediate problem facing the government was not an irate Pitt but a war with Spain. Newcastle, convinced that he could not *"out war Mr. Pitt,"* sought peace; Bute wished to press the Spanish war and reduce expenses by withdrawing from Germany. Defeated in the cabinet and betrayed by his own secretaries, the duke resigned in May, 1762, without reward for a life and a fortune spent in the service of the House of Hanover. Bute stepped into the Treasury, secured the assistance of the Duke of Bedford, whom he sent to Paris to conduct negotiations with France, and with Henry Fox at his elbow, he prepared to meet parliament at the end of the year.[51]

Secure withindoors, Bute took definite steps to secure popular backing for his peace policy. By 1762 he had learned the secret of organizing coffeehouse spies and was rapidly becoming proficient in the art of establishing a government press. Among others, William Guthrie, who had long enjoyed a pension from Newcastle, was granted a renewal of his £200 yearly upon the promise to deserve Bute's "future patronage and protection" by demonstrating "greater zeal if possible than ever."[52]

The most noteworthy acquisition was Dr. Samuel Johnson, who became the recipient of £300 yearly. Johnson's name was suggested to Bute by Alexander Wedderburn, and the negotiations were carried out by Thomas Sheridan and Arthur Murphy. That the pension carried any political implications was denied by all parties. When Johnson called upon Bute to express his appreciation, the earl insisted that "it is not given you for any thing you are to do, but for what you have done," and Wedderburn later told the indefatigable Boswell that the pension was granted without "even tacit understanding that he should write for administration."[53] So much for the disclaimers; eighteenth-century morals and manners required them of its Johnsons and its Gibbons.[54] Some time after the good Doctor's pension was granted, Charles Jenkinson provided him with certain papers concerning the peace negotiations. Johnson was well aware that it was intended he should put them to use. He failed to do so, however, and in 1765 returned them to Jenkinson with the pious wish "to see them employed . . . by a man so much more versed in publick affairs." Perhaps Johnson was piqued at the difficulties he experienced in collecting his pension. He certainly did not hold himself above such employment, but he proved a bad investment on the part of Bute's ministry—no more valuable nor useful than the poorest hack.[55]

Not all of Bute's propagandists were as prominent as Dr. Samuel Johnson. Charles Jenkinson, who was active in adding to the list of government writers[56] during the summer of 1762, secured the support of two obscure penmen. Edward Richardson seems to have had little to recommend him to the ministers except the support of Sir Matthew Blackiston, who was elected Lord Mayor of London in 1762, but that sufficed to secure him £50 a year from secret service funds. Richardson wrote for the *Gazetteer* as "Inquisitor," and although he declared to Bute that "Avarice constitutes no single part of my passion," he suggested that "if any assistance should be wanted by any visiting the print shops I could delight in that service." Such willingness was rewarded in October by appointment as controller of the Pepper Warehouse, and Richardson became one of Bute's agents in the City.[57]

Roger Flexman, clergyman, pamphleteer, and historian, also found his way to government employment through Jenkinson's interest. Flexman published a volume of *Critical, Historical, and Political Miscellanies* in 1752, and a second edition ten years later attracted the attention of Shute Barrington. On Jenkinson's inquiry if he could suggest some willing author, Barrington recommended Flexman as "extremely ready to undertake the employment." Arrangements were subsequently made through Barrington for an interview between Jenkinson and Flexman, and Barrington shortly congratulated the secretary on "having closed with Flexman, as I am convinced you will find his abilities adequate to any task you will assign him; and I believe his fidelity may be depended upon."[58]

So widespread and open were Bute's efforts to create a favorable press that they became the subject of considerable sarcastic humor. A broadside appearing in May, 1762, portrayed Bute distributing his dole among a flock of scribblers and etchers, and remarked that

> When his Lordship from Nothing was call'd into Power,
> Conscious Wits wou'd be squirting, and Writers wou'd lour;
> He got *this* a pension: and gave *that* a bribe.
> But this fortune can't silence the ill-natur'd Tribe.[59]

Throughout the year Dr. Philip Francis continued to pummel what was slowly growing into an opposition party. Fox admitted his chaplain's activity to the young Earl of Shelburne in January, but sought to keep his part in the pamphlet warfare a secret.[60] During the year, Francis wrote *A Letter from the Cocoa Tree to the Country Gentlemen* in which he attacked the opposition as "a formed design against his MAJESTY's independence" and called upon the country gentlemen to continue acting upon those principles of honor which had hitherto guided their conduct.

The total effect of Bute's occasional writers seems to have been satisfying to the ministry. It was at least possible for a moderate observer to declare in October that "if we may judge from the stile of these pamplets, the popular tide seems to have taken a turn favourable to the pacific measures of the present administration."[61] More sensitive observers, however, were becoming increasingly aware of the savage press attack which was unleashed against Bute in the summer of 1762. Walpole noted in June that his father, Sir Robert, "was not more abused after twenty years than Lord Bute is in twenty days," and by September he had counted "satiric prints enough to tapestry Westminster Hall."[62] Bute was unable to win the etchers to his cause and was defenseless against their attack.[63] As October rolled to an end, Newcastle and the old Whigs began to realize the completeness of Bute's victory, and in Walpole's words, "opposition ran stark mad at once, cursed, swore, called names, and has not been one minute cool enough to have a grain of wit." The leaders' attitude was reflected in the press. "Their prints are gross, their papers scurrilous; indeed the authors abuse one another more than anybody else."[64]

This rising wave of antagonism was in part a natural revulsion or reaction to Bute's own press policy. As one author expressed it, "I am no courtier. Thank God, I want no favour from that quarter, and would rather gain an honest livelihood by the sweat of my brow than enjoy any post his Majesty could give me, with the loss of freedom of speech and my integrity."[65] While he had secured much support, Bute had, with an "absurd stoicism . . . set himself up as a Pillory to be pelted by all the Blackguards of England, upon the supposition that they would grow tired and leave off."[66] His offensive had called forth the shock troops of the opposition, and he was to learn that a defensive position was not easily maintained. This surprised even Henry Fox, who, realizing that "nobody can prevent such clamour as was never before heard," could not account for the fact that a "young, civil, virtuous, good natur'd King" had not sufficient popularity to defend his Favorite. "To this pass are we brought," wrote Fox in September, "by newspapers & libels, & the encouragement given to the mob to think themselves the Government."[67]

As the French had formerly aided Bute against Pitt, the King of Prussia, wrathful at Bute's abandonment of his interests, now added to the anti-ministerial clamor. In August, Frederick II instructed his representative in London to "incite, so far as possible, the authors of the current pamphlets to decry the conduct of this minister, so as to come constantly nearer to hurling him from his place." The ministers intercepted these directions and objected strongly against such an attempt at interference by a foreign power, but the Prussian propagandists seem to have been little daunted by the warning.[68]

English pamphleteers were not less active. Bute's "Scothood" was a rallying cry as powerful as that of "Favourite." Johnson once said, "the noblest prospect which a Scotchman ever sees, is the high road that leads him to England,"[69] and the belief "that most places of Trust & Profit in England were engross'd by Scotchmen" became a national creed.[70] Dr. John Butler, later Bishop of Oxford and Hereford, replied to Francis' Letter from the Cocoa Tree with An Address to the Cocoa-Tree from a Whig, in which he attacked Bute as a Scot with no English interests. "The WHIGS therefore naturally dislike him; for WHIGGISM is a popular principle. The great object of it is the liberty of the people. . . . A KNOWN WHIG will of course enjoy popularity." The Weekly Magazine counteracted the government's plea for "extinction of party" by doing its utmost to blend "Butists and Tories."[71]

Upon Newcastle's resignation, John Almon hastily drew up a laudatory pamphlet which he called to his Grace's attention while praising the "distinguished Fortitude, and so inflexible Integrity" of the old duke.[72] Newcastle was not yet prepared for open opposition, however, and Almon dedicated his next effort, A Review of Mr. Pitt's Administration, to Earl Temple. That nobleman, already engaged in several projects of the opposition press, sent for the young pamphleteer and promptly attached him to his cause. Under Temple's patronage, Almon received Newcastle's thanks for the "warm friendship" shown earlier in the year and became a humble familiar in the political circle that included many of the great Whig lords and their followers.[73] As Almon was also an active writer for Charles Green Say's Gazetteer, Temple undoubtedly took advantage of the weekly visits he paid to Pall-Mall Street to secure the support of that paper in the campaign against Bute.[74]

The ministry, though annoyed and disturbed by the violence with which it was assailed, was unshaken and prepared to carry its great cause, the preliminaries of peace. Fox correctly predicted in September that with "Torys & Scotch" and those who "are in their hearts for peace, . . . after 2 or 3 angry debates, supported by no very great divisions, we shall get again into smooth water." As for the vocal opposition, Fox assured Bedford, "We are loudly threatened, but I see no reason why, like other threatened folk, we may not live long."[75]

Bute was less assured. As members came up for parliament, every effort was made "to silence or intimidate the printers of newspapers, libels, and satiric prints." Those who could be frightened were made aware of the strong arm of the government; those whom threats left unmoved were purchased whenever possible. The ministry was well on its way to spending the thirty or forty thousand pounds which it laid out in the course of three years in the attempt to mold public opinion.[76] Unfortunately for Bute, his prodigality had stirred up a hornet's nest among the periodical publications and brought to the fore the most virulent of his literary opponents, John Wilkes.

CHAPTER II

The War of the Weeklies

WHEN THE floodgates of paper warfare were lowered by the ministry in 1761, few realized the significance of what was to follow. The outpouring of pamphlets, letters, and articles stirred English political life in a manner hitherto unknown. This plethora of printed matter followed, inspired, and catered to public discussion which occurred at a social level and concerned itself with political problems which had had little place in English politics prior to the reign of George III. The broadening of English political consciousness and the deepening of the roots of English political activity was the work of the press.

The task would never have been accomplished had not the energies of the press been directed by men cognizant of its power, nor would they have succeeded without the opportune appearance of capable workmen. That the ultimate line of development was not the initial goal of a Temple or a Wilkes, is hardly surprising, for politicians are not prone to act upon general theories, but rather upon impulses of anger, jealousy, and the desire for power. Such stimuli moved one of the most exalted of Whig noblemen to link his interests with those of the most charming rascal in Georgian England. The combination produced a political convulsion from which arose the first glimmerings of a new interpretation of both the duties of the press and the liberty of the press.

Earl Temple once declared that "he loved faction, and had a great deal of money to spare."[1] It was an accurate self-appraisal. The fortune he spent on his estate at Stowe made it a show place in an age of extravagant landscaping. The money he poured into the political press as a result of his factiousness established Temple as the foremost propaganda master of his time. No contemporary knew better the path between pen and press, none realized more fully the political power which might be stirred into action by traveling that route. Personally less able than either his brother George Grenville or his famous brother-in-law, William Pitt, Temple taught them both the importance of the press in politics.

Upon his resignation in 1761, Temple's views found immediate expression in a weekly paper, the *Monitor*. Founded in 1755 by four political writers apparently backed by William Beckford, the *Monitor* was published by Jonathan Scott, a London bookseller, and edited by Arthur Beardmore and John Entick.[2] By 1762, the *Monitor* had an established reputation, and Beardmore had become Temple's lawyer and man of business in the City. The *Monitor* consequently reflected the attitude of the noble earl whom politics had shaped into an outspoken enemy of Bute and his ministry.

Beardmore and Entick, assisted by the lawyer's clerk, David Meredith, might suffice to call names and attack the ministry in general terms; other talent was called in upon special occasions, and through Temple the *Monitor* came to enjoy the services of John Wilkes. Politician, rake, and classical dilettante, Wilkes also held a colonelcy in the Buckinghamshire militia, and Temple, as lord-lieutenant of the county, frequently entertained him at Stowe. Although a follower of Pitt in the House of Commons, where he sat for Ailesbury, Wilkes was an opportunist, unashamedly admitting that "in this time of public dissension he was resolved to make his fortune."[3] That search once led him to Bute's levee at Whitehall, but after cooling his heels for two hours without even seeing Bute, Wilkes returned to his county patron.[4] By January, 1762, he was engaged in writing a typical Pittite pamphlet, *Observations on the Papers Relative to the Rupture with Spain*.[5] Some time in the next few months Wilkes began to contribute to the *Monitor* and may have penned the especially scathing attack on "the favourite" published on May 22.[6]

By that date Bute was anticipating Newcastle's resignation, and his pamphleteers were actively pressing his policy out-of-doors. He had accomplished the program elaborated at the onset of the reign except for the establishment of a periodical publication, a shortcoming which was remedied when novelist Tobias George Smollett undertook to bring forth a weekly sheet which bore the appellation *Briton*. The name was peculiarly significant. Reflecting those early words of George III, who "gloried in the name of Britain," the ministerial organ was intended to continue Bute's twofold propaganda effort: to support unity at home and peace abroad. Smollett appeared to be a good editorial choice. Experienced, known as "a hard hitting journalist," he had once admired Pitt but had recently veered toward Bute, and in the *Critical Review* he had praised the Great Commoner's critics.[7] Unfortunately for both Bute and his penman, Smollett was psychologically unfit for the burden which fell upon him. "My difficulties," he later wrote, "have arisen from my own indiscretion; from a warm temper easily provoked to rashness; from a want of courage to refuse that which I cannot grant without doing injustice to my own family; from indolence, bashfulness and want of economy."[8] Worst of all, Smollett was sensible of his own weakness, and in the rough-and-tumble of journalistic warfare only the strong survived.

Little is known concerning the founding of the *Briton*. Perhaps Lord Melcombe recommended Smollett to Bute,[9] but it seems more likely that Alexander Wedderburn had a hand in the negotiations which were concluded about May, 1762.[10] The first *Briton* appeared May 29, as Bute took up his duties at the Treasury. At least one man noticed that the paper bore the Royal Arms—though only as the sign of the printer John Coote of Paternoster Row.[11] The gage of battle had been thrown down, a rival to the *Monitor* found who would " 'pluck the mask of patriotism from the front of faction, and the torch of discord from the hand of sedition.' "[12] It was not an auspicious beginning, however. The *Briton*'s circulation, which never rose above 250, probably began much lower, and Smollett invited trouble when he challenged the *Monitor* to bring detailed rather than general charges against "the Favourite."[13]

It was not the place of the *Monitor* to accept the wager. That paper was well established, and neither Temple nor his underlings wished to attract the attention of the law.[14] But a reply was imperative and Temple resourceful. On June 5, the first number of a new weekly was published: the *North Briton*, planned and executed by John Wilkes, with Temple's approval.[15] The newcomer brought with him a fire and spirit which marked him as no common hack. He spoke the language of liberty and set his opponent on the defensive at one stroke of the pen. If his arguments were as old as Whiggery, they were the stronger for it and echoed familiarly in the minds of his readers. In John Wilkes the reign of George III discovered its first great propagandist, Temple the answer to Bute's control of place and pension, and the press a spokesman who, though he had many failings, was never silent.

Less than a week later a second government periodical reached the booksellers' stands. The *Auditor*, written by Arthur Murphy, was looked upon as a reply to the *North Briton*, a necessary antidote to his superiority over the *Briton*; but in all probability the *Auditor* was intended merely to reinforce that paper in overwhelming the *Monitor*.

Murphy, at any rate, showed himself to be a far better propagandist than Smollett; Wilkes balanced a hundred *Auditors* against a thousand *Britons*.[16] These were the men, these the weapons with which the in-fighting of the press war was conducted. Back of them stood the politicians; before them lay a summer of vituperation and the preliminaries of the Peace of Paris.

The general content of the four periodicals showed little originality on the part of any of the authors. The *Monitor* and *North Briton* attacked Bute's foreign policy and heaped odium upon all Scots in general—"the Favourite" in particular. Smollett did his best to defend the minister, while Murphy reversed the charge of "favouritism" by labeling Newcastle "the favourite of the *venal*" and Pitt "the favourite of the *Mob*."[17] In June the *Patriot* joined Wilkes and Beardmore for a short life of but five issues; he was even more briefly met by an *Occasional Writer* on the side of government.[18]

Personal abuse was the groundwork of the periodical struggle. Smollett and Wilkes had once been friends; just two months before the first *Briton* was published, Smollett had expressed his "warmest regard" for Wilkes and had assured him that "when I presume to differ from you in any point of opinion, I shall always do it with Diffidence and Deference."[19] Such terms were not to be found in Wilkes's vocabulary. He struck at author and patron indiscriminately and called to his aid Charles Churchill, sometime clergyman turned poet and political satirist. Already at odds with Smollett because of the manner in which the *Critical Review* had received his *Rosciad*, Churchill welcomed the opportunity to snipe at the *Briton* and point out that "what made Smollett write makes Johnson dumb."[20] William Hogarth came in for his share of abuse in September as a result of his print, *The Times*. Fearing the effectiveness and popularity of the engraver's work, Wilkes had urged Hogarth to withhold the print, but financial obligations weighed more than friendship, and *The Times* was published September 7. The *North Briton* struck on the twenty-fifth, and Hogarth, unable to defend himself verbally, waited patiently until the following spring, when he drew the famous caricature of a leering, squinting Wilkes. He thus became the unique victor over the patriot in the realm of personal abuse.*[21]

*Churchill also became entangled with Hogarth when, in defense of Wilkes, he published *The Epistle to William Hogarth*. The artist promptly portrayed the poet in a savage cartoon entitled "The Bruiser."

The liberated pen of Wilkes, while vastly strengthening the Pittite press, seems to have been almost too forceful in the eyes of its sponsor, Temple. With due regard to the fact that his correspondence was intercepted and read by the ministers, Temple urged moderation upon Wilkes as early as the second week in June. More interested in the criticism of policy than the personal squabbles of rival writers, Temple suggested to Wilkes that "the Briton left to himself is left to his worst enemy."[22] The earl's cautious attitude was soon reinforced by a paper which Wilkes proposed to print in the Monitor. Temple received an advance copy and refused to allow it to appear because of its reflections upon the royal family, whom he did not consider "lawful game." To "trespass within the bounds of royal manors" was apt to "start something of a delicate and personal nature, which should be avoided." He was ready enough "to defray the loss and expense of laying aside the paper" but insisted that his press should not embarrass "those it might mean to serve."[23] Wilkes was well aware that he was running close to the wind. On the fifteenth he asked Churchill to secure legal advice "for fear I have got too near the pillory," and promptly sought to soothe Temple's fears.[24]

Throughout the summer journalistic strife flourished. Amidst personal attacks and general abuse of all things Scottish, the great question of the terms of peace was debated. The Monitor held that both France and Spain must be crushed and stripped of their colonial possessions, while the Auditor declaimed against Pitt and Newcastle, war contractors, and West Indian planters. Murphy, in a more enlightened moment, countered the famous definition of the liberty of the press with which Wilkes had opened the North Briton with one of his own: it was "a free power, to deal about scandal and defamation on all ranks of men." He readily agreed that it powerfully attracted the "People of England," whom he identified as "the grand pensioner [Pitt], Lord Gawkee [Temple], Alderman Sugarcane [Beckford], Colonel Squintum [Wilkes], an illiterate bookseller [Sir James Hodges], a city attorney [Beardmore], a drunken parson [Entick], and a broken poet [Churchill]."*[25]

---

*Murphy erred when he included Hodges, an influential City politician, in his catalog of dissidents. A successful bookseller on London Bridge c. 1730–1758, Hodges entered politics in 1750, and was knighted in 1758. Although thought by some to have supported Pitt, he worked in Bute's interest from March, 1762, until the end of the earl's ministry.

As the weeks passed, the government became less tolerant of the abuse through which it waded toward peace with France. In August, proofsheets of the *North Briton* were scrutinized for possible legal action,[26] but prosecution did not follow immediately. Walpole suggested that the very indelicacy of the *North Briton* kept authority from wishing to publish it in courts of law.[27] Nonetheless, Wilkes found himself forced to pacify his publisher, George Kearsley, whose services had been secured with considerable difficulty and whose risks were as great as those of the author.[28]

Another sort of pacification was demanded by Lord Talbot, whose equestrian achievements Wilkes satirized in the August 12 *North Briton*.† Talbot paraded his injured honor and secured satisfaction in a bloodless duel which gave Wilkes subject matter for a very humorous letter to Temple—a letter which had serious political repercussions when it was published some years later.[29]

It was evident by late summer that ministerial writers alone could not turn public opinion from its anti-Scottish phobia or cry down the opposition to a Butean peace. In September Wilkes noted that Egremont had begun to exert pressure upon the London printers; Charles Say of the *Gazetteer* was specifically mentioned.[30] The approach of the parliamentary session concentrated attention upon the focal point of the peace, and as the pressure of politics and propaganda rose both Bute and Temple experienced difficulties within their respective press systems. Smollett, ill and overworked, complained of his journalistic troubles and sought recompense through appointment to some diplomatic post in a milder climate. Bute offered him a pension, but not the desired consulate, and in a moment of extreme bitterness Smollett declared that he was "traduced by malice, persecuted by faction, abandoned by false patrons."[31] The editors of both the *Briton* and the *Auditor* complained of their patron's lassitude in providing them with materials, and poor Murphy once accepted the bait of false information which Wilkes held out to him. The *North Briton* never forgot that coup—nor did it let Murphy forget, either.[32]

The *Monitor* ran aground early in October when Scott, the printer, quarreled with Beardmore and Entick. The paper of October 9 contained only scraps of a "History of England"; a week later two *Monitors* appeared, and it was acknowledged that the former proprietors

†William, Earl Talbot, was the unfortunate Lord Steward whose horse backed into the royal presence during George III's coronation ceremonies.

had parted company. Temple's agents transferred their printing to Jacob Wilson and Isaac Fell in Paternoster Row, while Scott attempted to publish a *Monitor* which now found Bute blameless. Scott's paper was discontinued about the first of November, by which time Temple's *Monitor* was experiencing the first effects of ministerial punitive action.[33]

The administration had turned its attention to the *Monitor's* susceptibility to legal attack early in October, perhaps because of the manner in which the paper had treated Bute's receipt of a Garter.[34] Formal steps were taken November 3, in accordance with the advice given by crown law officers, and Halifax issued warrants November 6, to Nathan Carrington, the senior king's messenger, for the arrest and seizure of the papers of Arthur Beardmore, John Entick, David Meredith, and John Medley, the printer of the *Monitor*. Action was also taken against Jacob Wilson and Isaac Fell, as booksellers advertising the *Monitor*, and all were promptly taken up.[35]

The direction of the thrust was quite obvious. Wilkes, who had written two of the *Monitors* of which complaint was made, was immediately concerned, and Temple was moved to inquire, "With what face can the patrons of the Auditor and of the Briton seize and confine the Monitors?"[36] Wilkes may have contemplated some drastic move in reply to governmental action but satisfied himself, under Temple's moderating influence, with visiting Beardmore and urging him to bring suit against the secretary of state for the false imprisonment of himself and his clerk. According to Wilkes, Beardmore refused to take this step until he had reason to believe it would be successful.[37]

The writer of the *North Briton* was himself in greater danger than he realized. On November 16, the attorney-general and solicitor-general had reported upon the libelous character of nine of the twenty-four issues of Wilkes's paper. A general warrant for the apprehension of the otherwise unidentified "Authors, Printers, and Publishers" of the first twenty-five *North Britons* was signed by Halifax two days later, and a second warrant, extending to No. 26, was also drawn up, though the paper did not pass into government hands until November 27.[38] The failure of the ministry to serve these warrants has been explained by assuming that they were put to another use. The printing of the *North Briton* had been done by Richardson of Salisbury Court, Fleet Street. Wilkes informed his coadjutor Churchill that Richardson had "absolutely refus'd the having any more concern in that paper."[39]

Dryden Leach of Eliot's Court was induced to print No. 26, which consisted chiefly of poetry, and the editors explained that the change was due to "the fears of a printer, who trembled at the thoughts of imprisonment, and smarted under a severe, *private* reprimand."[40] If the second warrant extending through No. 26 was shown to Leach and his printer, Peter Cock, it explains why the latter "had the terrors of the Lord of the Isle [Bute], so strong before him, that he was fallen ill to avoid printing the paper."[41] Kearsley was already negotiating with Richard Balfe of Old Bailey. Wilkes cleared No. 27 with his lawyer, Sayer, and Balfe printed the *North Briton* until its last famous number rolled off his press.[42] No. 27 consequently echoed Wilkes's first volley (although this one was written by Churchill) in defense of "the liberty of the press, that bulwark of the liberties of the people." Why, it asked, was not the *Monitor,* if criminal, suppressed long ago? The answer was forthcoming: because "at this important and critical juncture, it might be of excellent use to stop the mouths of those who imagine it possible to love their country, although they exclaim against the minister."[43]

The ministry had failed to intimidate the *North Briton,* and the case against the *Monitor* was not pushed. Bute, unable to silence criticism of the treaty he was about to present to parliament, might yet hope for success within those hallowed walls. There the effect of the pamphleteers and the war of the weeklies would be weighed, the result of Temple's policy evaluated. The process had already begun. The noble propagandist, who declared his disapproval of "this paper war, and the daily abominations which are published," for the prying eyes of the postal censors,[44] stood firmly behind public discussion of the peace. Pitt vacillated between open cooperation with Wilkes and warm opposition to " 'all kinds of political writing as productive of great mischief.' " As Wilkes observed to Temple, this was in character, for Pitt " 'ought to fear the shadow of a pen, . . . he was undoubtedly the best speaker and the worst writer of his age, . . . he would do well to harangue the 500 deputies of the people in the cause of liberty, and the *North Briton* wou'd endeavor to animate the nation at large.' "[45]

Grudging tribute was paid Temple's propagandists even among court circles. Bute notified his son-in-law Sir James Lowther of the signing of the preliminaries on November 17, but added, "War seems to be declared at home with the utmost virulence; I am the mark for the party, but the whole is in reality aim'd at the King himself, whose liberty is to be now decided on, liberty that his poorest subject enjoys, of choosing his own menial servants."[46] As Temple's old friend Lyttelton expressed it, " 'We have gott *peace abroad*, and I think, on the whole, *a good one*; but things seem to tend to *war at home*.' "[47]

Within Newcastle's circle opinion was confused and contradictory. The duke's informants advised him that Temple and Pitt were the authors of the *North Briton*, but they did not convince Hardwicke.[48] The vitriol that flowed from the press, like the satirical prints, had no place in Newcastle's system. "I am too dull to taste them," he wrote "and if they are not decyphered for me, I could not in the least guess, very often, what they mean. . . . *I detest the whole thing*."[49] Yet he expected a spontaneous press reaction when Fox and Bute joined forces and was surprised and disappointed when it was slow to materialize.[50] Newcastle was still thinking in terms of a parliamentary or even ministerial opposition. Hardwicke assured his son Charles Yorke, a member of the ministry in his office as attorney-general, "That there is no great ground at present for any public parliamentary opposition from measures." The unpopularity of *"the Scotchman,"* though widespread, offered no line of attack, and "there would be a difficulty upon the D[uke] of N[ewcastle] & his friends in shaping their opposition upon the conditions of the peace."[51] The difficulty was, of course, that the terms of peace which Bute asked, while less than British conquest warranted, were yet magnificent and equal to the expectations of moderate men. Even after the king demonstrated his disregard for Whig traditions by the abrupt dismissal of the Duke of Devonshire, Newcastle could think of nothing stronger than resignations to "strike terrors . . . in the proper place."[52]

December 9, when parliament considered the preliminaries, brought a rude awakening to many. The House of Lords did not divide; the House of Commons approved the terms by a majority of 254, in spite of Pitt's best efforts. The exploding bomb which Newcastle had threatened proved but the bursting of a bubble; "what had been the object of terror became a subject of derision."[53] "I think," wrote one member, "I have in no day for two months past heard less said against the peace than this day."[54] The definitive treaty was signed at Paris on February 10, 1763, and Bute's victory was well-nigh complete. The celebration in which the king and Fox indulged—wholesale purging of all office-holders who retained any ties with Newcastle—finally convinced the duke that new methods were needed to combat the strength of the ministry, and he recognized in the press which published the *North*

Briton the means by which opposition might express itself.[55] He could hardly avoid it when Wilkes wrote, "It is generally believed, that every person *brought in* by the Duke of Newcastle, is now . . . to be *turned out*—except the King."[56] Completely humiliated in parliament, the press spontaneously reflecting a declining public interest in the peace,[57] there was little else to choose.

With the definitive peace, Bute released his chief writers, Smollett and Murphy. The *Auditor* expired February 8, the *Briton* two days later. Their usefulness was over, but they left the field while their opponent was still active. Murphy retired to his place and pension, but Smollett, sick in mind and body, fled from England and from "a scene of illiberal dispute . . . where a few worthless incendiaries had, by dint of perfidious calumnies and atrocious abuse, kindled up a flame which threatened all the horrors of civil dissension."[58] To the less sensitive soul of George III, the situation appeared far less threatening. The "machinations of faction" had been frustrated, and the hour for which he and Bute had long waited was at hand, a time "when men see no other resource" than the crown and "rather than be driven out" would join in "a reformation in Government."[59]

While Newcastle's followers cried for vengeance, they were slow in gaining Pitt to their side, and not until the debates on the cider bill in March was even an approximate concert of interests established.[60] Yet the weakness of opposition in parliament might never have been guessed from the pungent paragraphs of the *North Briton*. Walpole remarked at the time that "no citadel was ever taken by popguns," but he later realized that the seeds sown in this period took deep root.[61]

The significance of Walpole's post facto judgment was shown when Wilkes published a supposititious letter from the Pretender, February 19, as the thirty-eighth number of the *North Briton*. A brilliant satire, this issue promptly attracted the attention of the government. George III took a personal interest in the report of the solicitor-general that No. 38 was actionable and informed Bute that he hoped prosecution would be undertaken.[62] No action was taken, however. On April 18, Hardwicke wrote to his son Charles Yorke, the attorney-general, and pressed upon him the desirability of calling upon Lord Bath to give him an account "of what passed between you and the Solicitor Gen[eral] about prosecuting the *North-Briton* for the Letter from the Pretender."[63] From the king's letter to Bute it appears that the solicitor-general, Sir Fletcher Norton, strongly supported a prosecution; Hard-

wicke's letter suggests that a difference of opinion arose between
Norton and the attorney-general, and Yorke may have been directly
responsible for stifling the proceedings at an early stage. There was
something about his action which Hardwicke later felt needed explanation, and if Yorke so acted in February, it would explain in part his
embarrassment over the attack upon No. 45 in April. This was the
first of many instances in which the political alignment of the House
of Yorke—the father Newcastle's closest friend, the son dependent upon
crown support for future honors in his profession—came into conflict
with the press in politics.[64] The Woolsack, which Hardwicke once
occupied as Lord Chancellor, was the goal set by him for Charles
Yorke. Occupancy depended upon both crown and ministry. The
former might be presumed to favor Yorke's advancement in light of
his retention of office in opposition to those bonds of friendship and
interest with which Newcastle had sought vainly to bring about his
resignation.[65] George had, in fact, designated Yorke as the next lord
chancellor in August, 1762, and there was but one possible rival, Pitt's
protégé Charles Pratt, who had risen to the chief justiceship of the
Common Pleas and would be Pitt's candidate for the Woolsack should
he return to power. By the end of February it was apparent that Pitt
and Newcastle were approaching a common opposition. If Bute fell
and Pitt entered a new coalition ministry, he would, in all probability,
demand Pratt's advancement; particularly would this be true if Yorke
headed the prosecution of the paper which had most consistently and
daringly upheld Pitt throughout the recent months. It behooved Hardwicke to mend his fences, and he did so early in the year.[66] If in regard
to *North Briton* No. 38 Yorke sought his father's advice as he did in
the case of No. 45, that advice might well have been to avoid any action
until the shifting political stage was better illuminated. Yorke would
have followed Hardwicke's instructions, and Wilkes, consequently, escaped prosecution.[67] As Devonshire sagely predicted, "Perhaps when
[the Yorkes] find out that Mr. Pitt etc. are coming to a right understanding with us, they may . . . be more disposed to take a proper
part."[68]

While the opposition was slowly forming, Wilkes continued to
attack the most vulnerable points in Bute's armor; the resurrection of
Tories, Henry Fox's millions, abuse of the financial administration—
each served in turn as targets for Wilkes's steel. Walpole declared late
in March, "The saddest dog of all, Wilkes, shows most spirit. The last

North Briton is a masterpiece of mischief."[69] This issue, No. 42, dealt with a new loan of £3,500,000 which was let out with a fine eye to political considerations. Wilkes's disclosure of the profits of the subscribers, whom he named, almost embroiled him in further legal troubles. Peregrine Cust, one of the merchant profiteers, employed Sir Fletcher Norton to move the Court of King's Bench against the printer, George Kearsley. Norton cheerfully undertook the task; preliminary steps were taken on April 20 against the printers and publishers of the *North Briton* of March 19,[70] " 'but the ridicule attending it soon stop'd all the proceedings. Mr. Wilkes however was at the expense of feeing Councel to defend the Printer.' "[71] It was difficult for Cust to claim damages when he had just pocketed £20,000 on the negotiation!

The furor raised in parliament and the western counties by a tax on cider seemed to foreshadow a crisis in the first days of April. Walpole overstated the case as usual when he wrote, "If Mr Wilkes will turn patriot-hero, or patriot-incendiary in earnest, and put himself at their head, he may obtain a rope of martyrdom before the summer is over,"[72] but the increasing strength of the opposition lent courage to the publishers of the *North Briton*. Although private affairs took Wilkes to France on March 27, No. 44 was already set up, and on April 2 it admonished the government in terms that ominously foreshadowed coming events: "the liberty of communicating our sentiments to the public freely and honestly, shall not be tamely given up. . . ." Nor shall it be forcibly seized by courtiers who "if they know their own interest . . . will not attempt it."

> Inclination there is, no doubt, to silence the *North Briton*, but a consciousness of guilt prevents its being carried into execution; and however they may deal out large promises, and thunder forth empty threats, that impudent libeller, as they are pleased to call, but cannot, or dare not prove him, shall still pursue the path in which he hath hitherto trod. . . .[73]

No ministry could ignore such a challenge and hope to retain any semblance of public respect. Wilkes may have guessed, but could not know, that Bute had determined to withdraw from his exposed position. Although Fox knew as early as March 11 that the Thane was prepared to resign his staff, the secret was kept remarkably well. Bute was physically ill, mentally harassed, and aware that his continuance in office was a disservice to the king, for the abuse cast upon the min-

ister inevitably splashed his master. Unable to secure either Fox or
Pitt in active cooperation, he turned to George Grenville, who agreed
to fill the gap. On April 8, 1763, the Earl of Bute resigned. As Grenville
drew the lines of his cabinet, Walpole wrote, "There are many ifs in
this arrangement; the principal if is, if they dare stand a tempest which
has so terrified the pilot."[74] That the new ministry was Bute's, despite
his absence, few doubted as yet—the earl included.[75] That it was an
intended stopgap all admitted. No one seems to have known George
Grenville, a man who dared anything he believed right, and believed
himself always right.

North Briton No. 45 was not published April 9; Wilkes reached
London on the eleventh, and finding that uncertainty prevailed, he
announced in a handbill, published two days later and widely reprinted, that "in the present unsettled and fluctuating state of the
administration, he [was] really fearful of falling into involuntary
errors." If, however, the new triumvirate of Grenville, Egremont, and
Halifax was but "the Scot" in another form, a triple-headed Cerberus,
then the *North Briton* was ready as ever to assert "the rights of his
fellow-subjects, and . . . the liberties of WHIGS AND ENGLISHMEN."

Another Saturday passed without indication of the complexion of
the new administration, but on April 19, the king's speech from the
throne, closing the session, displayed the colors of Bute and Grenville
flying together. According to John Almon, Temple secured a copy of
the speech on the eighteenth, and that evening, while Pitt and Temple
were discussing its contents, Wilkes called upon the earl, learned the
tenor of the speech, and thereupon set out to write the *North Briton's*
reply.[76] The words were Wilkes's, the spirit that of Pitt, and Temple
must have approved the condemnation of his brother. In general the
paper which Wilkes drew up differed little from earlier *North Britons*
except that it struck directly at the seat of power: "The *King's Speech*
has always been considered . . . as the *Speech of the Minister,* [but]
every friend of his country must lament that a prince . . . can be
brought to give the sanction of his sacred name to the most odious
measures, and to the most unjustifiable, public declarations, from a
throne ever renowned for truth, honour, and unsullied virtue." The
King of England is "responsible to his people for the due execution of
the royal functions" and his prerogative is not to be exerted with
"blind favour and partiality. . . . The people too have their prerogative, and . . . Freedom *is the English subject's* Prerogative."[77]

"Nothing could be more just than the satire," observed Horace Walpole, "nothing more bold than the unmeasured liberty with which it was uttered."[78] When asked in France how far the liberty of the press extended in England, Wilkes had replied, " 'I cannot tell, but I am trying to know.' "[79] The *North Briton* published April 23 bore the number *45*.

CHAPTER III

The General Warrant in Politics

THE REIGN of George III had been marked by few cases of legal prosecution of the press prior to 1763, and those, with the exceptions already mentioned, had been based upon religious or moral objections to the matter printed. Bute had been lavish in the construction of his press, but he had not drawn upon the resources of the law to destroy his opponents' system, and threats only encouraged Wilkes and Temple. Silencing the *Monitor* simply concentrated the *North Briton*'s venom. Yet the scourge which Bute so long endured did not enjoy universal approbation. Murmurs of dissatisfaction with the license of the press were often heard. William Warburton, Bishop of Gloucester, declared in July, 1762, that "the licentiousness of party scribblers is the greatest dishonour a learned nation can suffer. I leave it to our superiors to prevent or punish the civil mischief they occasion," and by April, 1763, a moderate man might ask, "Are the people . . . all gone mad? I never read such shocking stuff in my life as the political papers . . . ; they are even a disgrace to Grub Street, and nothing can exceed the folly of losing time in their perusal but the wickedness of writing them."[1]

If ministerial weakness was a reflection of Bute's personality, vigorous action might be expected under his successor, George Grenville. Not only was the administration's honor at stake, the *North Briton* was extending its influence to the country at large. A friend of the ministry, facing a by-election in April, 1763, cried for governmental support in the face of an opposition

> carried on with great violence and open bribery. Ribbons with Liberty, Property, no Excise are the ornaments of my opponents. . . . Guineas and scraps of North Britons are scattered all over the town and I can assure you that the opposition is founded by that ingenious gentleman Mr. Wilkes and his crew and is more immediately at Government than me.[2]

The situation demanded action on the part of ministers, and they responded readily. *North Briton* No. 45 was published on Saturday,

April 23; the next day Edward Weston, under-secretary of state, brought it to the attention of his superior, the Earl of Halifax, who immediately replied, "I had read the North Briton before I received Your Letter, and formed the Same Opinion of it which you have done. I would by all Means have it referred to the Attorney & Solicitor generals for their Opinion."[3] This step was taken on Monday, April 25, and on Tuesday, Halifax signed a general warrant directing Carrington and three other messengers, John Money, James Watson and Robert Blackmore, "to make strict & diligent Search for the Authors, Printers & Publishers of a Seditious, & Treasonable Paper intitled, The North Briton, Number 45, . . . printed for G. Kearsley . . . , to apprehend & seize [them] together with Their Papers."[4] It has long been maintained that George III personally instigated the action against Wilkes, but the initial step was taken by Halifax in accordance with the regular procedures of his office.*[5]

Ministers delayed further action until they received the attorney and solicitor-general's report on the legal aspects of the case. Although the general warrant which Halifax had signed was based upon long usage in the secretary's office, he was aware of the dangers involved. The name of the author of the *North Briton* was an open secret, but John Wilkes was a member of parliament, and breach of parliamentary privilege might have serious repercussions.

The law officers reported on April 27 that the paper was libelous and punishable as a misdemeanor by "due course of law." At the same time Charles Yorke submitted an opinion on the question of privilege which was sure to arise if Wilkes were arrested. He declared in effect that the plea of privilege did not apply to cases of treason, felony, or breach of the peace.[6]

As the warrant already included the word "treasonable," Halifax felt free to proceed. The messengers received the warrant and their instructions on Thursday, April 28, but the incapacity of the senior messenger, Carrington, delayed action until Friday morning.[7] In the

*Most authors follow Lecky (*History of England*, III, 244), who placed the initiative with the king, but Lecky's sole contemporary authority, Grafton's "Journal," does not support his conclusions. Nobbe (*North Briton*, p. 213) takes the same position and cites Grenville's complaint that the king had sacrificed his servants in the Wilkes affair, "though acting by His Majesty's commands." As Grenville obviously refers to events *subsequent* to Wilkes's arrest, royal intervention is still not demonstrable prior to April 30, when Egremont informed the king of the preceding day's occurrences.

early hours of April 29, the arrests began. A wholesale collection of printers, together with their journeymen and their papers, was carried out; by evening forty-eight arrests had been made. George Kearsley, examined at about four o'clock, implicated Wilkes and Churchill, and named Balfe as their printer. Balfe, who was shortly apprehended, declared that No. 45 was delivered to him by Wilkes and that the manuscript was in Wilkes's handwriting. None of this information was given under oath, but the secretaries felt that it offered sufficient grounds upon which to arrest Wilkes as the author of the *North Briton*. Once more the law officers were consulted. They reported that Wilkes's arrest would be legal notwithstanding his privilege, and at midnight the messengers were verbally instructed to seize him. Grenville had suggested confining Wilkes in Newgate, but after spending the evening at the home of the messenger Robert Blackmore, in conference with Dryden Leach, the first of the printers arrested, Wilkes disappeared and was not to be found until the next day.[8]

Blackmore met Wilkes returning to his house in Great George Street, early Saturday morning. After a brief exchange Wilkes indicated that he would not submit to arrest, and Blackmore satisfied himself by accompanying Wilkes homeward and sending for reinforcements. Within a couple of hours other officers arrived in Great George Street and Wilkes was surrounded by a veritable bodyguard. The activity of the preceding day had warned Temple and his friends what to expect on Saturday. John Almon called on Wilkes around nine o'clock, and quickly learned of his plight. At Wilkes's request, Almon hastened to inform Temple of the arrest. Temple promptly dispatched Almon to Arthur Beardmore with instructions to secure a writ of habeas corpus and himself hurried to the scene of action. Ironically, Charles Churchill also called on Wilkes that morning, but being warned of his imminent danger, the poet fled from the house and the city with the greatest alacrity.[9]

While Wilkes was baiting the arresting officers into carrying him the four doors to Halifax's house, where the secretaries were sitting, his friends were moving the Court of Common Pleas for the desired writ of habeas corpus. Chief Justice Pratt promptly granted the writ, but an accidental delay in drawing it up allowed Wilkes to achieve the laurels of martyrdom. Despite knowledge that the writ had been granted—or because of it, as Wilkes's supporters claimed—the secretaries drew up a new warrant committing their prisoner to the Tower—

and there John Wilkes spent the weekend.[10] While the ministry collected Wilkes's private papers, the complications of politics began to assert themselves.

No one was more concerned by the events of April 30 than the Earl of Hardwicke, even though he played no official part in the action against Wilkes. Charles Yorke was the link between the earl and the ministry. Before Wilkes was arrested, the secretaries inquired specifically of the attorney-general if libel was a breach of the peace and consequently not subject to privilege. Yorke drew up an affirmative opinion and Philip Carteret Webb carried it to Hardwicke for his approval.[11] The old earl felt that "the point of privilege is always delicate; and therefore, we used to avoid giving opinions in writing." He urged Webb to return the document to Yorke and, without mentioning his name, to suggest that the secretaries consult the speaker of the House of Commons.[12] In spite of Hardwicke's advice, Webb transmitted the written opinion to the secretaries, and Wilkes was consequently apprehended. Later in the day Hardwicke was informed of the wording of the warrant, and with evident relief he wrote to the attorney-general, "I see now the reason of insisting so much on that word [treasonable], which I suppose was to take it clearly out of the case of *privilege,* which certainly cannot extend to *treason.*"[13]

Convinced that his son's position was impregnable, Hardwicke turned to Newcastle, to whom he wrote a calming epistle which ignored his own part in the affair and questioned the forwardness of Temple. The duke was flustered. He agreed with Hardwicke that No. 45 was "wrote with very little consideration or caution," but he was more influenced by public manifestations: "the city and suburbs are in the utmost alarm at these proceedings, which they call illegal and oppressive." He found Lord Temple "very full of taking the strongest part," and his reply to Hardwicke closed typically, "For God's sake turn these things in your thoughts and consider what it may be right to do." The elder Yorke replied the same day, cautioning Newcastle "not to suffer yourself to be too much possessed and warmed by the discourse of the zealous young gentlemen," and assuring him of the rectitude of governmental procedure, Chief Justice Pratt notwithstanding. "All I mean," he summed up, "is that we should not too hastily make *cause commune* with Mr. W[ilkes]."[14]

Proximity to John Wilkes was even less desirable in the eyes of George III. Egremont informed the king of the progress of events on

Saturday evening. During their interview the king intimated his intention of having Wilkes removed from his militia command. The suggestion was enthusiastically received by the secretary of state, who only wished to defer acting upon it until Wilkes's papers might be examined. He hoped thereby to incriminate Temple, so that his "demission" might accompany that of his penman. The king promptly notified Bute of all that had passed and asked his advice concerning Temple. Bute suggested that Temple be forbidden the right to appear at court.[15]

One act of pacification was undertaken by the ministry. Warned by Hardwicke of the dangers of falling afoul the House of Commons, Edward Weston visited Sir John Cust, the speaker, and explained that Wilkes had been committed to the Tower for "a Breach of the Peace, to which Privilege of Parliament does not extend." Cust was given to understand that his Majesty would bring the matter to the attention of the House when it next convened.[16] Grenville kept that promise with vengeful exactitude.

The two days which John Wilkes passed under close confinement in the Tower of London sufficed to make him a martyr and raised a new wave of criticism against his tormentors. Throughout the first week of May as Wilkes's case was laid before the public and awaited judgment in the Court of Common Pleas, numerous prints, broadsides, and verses were scrutinized by the law officers and found actionable.[17]

The setting of the next scene of the drama was most unusual. Application to Pratt, the friend of Temple and Pitt, was quite logical, but application for a writ of habeas corpus in the Court of Common Pleas was unique. " 'Such a writ has not been moved in that court since the reign of Charles II,' " declared one observer.[18] The decision to defend Wilkes in Common Pleas was based upon the reasonable assumption that Pratt would be far more kindly disposed toward Pitt's propagandist than would Chief Justice Mansfield in the Court of King's Bench, where the case would normally have appeared. The great Scottish law-lord had not yet won infamy as the persecutor of the press and pressmen, but his nationality alone would preclude him from friendship toward Wilkes.

The case, which was heard between mid-morning and mid-afternoon on May 3, raised Pratt to the Woolsack and Wilkes to the first step of the Lord Mayor's carriage. John Glynn spoke for Wilkes, and in the absence of either the attorney or solicitor-general, the crown was represented by four serjeants-at-law. Glynn opened by moving the court for

Wilkes's immediate discharge without bail on grounds that he had been arrested on unsupported evidence, that the warrant was too general, and more particularly that libels might tend toward a breach of the peace but were not such in themselves—consequently Wilkes might plead his privilege as a member of parliament. Serjeant Hewitt replied to Glynn's first points with ease, but forced to admit Wilkes's membership in the House of Commons, he could not bring himself to declare that libel was a breach of peace or that Wilkes's arrest was not a breach of privilege. As the attorney-general commented, "This point of privilege ... [was] spoke to without learning on either side."[19]

The pleading was dull, and Wilkes did little to enliven it when he spoke in his own cause. His remarks were directed against the ministers—a favorite topic—but only his concluding remark showed a spark of that defiance and humor mixed with platitude which filled the *North Briton.* "Their bribes I rejected, their menaces I defy," he said; "and I think this is the most fortunate event of my life, when I appear before your lordship and this court, where innocence is sure of protection, and liberty can never want friends or guardians."[20] As the prisoner was conducted back to the Tower—the court being desirous of a few days to consider the case—the hall was filled with cheers and shouts until, said Charles Yorke, "you would have thought the Seven Bishops had been acquitted."[21]

While Pratt pondered and Wilkes waited for Friday and the chief justice's decision, the heads of faction were considering Wilkes as a pawn in the game of politics. Temple had played his part well; he had done everything possible to aid Wilkes and had secured the support of a number of others, among them the young Duke of Grafton. They had been witnesses to Wilkes's close imprisonment, and Wilkes looked to both for support should he be called upon to offer bail. Grafton, however, drew the line at moral support and excused himself to Temple. The earl recognized the man who would not support a cause for fear of "the shadow of offence" against the king, as a potential enemy, and his reply was a masterpiece of frigid politeness.[22] The difficulty of separating the individual from the issues he came to represent had far-reaching consequences. Wilkes himself preferred a fusion of identity; his personal success well-nigh defeated the movement which he came to head.

On Friday morning, May 6, Wilkes was brought to the Court of Common Pleas to hear the chief justice's decision in his case. Pratt delivered his opinion at about ten o'clock. He threw out the first two objections which Glynn had raised, but the plea of privilege he upheld. "We are all of opinion that libel is not a breach of the peace, and that is the utmost. . . . Mr. Wilkes must be discharged from his imprisonment."[23] Wilkes thanked the court and his counsel and, as he turned to leave, bowed low to the audience crowding the hall. An explosive roar of cheers and applause greeted him. His auditors, stirred up by handbills circulated industriously about the courtroom, accompanied Wilkes to his home, and celebrated the occasion well into the night. England had found her patriot.[24]

A taste of the Tower had whetted Wilkes's appetite. No sooner had he arrived in Great George Street, than he sent to the secretaries of state demanding the return of his sequestered papers—"stolen goods"— which he believed their lordships to possess. Egremont and Halifax no less promptly reminded Wilkes that he was still charged with being the author of a seditious libel and that "his Majesty had ordered you to be prosecuted by his attorney-general." The secretaries may have spoken truthfully in representing the royal wish to continue prosecution, but it appears that no official action was taken until May 9, when Halifax ordered the attorney-general to proceed by information to the case of Wilkes and Kearsley as author and publisher of No. 45. Scarcely rebuffed by the threat of prosecution, Wilkes called the secretaries' letter "Billingsgate," thereby scoring a very palpable hit. Halifax, irate at such treatment, inquired of the law officers as to the actionable character of Wilkes's first letter, which he personally found "very abusive" toward secretaries, privy councilors, and peers of the realm in general.[25]

Yorke preferred to leave Wilkes to the tender mercies of Hogarth, whose satirical print of Wilkes, the Champion of Liberty, ran through its first printing of 4,000 so rapidly that the printer was forced to work his presses day and night.[26] Solicitor-general Norton reported, May 11, that the granting of an information against Wilkes in the King's Bench would only raise the question of privilege once more. Nevertheless, against the advice of the law officers, a new prosecution was begun. Wilkes stood upon his privilege; Yorke refused to precipitate matters by forcing his attendance, and the case dragged on until political events intervened.[27]

Pratt's decision pleased many, but it failed to convince Hardwicke: "After having been Attorney-General ten years, Chief Justice between three and four years, and Chancellor almost twenty, I shall not now contradict all the principles, and all the rules of law and order, which I have been maintaining all my life." The whole affair gave cause for "very serious reflexions," and when Egremont called on him, May 13, he found the secretary "very sore" on the subject of Wilkes, and "his Master . . . extremely hurt and provoked with it." The effort to bring Hardwicke and Newcastle into the court ranks was unsuccessful, however, and the earl shortly retired to the country, where, he wrote his son, "one of my greatest pleasures . . . is being free from the noise and eternal talk about Mr. Wilkes."[28]

Just as Hardwicke had reminded Newcastle that in his day the duke had issued warrants similar to that under which Wilkes was arrested, so Pitt realized his own complicity and made queries. To solve his doubts he turned to Pratt. The point in issue was the legality of the warrant—a point which had not entered largely in the hearings of May 3 and 6, but which lay dormant in the process by which Wilkes had been apprehended. The chief justice pointed out to Pitt that the warrant was not defensible, particularly in regard to the seizure of papers. Only in the instance of stolen goods was search and seizure admissible; in certain cases forcible entry might be allowed, but the officer could apprehend nothing but the person. Recently, said Pratt, general warrants had been issued against printers whose papers provided evidence of their guilt, " 'but only now and then upon extraordinary occasions.' " The practice lacked the force of immemorial custom, however, and secretaries of state possessed no authority beyond that of a common magistrate. Finally, Pratt warned, reason of state was insufficient cause for overriding the law and past actions ought " 'never be too much scanned or defined.' "[29] It is to Pitt's credit that, knowing his vulnerability, he adopted Pratt's arguments wholeheartedly; at the same time, the popularity of the stand taken by Pitt and the chief justice was sufficient insurance against any possible retroactive condemnation.

Similar advice was given to the Earl of Shelburne, possibly by John Glynn, and provided one more thread to eventually bind that young nobleman to Pitt. Although a member of the administration, Shelburne's loyalty lay with Bute rather than Grenville, and he was already at odds with the secretaries of state upon colonial matters.[30] Before the year was out he would embark upon that tortuous political course which won him the distrust of every faction and party except his own.

Throughout the summer of 1763, the question posed by John Wilkes lay unhappily between the two major opposition groups: that headed by Pitt and Temple, and the bevy of great lords who associated themselves with Newcastle. The dividing line between them was one of law—on one side stood Charles Pratt, on the other Charles Yorke. Behind the champions filed the politicians, ahead for one of them, lay the chancellorship. For Grenville's ministry this division was opportune; it assured the political isolation of Pitt and cost ministers no effort, for Wilkes and Temple sustained the fires of legal action which kept the issue at white heat.

Following Egremont's initial overtures to Newcastle and Hardwicke in May, a serious effort was made to establish a working union between the Pittites and the Whig lords. Charles Yorke's hesitancy in prosecuting Wilkes in the Court of King's Bench provided a possible opening, and both Pitt and Temple seemed conciliatory. The earl represented to Newcastle that his brother-in-law was "highly pleased with the House of York," and Newcastle, acting on the hint, urged that Hardwicke move his son to visit Pitt's estate at Hayes. The interview was arranged for June 7. The preceding day, Temple called upon Newcastle at Claremont and dwelt at great length upon the possibilities of union. He was, the duke advised Charles Yorke, "enthusiastic as you know about Wilkes, but that will signify nothing." More important was Temple's expression of his and Pitt's friendship for Yorke, a friendship which might be combined with "their good dispositions to my Lord Chief Justice Pratt." Newcastle was convinced by his guest that "what related to the Attorney General was *their first object*." Admitting that nothing could be done without Pitt, the duke entreated Yorke to open his heart to the Great Commoner: "his vanity will be flattered, and give him his due he is incapable of making an ill use of it."[31]

Perhaps Newcastle judged Pitt rightly, but it is evident that Temple presented an overly optimistic picture of things at Hayes. The Duke of Devonshire warned Yorke of just such a contingency on the morning of his visit: Pitt "did not intimate in the least to me, as if any bargain or agreement was to be made between you and my Lord Chief Justice Pratt" in the event of the Great Seal falling vacant, but only accommodation for the disappointed party.[32]

At Hayes, Yorke found a loquacious Pitt full of Revolution principles, the Whig party, and consideration for the Tories and country gentlemen. His charm won the attorney-general's favor, as did his deprecation of the problem of the Great Seal. It had been placed before Yorke's eyes, and he supposed it was an object at court. Should he have any influence there, and the king be so inclined, "it would have his approbation." His friendship for Pratt made him wish that the chief justice might appear to acquiesce and approve. This "would be of great utility to the public [and] would discourage those at Court from setting up one against the other." If Yorke would trust him, "he believed that he could bring the matter to bear." Pitt "shadowed out by way of compliment" that the attorney-general might be fitter for such high office than Pratt and blinded the younger man to his repeated reservations in Pratt's favor. "All he wished was, that when the event should happen, it might be . . . [adjusted to] the satisfaction of my Lord Ch[ief] J[ustice]."

In all of this Yorke readily concurred and assured Pitt that his ties to Newcastle were stronger than those with the court. He had only the highest regard for Pratt, and felt sure that Pitt could "make his friend do right." As to the Wilkes affair, that was "a very unfortunate event, which gave some advantage to the enemy, and produced disagreeable consequences." Pitt "interposed very decently" to explain that he had not touched upon the subject out of respect to Yorke's official connection with it. Yorke then pointed out that he had raised the matter only because of the possible political consequences. Sensing the turn of the conversation, Pitt quickly shifted the emphasis. A great noise had been made about Temple's relations with Wilkes, and what did it amount to? Wilkes was simply "a Buckinghamshire neighbour, an old acquaintance, in distress!" There was something to be said on both sides.[33]

It is almost incomprehensible that the attorney-general should be taken in by such a misrepresentation of fact, yet he seems to have accepted Pitt's obvious falsehoods at their face value and returned to London in high spirits. Hardwicke called upon his son the next day to learn what passed at Hayes. The old earl was less easily deceived. Writing to Newcastle he remarked, "It may be all very sincere; but I own it smells a little of that holy water, which great men are apt to sprinkle when they have a mind to baptize others into their political faith." Pitt's observations simply confirmed his own opinion of the dangers lying ahead. The chasm between the two factions was deep, and if Temple, having cooled a little, talked more calmly, neither he nor his relation was blind to political reality. Without Newcastle and his friends, they would be left naked and unsupported. Hardwicke reminded Newcastle of the low character of Temple's followers: "These are fellows who would have hanged your grace and me a few years ago, and would do so still, had they the power."

"Indeed, my dear Lord, I cannot help looking upon this affair of Wilkes as big with very mischievous consequences," and those with regard not to Wilkes, but to the part Pitt might take. Rockingham had recently visited Pitt and the master of Hayes had made his position quite clear. Wilkes was entitled to privilege, and No. 45 was no libel; to hold it so would be to infringe in a high degree upon the liberty of the press to censure ministers. Pitt would leave to a jury the determination of whether the *North Briton* was or was not a libel.

These were Pitt's own declarations—of far more weight than "all my Lord Temple's loose and vague professions of thorough union etc." Hardwicke foresaw (and with perfect accuracy) that Pitt would "set himself up as a premptory judge of constitutional law" as he had in 1758 when he declared, *"Lawyers are not to be regarded in questions of liberty."* "I did not give way to him then," said Hardwicke, "nor will I do so now. . . ."

> In political points I can show a deference for his opinion; but I will never act so mean a part as to give up all my knowledge and experience in the law, and all the principles about the legal prerogative of the Crown and public order and good government, which I have been endeavouring to support all my life, in complaisance to any man.[34]

Charles Yorke's family ties and political relations were scarcely less embarrassing to the government. Having failed to punish Wilkes through the courts, Grenville determined upon expelling him from the House of Commons and naturally turned to the attorney-general for legal advice. The project was known to Pitt and Newcastle by the first of June and was denounced by both. Hardwicke warned his old friend that such action could be carried out by the House, but assured him that no rumors of such a step had reached his ears. Consequently, while Newcastle rejoiced at the coming union of the house of Yorke with Pitt and Temple, the attorney-general was declaring to Grenville that he would "examine the properest modes of proceeding" to the expulsion of John Wilkes. In the course of their discussion, however, Yorke indicated quite plainly that his own position was subject to change; ". . . in the present perplex'd state of affairs it was impossible to say what any man might from habitudes be forced to."[35]

As July passed into August, a clarification of political alignment seemed imminent. The king was dissatisfied with Grenville, and Bute was ready to help his master probe the possibilities of change. By the first of August, ministers felt themselves not only deprived of the "support and confidence" necessary to carry on government, but personally insulted by the king. At the royal command, Egremont approached Hardwicke once more; he offered to accommodate Newcastle, but Hardwicke refused to speak for his friend or consider anything for himself unless the door were opened to Newcastle's new "connexions," Pitt and Temple. No greater success attended the efforts of Shelburne to secure the Duke of Bedford, and Pitt alone remained untried.[36] If he remained firm in conjunction with Newcastle, the king would be left no choice but to return to Grenville or lose every victory gained in the past three years.

Pitt was aware of his advantageous position; his hauteur and his demands rose accordingly. Newcastle, in two very long conferences with Pitt, soon got to the heart of the problem: "it all centred in the conduct of the Yorke family, [and] my Lord Chief Justice Pratt's opinion with relation to the point of privilege." Pitt spoke of "Whiggism, the Constitution and the liberty of the subject." He knew what liberty was, and the liberty of the press was essentially concerned in this question. True, he disapproved of the *North Briton,* but when parliamentary privilege was denied in order to stifle the expression of opinion, "the liberty of the press was taken away." He would uphold Pratt's opinion, and would never act with anyone who opposed it. Those who would "humour the Court and . . . extend the power of the Crown to the diminution of the liberty of the subject, he should never call Whigs."

Before Newcastle, Pitt held a far different opinion of the merits of Pratt and Yorke than he had to the attorney-general. Pratt was "the first and ablest man" at bench or bar, "he was the man for the support of the law and the Constitution, and if . . . [Pitt] could prevent it . . . Pratt should never be run down." The attorney-general had received his overtures "so coldly and in such a manner," complained Pitt, that he had "returned to his old friendship and predilection for . . . Pratt, and must, if the case ever existed, give him the preference to the Attorney-General."

The duke was taken aback—as well he might be. "Nothing could be so strong or so violent upon this whole affair as Mr. Pitt was. I

lamented it extremely and did all I could to bring him back to his own
former position of accommodating the affair between them, but to no
purpose." Failing in this, Newcastle pointed out to Pitt that the Great
Seal was not at the moment in question. "Our business was to form
such a plan of administration as should be most for His Majesty's
service." Pitt was adamant, and Newcastle could only express his
candid preference for Yorke.

That subject exhausted, Pitt launched forth upon "his own grievances and his apprehensions of playing a solo with my Lord Temple."
Nothing could have been more typical of Pitt or more sharply illuminated his great weakness than the words which Newcastle recorded:

> If I am so necessary, as you all tell me I am, why should there be
> any difficulty in giving me proper support in the formation of the
> ministry and council? If I am in this desperate situation to answer
> for everything, is it unnatural in me to desire, that the Great Seal
> may be put into the hands of a friend of mine?[37]

The interview closed on a more cheerful note, but the truth had at
last appeared. Compromise, understanding, union—these were not
Pitt's words. In one flash of supreme egotism he could lay bare his own
power and his opponent's weakness, never aware that the flaws in his
own armor were thereby exposed—never aware that in maintaining his
own purity he destroyed the very object of his desires. In his sweeping
generalizations concerning law, privilege, and liberty, Pitt exposed the
touchstone of the problem. Great enough to be aware of the interrela-
tionship between the press, parliament, and the people, he was not
small enough to grasp the separate parts and place them in their
proper order. His inability to do so would plague the English press in
politics for a decade and block nearly every effort to revise common
and constitutional press law.

Charles Yorke was rightfully hurt when he heard of Pitt's *volte
face,* but a night's meditations and Newcastle's sage advice calmed him
and brought to mind those details of his own discussion with Pitt
which he had hitherto overlooked. To Newcastle he now openly—and
for the first time—declared his political allegiance. He had retained
office only to smooth the way for the return of his friends; if that
proved impossible in the present juncture, "he knew what his honour
required of him." Newcastle had succeeded in strengthening the integrity of his own faction, but he realized fully that unless Pitt's fears and

suspicions could be dissuaded, "it is in vain to think of engaging Mr. Pitt to take an active, confidential part with us."[38]

Negotiations toward a change of government had been carried on deliberately through the middle of August. On the twenty-first Egremont died, and a crisis was precipitated. Grenville and Halifax informed the king that he must in some way strengthen his present ministers or "throw the Government entirely into the hands of Mr. Pitt. . . . The King said the last was what he never could consent to." By the end of the week Pitt and Bute met in London; George announced that he intended to call in Pitt, and when Grenville came to court, Saturday the twenty-seventh, he found Pitt closeted with the king. Pitt outlined the ministry he wished to establish: Temple at the Treasury, Newcastle as Privy Seal, Hardwicke as Lord President, the Duke of Devonshire to be Chamberlain. Pratt should receive a peerage and be brought into the cabinet; nothing was said concerning Yorke. Both Pitt and Newcastle believed the change to be assured, but at the last moment the project collapsed. Newcastle had succeeded in binding Pitt to him, and Pitt had presented to the king a ministry as strong and of the same complexion as that which he had led at the outset of the reign. Although Pitt excluded only those most closely associated with the Peace of Paris, his proposals left Bute totally unprotected within the cabinet. According to Grenville, when Bute was made to realize the possible consequences of the step he had advised, the earl reconsidered and advised George to recall his present ministers. On Monday the king found Pitt unchanged in his determination and dismissed him, saying, "Well, Mr. Pitt, I see this won't do. My honour is concerned, and I must support it." Thus ended a negotiation which might have established a ministry capable of turning the course of English history from the path it followed for the next quarter-century.[39]

During the critical weekend of August 27–29, the problems raised between Newcastle and Pitt by their favorite lawyers were suppressed in a most commendable manner. Pitt's request of a peerage for the chief justice was reasonable and in keeping with his earlier declarations. Both Newcastle and Hardwicke foresaw it, but by pointing out that they must have Pitt if they hoped to succeed, Newcastle was able to win the earl's support. Hardwicke hurried up to London in anticipation of a change, only stopping to send before him a hearty wish for success and satisfaction for his friends.[40]

Grenville took advantage of the king's failure to form a new ministry to rid himself of the traitor Shelburne and to secure the royal promise that Bute would no longer interfere. To his aid he called the Duke of Bedford, whose follower, the Earl of Sandwich, became secretary of state. These allies brought the ministry little strength and, in light of Sandwich's character, little honor. Newcastle and his friends might yet hope to overthrow Grenville in the near future.[41]

All depended upon Pitt's willingness to cooperate in a vigorous opposition—but that he would not. Believing that "the Subversion of the administration was not to be brought about by Parliament; that nothing could be done in the House of Commons," Pitt "was ready to fight a series of duels, but was not prepared to carry on a campaign." The matter of "the law" did not come up between Newcastle and Pitt during September; the duke even hoped that it would disappear completely, for by October 1, Yorke had determined to resign. Hardwicke's mistrust of Pitt gave Newcastle momentary qualms, but early in October, Pitt was "more reasonable about the Attorney than he had been." At the same time the Great Commoner "exclaimed against Wilkes and the *North Briton*" with the most vehemence Newcastle had ever heard.[42] His Grace scarce expected the debacle which was preparing.

Pitt had, in the course of discussions with Newcastle and the Duke of Devonshire, expressed some dissatisfaction with the part Yorke was playing. To settle all doubts, the attorney-general called upon Pitt, October 12, intent upon giving full satisfaction to his critic. This he did, as far as his personal actions were concerned. On the point of privilege, which was sure to arise when parliament met, Yorke could only say that he would respectfully but firmly maintain the rectitude of his original opinion. Pitt promptly declared that the attorney-general was thereby excluded from among his political friends.

Newcastle learned this disheartening news from Yorke; Pitt did not soften it. Disclaiming any previous knowledge of the attorney-general's opinion on privilege, Pitt stated bluntly that "solid union upon real revolution principles and an assertion in earnest of the freedom of the Constitution [was a] vain dream." He blamed Yorke explicitly, for "how after all could a lingering on in a Court situation under a rash and odious ministry be brought to square with the public views of those, who openly resisted the dangerous power of it?" Under no conditions could Pitt be classified in the latter category, but he realized the significance of his own present actions. "The fatal consequences of this inevitable disunion are too obvious to admit of much observation." Yorke had delivered the fatal stroke, and Pitt despaired of doing "anything material for the public good"; he now relinquished all hope "of seeing Mr. Attorney-general upon one ground with me . . . in the notions of liberty and of the great landmarks of the Constitution."[43]

Newcastle could do little more than regret that "an amicable discussion and consideration of such points" could not reconcile these differences. No less than Pitt he saw the fatal consequences of disunion, but, he added, "I have done, and shall do, everything in my power to remove all obstacles which might create any coolness or difference amongst those, who alone . . . can save this country and this government . . . from contempt and insignificance." As Hardwicke observed, what Pitt meant by an understanding between Pratt and Yorke was that the latter should completely adopt the chief justice's opinion in regard to the point of privilege—"as if the differing in opinion upon a question of privilege of the House of Commons, never yet determined by that House itself . . . was of the essence of Magna Charta and . . . the Revolution." If, after giving his opinion to the king as his attorney-general, Yorke should concur in such a proposal, "he should be the last of men."[44]

Newcastle was sufficiently versed in politics to see that the schism might not be entirely disagreeable to either party. Yorke might well be maintaining his court contacts; the king had informed his attorney-general of Pitt's demand of a peerage for Pratt and had told Yorke that he should have a peerage whenever he left that office—if he would continue at present. In a moment of candor Pitt had admitted to the duke "that there was not a moment since the King came to the Crown when he would not have preferred my Lord Chief Justice Pratt to Mr. Yorke."[45]

The attorney-general did nothing to ease the situation. On October 21, he told Newcastle that he intended to resign shortly. Yorke apparently felt that this long-delayed step would blast his future hopes and blamed the duke for placing him in so difficult a position. He wished his determination to remain a secret, but it was badly kept. Newcastle promptly informed Devonshire of the conversation, and Grenville knew of Yorke's plans within a week. For the ministry, this was timely aid, coming as it did just prior to the opening of the session. Newcastle did his best to heal the wounds of both parties; he urged the necessity of union and agreement upon the Duke of Cumberland, who came to

London to consult with Pitt, and advised Cumberland that Yorke had determined to resign.[46]

Once more Pitt remained adamant. The Marquis of Rockingham informed Newcastle that Yorke's resignation had no effect upon Pitt, that he considered it immaterial. Pitt's determination to advance Pratt was the insurmountable bar to union. A meeting between Pitt and Charles Townshend ended explosively; as Townshend declared to Newcastle, Pitt "would do nothing, would concert with nobody, expected that everybody should follow him and his measures, without vouchsafing even to give his reason for his opinion." To Cumberland the Great Commoner gave "an absolute negative" to any suggestion of cooperation and informed his royal highness that he felt he had made an impression upon the king during their recent interview. Cumberland assured Pitt that, on the contrary, he was *the obnoxious man at Court.*" But to no avail. Pitt believed he would be sent for again, and so would not compromise his chances by a single step toward the old Whigs.[47]

The long-awaited resignation of Charles Yorke took place November 2, in the course of a lengthy and painful audience with the king. The attorney-general departed with tears and obvious reluctance. He entered the opposition camp with qualifications, for he insisted upon freedom to speak against the point of privilege. Efforts at reconciliation were continued throughout the week preceding the opening of parliament. Newcastle feebly attempted to pacify Yorke, while Rockingham sought a belated rapprochement with Pitt through Temple's mediation. The earl was highly pleased by Yorke's resignation, but nothing could move either side.[48] Pitt, determined to avoid a formed opposition upon principle, unwilling to support the person of John Wilkes, although he would fight for the principles involved, stood alone, unattached, and responsible to none. Newcastle and his friends found themselves entering the session without the spokesman they sorely needed, encumbered by a recent ally whose views they could only partially accept. The king and his ministers had reason to believe that all would go well and that the destruction of John Wilkes was at hand.

CHAPTER IV

The General Warrant in the Courts of Law:
The Cases Arising from North Briton No. 45

WHILE THE rival ambitions of Pratt and Yorke clashed on the stage of politics, other aspects of the problems arising from the arrest of John Wilkes were being debated in the courts of law. The decisions handed down in the cases initiated on behalf of the printers and publishers arrested under the general warrant of April 26, 1763, supported a new interpretation of the powers of government and of the liberty of the press based upon a growing realization of the power of public opinion as expressed by a jury of freeborn Englishmen. These developments did not originate in the summer of 1763, nor most certainly did they win complete acceptance at that time, but the transference of political authority from government and law to the people and the law may be dated from the cases revolving about *North Briton* No. 45.

Wilkes had urged the publishers of the *Monitor* to begin actions for false arrest when they were seized, and when he found himself in a comparable situation he acted upon his own advice. Here was not one but many clubs with which to belabor the government. As soon as Wilkes was released by the Court of Common Pleas, prosecutions against the king's messengers were begun in behalf of the various printers. Back of these men, who could hardly meet the expense of lengthy legal proceedings, stood Earl Temple. His was the "long purse" which contended against the public treasury and perhaps his the initiative in starting the series of actions that dragged on for two years. Almon correctly stated that "in this [Temple] was alone—even Mr. Pitt thought his spirit was too high." But it was Wilkes who profited most from every action and made certain that they "were prosecuted in such a manner, that the public attention to them was kept continually alive."[1]

The Patriot himself began actions against the secretaries of state, Robert Wood, and Philip Carteret Webb for his arrest and imprisonment and the seizure of his papers. Serjeant John Glynn he retained

59

as his counsel, along with Temple's agent Arthur Beardmore. By the middle of June, Wilkes advised the earl that "everything legal wears the most smiling aspect," and he was "charmed with the account Serjeant Glynn gave me of the state of the cause." On the sixteenth, eight special juries were requested to handle the prosecutions, and two days later, after a lengthy conference with his legal advisers, Wilkes exulted, "I believe that I shall experience all the douceurs of the law, without either the smart or the delay of it." As to the printers' cases, he added, "There is but one opinion respecting [the outcome of] all those actions."[2]

The first cause to reach the bar was that of William Huckell, a journeyman printer employed by Dryden Leach. Huckell had been seized and detained for some hours in the messengers' custody on April 29, although in no way implicated in the publishing of No. 45. His case came on before Chief Justice Pratt at the Court of Common Pleas in the Guildhall, July 6; the hearing began at 9:00 A.M. and lasted until eight o'clock that evening. The jury considered the case only a few minutes before it returned a verdict in Huckell's favor and set his damages at £300 and costs.

The weight of argument fell upon John Glynn and Charles Yorke. After witnesses had established the basic facts in the case, the attorney-general opened his defense with an attack upon the licentiousness of the *North Briton* and a panegyric on the king's personal virtues. It was, as Pitt's solicitor wrote, "A very good speech upon the whole, if addressed to the King himself, but a very injudicious one to a jury of citizens of London." The defense was nonetheless well planned to avoid bringing into question the legality of the general warrant itself. Yorke held that the plaintiff's procedure was technically incorrect: constables must be sued together with justices of the peace, and as no action had been brought against the secretaries of state, this case could not be supported. The attorney-general and the solicitor-general also maintained that there had been sufficient probable cause to warrant the apprehension of the printer. They stressed the antiquity of the practice and powers of the secretary's office and defended the messengers as acting under their lawful authority. In a final maneuver to protect their superiors, the crown law officers requested a special verdict which, if granted, would allow another hearing before a full bench.

Glynn merely appealed to the jury upon the grounds of the harsh and arbitrary actions under which his client had suffered; it was Pratt who blasted the defense position by refuting the attorney-general's arguments. The chief justice held that secretaries and messengers were not justices of the peace and constables, and they had not carried out the instructions of the warrant by arresting Huckell; hence they were not entitled to the protection of the warrant. As to the grounds upon which Huckell was apprehended, they were plainly insufficient to form any defense.

Pratt at first favored a special verdict, desiring further time to consider certain points of law, but the jury insisted upon bringing in a general verdict under his direction. Following the chief justice's lengthy summation, Webb handed Yorke a bill of exceptions which was presented before Pratt instructed the jury to find the defendants guilty and determine damages. This step, though quite legal and designed to allow further hearings for the defense, was at best ill-considered. Counsel for the plaintiff promptly and successfully urged the jury to find liberal damages, since arguing the exceptions would probably cost his client £200, and it was patently clear that the crown had anticipated Pratt's opinion. As the chief justice remarked to Yorke, "I find you don't care to trust either me or the jury."

The verdict was well received. Wilkes attended the trial and departed amidst hearty cheers; Sir Fletcher Norton drew the wrath of the mob and was hissed from the court to his chariot. The damages awarded, admittedly high, were neither in keeping with the plaintiff's sufferings nor his station. They reflected accurately, however, the opinion of the London citizenry upon every aspect of the case. On July 7, the scene was repeated. James Lindsay received £200 and costs, and the crown agreed to recognize this decision as determining the twelve actions still to be heard. The court was undoubtedly disgruntled at the turn of events, but the city overflowed with joy. Wilkes congratulated Temple on "the glorious verdicts," and added, "the Chief Justice is adored, and Serjeant Glynn has increased a very great stock of reputation." Seven more printers, he observed, were commencing actions.[3]

Hardwicke felt that Pratt had allowed too much freedom to the jury, tending to make them "judges of law as well as of fact, which, if it comes to be established, will have extraordinary consequences." He also felt, with "many cool-headed impartial persons," that the damages were excessive. In Scotland it was at first believed that the decision was an acquittal of No. 45; Bute's friends urged the ministry to counteract such an opinion before it became general. As the government was quick to point out, these cases condemned the action of the messengers in arresting the printers; the legality of the general warrant was purposely avoided and in no way affected by them.[4]

The printers' cases were by no means ended. Although the government had apparently conceded defeat, the bill of exceptions remained, and Temple, at least, wondered whether new actions should not be undertaken in conformity with the steps the attorney-general had outlined as technically correct. The earl felt that such a course would insure the printers, for "the whole fund of their damages, if successful, will abundantly answer even all the expenses which Webb can accumulate." Another observer of the cost of the administration's errors posed the question, "And I ask you, how like you the present times? whether you had not rather be a Printer's Devil, than a Secretary of State?"[5]

The bill of exceptions was not pressed. A motion was made in Common Pleas, however, to set aside the verdicts because of excessive damages. The court granted a rule to show cause why new trials should not be granted, but after counsel was heard the motion was set aside, and on November 26, 1763, the verdicts were confirmed. There remained only the payment of the damages, and this was delayed another six months. On Monday evening, June 25, 1764, fourteen printers with verdicts against the messengers received their damages from Carrington and Blackmore. Huckell, who had been awarded £300 was paid £170; the others received £120 of their £200, and their attorney fees were paid. It was noted that "from the long delay in the payment; their attorney's bills, and the roguery of some of them, who absconded with two of their shopmates shares, they are supposed to have received very little benefit."[6]

One other case of a supposed printer of No. 45 was yet to be fought out. Dryden Leach, the master of several of the journeymen whose cases were heard in July, 1763, was the first man seized under the general warrant. He did not carry his cause along with his journeymen but supported a separate action of trespass against the three messengers, Money, Watson, and Blackmore, who had entered his house and seized his belongings. His case came on at the Guildhall before Pratt and a special jury on December 10. The defendants pleaded not guilty and sought to justify their action under the order of the secretary of state. After a hearing of seven hours' duration, the jury found for the plaintiff in £400 and costs. A bill of exception was at once entered on the basis of the statute protecting justices of the peace and constables

while acting in obedience to their warrants. The issue of Leach's case
had been foreseen by the ministry.*7

Judgment was given for the plaintiff on June 16, 1764, and two
days later arguments were heard on the writ of error in the Court of
King's Bench. Solicitor-General William De Grey argued that the
secretary was a justice of the peace ex officio, and the character of the
warrant was sanctioned by long usage, consequently the messengers
were protected by law. John Dunning, representing the plaintiff, held
that as Halifax was not a justice, the messengers were not protected
under the terms of the act. Nor did he hesitate to declare that

> . . . the warrant itself is illegal. It is against the author, printer,
> and publisher of the paper, generally, without naming or describ-
> ing them; and not founded on any charge upon oath. . . . No jus-
> tice of peace has power to issue such a warrant. . . . Nor is there
> any pretence of usage to support such a claim. . . .

In summarizing the case Chief Justice Mansfield upheld Dunning's
argument. "This is only the usage of a particular office, and contrary
to the usage of all other justices and conservators of the peace. . . . A
usage," he declared, "to grow into law, ought to be a general usage."
The messengers were therefore held to be unprotected by the act of
parliament, and the exception was not allowed. A reopening was begun
by Charles Yorke on November 8, 1765, but he confessed himself unable to carry the argument, and judgment was confirmed. His surprising withdrawal demonstrates the effect of politics upon legal action.
Having begun the messengers' defense as attorney-general, Yorke had
resigned toward the end of 1763, only to return to office with Rockingham and Newcastle two years later. The Rockingham ministry had no
reason to defend such actions as Leach's to the last, and Yorke advised
Rockingham that it was clearly impossible to protect the messengers
any further: "The true complaint of all these verdicts is the *excess of
damages*, which cannot be set right; and . . . it is impossible to avoid
the payment of them." He therefore urged that an end be made to all
actions. "Though the King may think, as the impartial world does, the
damages too great, yet his servants must submit to the course of law

---

*Several other printers also brought suit at this time, but when the verdict in
Leach's case was rendered, they declared themselves willing to accept nominal
damages and costs. Crown counsel readily accepted the offer which was commended
by the court and applauded by the crowd.

and justice."[8] Yorke's request for a free hand to settle these matters was apparently granted.

The practical effect of the case of Leach v. Money et al. was to end the use of general warrants for arrest. It should be noted, however, that Mansfield's declarations concerning the illegality of the general warrant appeared only in a prejudgment dictum and the attorney-general gave up his case on another point; consequently, general warrants for arrest were never formally condemned. The unanimity of the Court of King's Bench and the weight of Mansfield's opinion was sufficient, nonetheless, to have the effect of a formal declaration.[9]

A second set of legal cases rising from the publication of North Briton No. 45 concerned the authors, printers, and publishers of the Monitor. The circumstances under which Beardmore, Entick, and their associates were arrested have been noticed earlier. The ministry, having won its point by silencing the Monitor, failed to press actions against the men concerned, and on June 22, 1763, they were discharged from their recognizances by the Court of King's Bench. No doubt the recent developments in the Court of Common Pleas influenced government to display a leniency which Beardmore and his friends did not share. Having taken part in Wilkes's trial, Arthur Beardmore saw the possibilities of counterattack, and after the success of the journeymen printers in July, actions were begun against Lord Halifax and the king's messengers. The first of these cases to be heard in the Court of Common Pleas was that brought by Beardmore against the messengers for entering his house and seizing his papers. The attorney-general noted that an action for false imprisonment was also pending and proposed that the cases be united. Both the plaintiff and Chief Justice Pratt agreeing, a new trial was scheduled.[10]

On May 4, 1764, after a hearing of seven hours during which the arguments of the attorney-general and the solicitor-general were matched by those of Glynn and Dunning, the jury retired for fifty minutes and returned with a verdict for the plaintiff with £1,000 damages. Toward the end of May counsel was again heard as the crown law officers attempted to secure a new trial because of excessive damages. Arguments were extended throughout two days, and in the course of the motion Beardmore offered to forego this verdict if Halifax would consent to the case against himself coming to trial and would abide by the decision in that case. The defendant's counsel had no authority to accept such a proposition, and the original verdict was maintained by the court.[11]

The secretary of state's efforts to escape prosecution (successful in Wilkes's case) by delaying his appearance in court, served only to bind him more firmly in the tentacles of the law. William Meredith, Beardmore's clerk and a probable contributor to the *Monitor*, found his action against Halifax put off for almost a year. His counsel therefore moved the Court of Common Pleas, June 27, 1764, to increase the issues on the return of a writ of *distringas* against Halifax. In view of the protracted delay caused by the defendant, the court ordered £500 issues on the *alias distringas*.*[12] By the end of the year the secretary was at the mercy of the entire *Monitor* staff.

Wilson and Fell, the booksellers who published the *Monitor*, brought action against three of the messengers for trespassing and seizing their papers. Beardmore acted as their attorney and John Dunning as their counsel. The inquiry of damages was made on June 21, at the Guildhall, and the jury returned £600 damages for Wilson and Fell.[13]

John Entick next brought suit against Carrington for the seizure of his papers as the supposed author of the *Monitor*. Entick *v.* Carrington was heard July 20, 1764, at Westminster Hall before Chief Justice Pratt and a special jury. The erstwhile printer of the *Monitor*, Jonathan Scott, was the star witness for the crown, but he could not sway the jury. The defense plea was, as usual, action under the secretary of state's warrant, and it was no more successful than before. After an hour, the jury found for the plaintiff—not the £2,000 damages he asked, but £300 and costs.[14]

The actions against the Earl of Halifax came on in the second week of December. Beardmore's case was argued for eight hours, and after forty-five minutes the jury returned a verdict for Beardmore with £1,500 damages including the £1,000 previously awarded in the case against the messengers. The next day the actions of Entick, Fell, Wilson, and Meredith against the secretary were heard by four different juries which found damages of £20, £10, £40, and £200 for the respective plaintiffs. As in preceding cases, the legality of the warrant was not in question, and the verdicts were based upon the improprieties of

---

*A writ of *distringas* was designed to force the appearance of a defendant in court by placing his chattels at forfeit in the amount named if he failed to obey the order to appear. The court order of *alias distringas* indicates that one writ had already been issued in Meredith's behalf.

execution. The actions of December 11–12, 1764, were reviewed February 7, 1765, on motions to show cause why the verdicts should not be set aside, and the Court of Common Pleas upheld the decisions for Beardmore, Meredith, Wilson, and Fell.[15]

Entick *v.* Carrington remained undetermined until the Easter term. Serjeant Leigh argued for the plaintiff on May 13, and was seconded by Glynn on June 18, 1765. They held that the secretary of state was not a justice of the peace, and that "a power to issue such a warrant is contrary to the genius of the law of England." If in the past secretaries had acted in such a manner, it was high time to put an end to such practices. "No power can lawfully break into a man's house and . . . search for evidence against him. This would be worse than the Spanish inquisition."

The chief justice, now Lord Camden, delivered his opinion November 27, 1765. It was a lengthy and notable decision, one which marked Camden as a worthy successor of Coke, Hale, and Holt in the work of "so adjusting the claims of the Crown and the subject that both the authority of the state and the liberty of the subject are preserved."[16] Camden maintained that a secretary of state was not a justice of the peace, and consequenly he and those employed by him were not protected by act of parliament. The general warrant, he declared, had not been carried out properly, but more important was the question of the warrant's legality.

> This . . . is the most interesting question in the cause; because if this point should be determined in favour of the jurisdiction, the secret cabinets and bureaus of every subject in this kingdom will be thrown open to the search and inspection of a messenger, whenever the secretary of state shall think fit to charge, or even to suspect a person to be the author, printer or publisher of a seditious libel.

After stating in detail the defense of the practice of issuing general warrants—the usage of custom and the necessity of such a power for the maintenance of peace and government—the chief justice struck at the heart of the case. "The great end, for which men entered into society, was to secure their property. That right is preserved sacred and incommunicable in all instances, where it has not been taken away or abridged by some public law for the good of the whole. . . . Papers are the owner's goods and chattels; they are his dearest property." There is no written law that gives any magistrate the power of seizure and inspection: such a practice "would be subversive of all the comforts of society." If this practice began with the Revolution, "it began too late to be law now. . . . I could have wished, that upon this occasion the Revolution had not been considered as the only basis of our liberty. The Revolution restored this constitution to its first principles. It did no more." If victims have submitted to such warrants heretofore, "there has been a submission of guilt and poverty to power and the terror of punishment."

Camden next traced the history of the control of the press by government, noting that "whilst the press is free, I am afraid it will always be licentious, and all governments have an aversion to libels." However, no respectable authority could be cited to justify the seizure of libels. As the power of search must follow the right of seizure, and as "no authority in our books can be produced to support such a doctrine . . . I cannot be persuaded, that such a power can be justified by the common law." Reason of state had been raised in defense of general warrants, but "the common law does not understand that Kind of reasoning." Finally, declared his Lordship, "We are all of the opinion, that the warrant to seize and carry away the party's papers in the case of a seditious libel, is illegal and void."[17]

The uniform determinations of both the Court of Common Pleas and the King's Bench placed no small burden upon the parties who were found at fault in the eyes of the law. Precedent and practice in the secretary of state's office was not acceptable to the chief justices, but politicians in office appreciated the vicissitudes of public condemnation. As the dangers grew in number and magnitude, the Grenville ministry took steps to recompense the secretary and his staff for their losses. In accordance with his Majesty's pleasure, Grenville announced to his ministry, May 31, 1765, that the crown had agreed to defray all expenses incurred in actions against Halifax, the undersecretaries, messengers, and solicitors for "proceedings had by them in executing the business of their respective offices." A list of expenses was drawn up by P. C. Webb; an additional estimate of £3,000 was submitted, and steps were taken to assure the issuance of the allotted funds.[18] It has been claimed that the actions arising from No. 45 cost the government £100,000; it seems certain that no individual bore any part of that sum.

While authors, printers, and publishers who had suffered under a general warrant were refreshing themselves at the fount of the public purse, John Wilkes was enjoying both the "douceurs" and the harshness of the law. Wilkes was, at this time, unable to level his legal sights on either of the secretaries. Egremont played him "a scoundrell trick"[19] by dying in August, 1763, and Halifax used his influence and a bold disconcern for the law to avoid Wilkes's efforts until political persecution had forced the Patriot to seek refuge in France, and he was nonsuited by being declared an outlaw.

Against the lesser lights of the ministerial camp Wilkes experienced greater success. He brought action against Egremont's secretary, Robert Wood, for trespass and illegal seizure of his papers. The case was placed in the able hands of Glynn and Dunning, and Wilkes, always ready to call the press to his aid, prepared to distribute copies of an inflammatory pamphlet to the members of the jury.[20] Wilkes had hoped to secure an early hearing but was forced to wait until December 6, 1763, when he appeared before Pratt in the Court of Common Pleas. The plaintiff asked £5,000 damages, and Glynn supported that astronomical figure by enlarging upon the implied threat to "the liberty of every subject of this country." Denying the validity of a general search warrant, Glynn urged, "When we consider the persons concerned in this affair, it ceases to be an outrage to Mr. Wilkes personally, it is an outrage to the constitution itself." The solicitor-general replied, "This was the first time he ever knew a private action represented as the cause of all the good people of England." Counsel for the defense tried unsuccessfully to prove that Wilkes was the author of the *North Briton,* and Glynn, in rebuttal, described the general warrant as the sort of thing that may "creep into our constitution, subversive of its very foundation."

In summing up, Pratt declared that Wood's justification rested upon Wilkes's authorship; this failing of proof, Wood must be found guilty. The chief justice denied the power of the secretary to issue such a warrant; his action in so doing aggravated the damages which, if placed high, would "deter from any such proceeding for the future." The jury found for Wilkes in less than thirty minutes and awarded £1,000 damages. Pratt refused to allow a bill of exceptions, and the entire action was completed in less than three hours.[21]

Pratt's decision in Wilkes *v.* Wood, followed as it was just four days later by that in Leach *v.* Money, marked him as an ardent juridicial foe of the ministry. Lord Mansfield, though a personal friend to the ministers, declared that "no man had ever behaved so shamefully as

Lord Chief Justice Pratt had done . . . for that he had denied to His Majesty that justice which every petty justice of the peace would have granted to a highwayman."[22] The popularity he lost at court, Pratt won back tenfold in the City. As case after case passed before him Pratt demonstrated his willingness and ability to interpret constitutional points; he was the sole justice of his era to recognize and put into action the reinterpretation of the constitution which was being effected in the late eighteenth century.*

The cases which arose from the publication of *North Briton* No. 45 raised three significant constitutional questions: the measure of the secretary of state's power to make arrests, the validity of a general warrant, and the legality of a warrant to seize the papers of the author, printer, or publisher of a seditious libel. Camden's refusal to recognize a secretary as a justice of the peace or to accept the arguments of custom or reason of state in the case of Entick *v.* Carrington brought abrupt limitation to the powers of that office. The reiterated opinions of both Pratt and Mansfield against the legality of the general warrant found final expression in the Court of King's Bench in the case of Leach *v.* Money, although the warrant escaped explicit condemnation. The cases of Wilkes *v.* Wood and Entick *v.* Carrington gave to the seizure of papers a judicial airing well beyond any previous example. The result was a flat denial of that power in the secretary of state's office. In all these cases the courts reflected the traditional attitude of the common law toward the executive, amply illustrating the reason why "in all the ages, Englishmen have turned to the rules of the common law as their best protection against arbitrary government."[23]

---

*Pratt's biographer, H. S. Eeles, has suggested that "it must have been a distinct temptation to Pratt to come down in favour of the Government . . . he could have dispelled at one stroke the suspicion with which . . . he was regarded in high places." *Lord Chancellor Camden and His Family* (London, 1934), p. 78. To have done so would have amounted to political and professional suicide, for Pratt's one friend in politics was Pitt, and his only rival for higher office was Charles Yorke: the temptation cannot have been very great.

CHAPTER V

Press, Parliament, and Privilege, 1763–1764

IT HAS often been maintained that had government left John Wilkes to his own devices he would soon have fallen from the pedestal of patriotism. This argument ignores the characters of two of the principal actors in the events of 1763–1764: John Wilkes and George Grenville. Wilkes was an adventurer, an opportunist, and a demagogue; he was also a propagandist who knew how to keep himself squarely in the public eye. Once he stepped upon the political stage, only with his own cooperation could he be driven to the wings. George Grenville offers a striking contrast to his witty antagonist. Coldly formal, eminently competent but not brilliant, Grenville possessed personal virtue without a single enlivening vice. That the personalities of these two men should clash was natural, that they should meet upon constitutional grounds was inevitable, for no man appealed more often to the constitution than Wilkes, and no one took the constitution more seriously than Grenville. As the head of his Majesty's government he represented authority and embodied legalism. This aspect of Grenville's character explains the tortuous but steady effort which drove Wilkes from England. As Walpole observed, "It was rage to see authority set at nought while *he* was the minister."[1]

When John Wilkes achieved his freedom he promised that he would dedicate himself to the cause of all Englishmen. He did not lose sight of that objective, for in it lay his hope of future rewards. Having won fame through the press, he turned to it once more, established a printing press in his house in Great George Street, and introduced a number of workmen to print whatever might be profitable. Wilkes took this step in the face of warnings from his friends. "They repeatedly represented to him the great and imminent danger of putting a set of low, illiberal fellows into the possession of some of his most valuable secrets, at a time . . . when it behoved government . . . to get at him, if possible." Temple told Wilkes, "You ought not to furnish your enemies now with the means of obtaining that evidence which you have hitherto had prudence to prevent," and offered Wilkes any amount he might name if he would but remove the press.[2] Wilkes's refusal to accept the advice (he did accept the money) marks the patriot's first step toward independence.

One of the first productions of Wilkes's press was *A Letter to the Right Honourable the Earls of Egremont and Halifax, His Majesty's Principal Secretaries of State, on the Seizure of Papers*. Probably sketched by Temple and revised by Wilkes, the *Letter* possessed timely interest and struck hard against the secretaries' practice of intimidating printers by threatening them with legal action. The authority of a secretary of state and the power of the public purse "will soon conquer these poor men's ideas of liberty," wrote the author. "How far that is consistent with the LIBERTY OF THE PRESS, or for the advantage of the public, is another question."[3]

More important to John Wilkes was the possibility of financial success offered by his press. Toward this end he reprinted the *North Briton*, including No. 45, and sought to raise a subscription to cover his expenses. He could find only 120 subscribers, however, and so determined to sell his volumes at half a guinea. "I am not a little out of pocket by such a bold undertaking," he wrote Temple, "but North Briton and Wilkes will be talked of together by posterity." The financial failure of his publishing venture and the expense of legal fees allowed Wilkes to play a merry tune upon Temple's purse. Between May 25 and July 9 he asked for £1,200 and probably received most of that sum.[4]

It was audacious of Wilkes to republish the *North Briton* at a time when court actions against it were pending, but it was a most unfortunate error of judgment to utilize his private press for the printing of a set of obscene verses. Foremost in this collection of ribaldry was *An Essay on Woman*, probably written by Thomas Potter, and inscribed to the famous demimondaine Fanny Murray. Appended to the text of this parody on Pope's *Essay on Man* were notes attributed to William Warburton, Bishop of Gloucester.[5] Wilkes may have intended to circulate copies among his rakish friends of the Medmenham Abbey Hell-fire Club, who would have appreciated it fully, or perhaps the printing simply represents a slight touch of bibliomania aggravated by the proximity of printer's ink. Wilkes certainly did not intend to make the *Essay* public, and he failed to realize his danger should it fall into the hands of his enemies. George Kearsley had arranged to have the poem printed for Wilkes in 1762, and it was sent to Temple for his amusement.[6] This form of the *Essay* probably fell into the hands of the ministry when Wilkes's house was ransacked. Realizing the political effectiveness of damning Wilkes's character, ministers set to work to add a case of blasphemy to charges of seditious libel. Bribery, intimidation, forgery, and fraud were used by the Earl of Sandwich and Philip Carteret Webb to play upon the "low, illiberal fellows" who worked the press in Great George Street.[7] The Reverend John Kidgell, chaplain to Sandwich's friend the Earl of March, contacted Wilkes's printers; they betrayed their master for a price, and Sandwich enthusiastically prepared his trap.

The *Essay on Woman* was to be presented to the House of Lords on the ground that mention of Warburton's name had infringed upon the privilege of a peer. The good bishop, already antagonistic toward Wilkes because of the *North Briton,* agreed to the plan when Sandwich assured him that "the King desired it as for his service." Warburton's cooperation removed the objections raised by the lord chancellor to "the impropriety of bringing the matter before the House merely as a blasphemous and impious work."[8] The solid majority enjoyed by the government among the Lords assured success in that house, but as Wilkes was a member of the lower chamber, a second line of attack was also needed.

Threats and rumors of threats to expel John Wilkes from the House of Commons were current throughout the summer of 1763. The government's plans were formulated by the latter part of September, and the ministers looked eagerly toward the meeting of parliament in order to forestall Wilkes's pending legal action. Their plan was to secure parliamentary censure of *North Briton* No. 45 before Wilkes could present his complaint of breach of privilege. Grenville experienced some little difficulty in securing an aide to guide the measure through the House, but by the end of October, Halifax had won the support of the complaisant Frederick, Lord North. The junior lord of the treasury was not entirely happy with his decision. On October 30 he wrote to Halifax asking that he might be relieved of the duty of seconding whatever Grenville might propose. North put forward the civilities he had received from Wilkes and balanced against them the rather slight "marks of favour received from His Majesty by my father and myself [which] are not such as to make the world expect that we should be the first in this declaration of duty." Halifax immediately informed Grenville of this tergiversation and urged him to work subtly to persuade North of the rectitude of his original agreement. Grenville succeeded in this task, but North was never thoroughly satisfied with the part marked out for him. In a long letter to his father, Lord Guilford, North declared, "Nothing can go more against me than the business I am now upon, but while things stand in their present ticklish situation it is impossible to avoid it." He wished he had followed Newcastle out of office, and in an admirable passage which throws much light upon his later career, he concluded, "From the time one engages one draws closer and closer, until one has so far engaged that one cannot in honour decline taking a part in a thousand affairs wherein one would choose to be quiet."[9]

While the chiefs formed their schemes, the clans literally gathered. The government's plans were kept secret from the opposition despite the apparent widespread knowledge of coming events among the friends of the court. Grenville and the two secretaries informed Stuart Mackenzie of their plans in October, and he immediately set out to whip up the attendance of the Scottish members. "I hope to God no one Member of the north of the Tweed (except the scabby sheep) will be absent at the opening of the session," he advised a friend, and at the same time warned him to "say nothing, for God's sake, but in confidence, and to excite any backward member to attend, of what I have told you about our intended proceedings at the opening of the Session." Among the Scots the anticipated crushing of John Wilkes was an affair of national honor, and men like Gilbert Elliot looked forward to "some pretty interesting points" when parliament should convene.[10]

November 15, the two houses met. It became immediately apparent that l'affaire Wilkes was foremost in the minds of all parties. Grenville and Wilkes clashed in the opening moments of the session, the first acquainting the House that he had a message from the king, the latter raising a point of privilege. As it was customary to begin the session by reading a bill, both sides tried to secure priority by amending the motion for the bill. The ministry carried their point by a division of 300–111, and Grenville presented the royal message. He informed the House that John Wilkes was the author of a most seditious and dangerous libel, that he had been arrested and discharged by the Court of Common Pleas on his privilege as a member and had since refused to appear in answer to charges laid against him in the Court of King's Bench. He therefore brought the case before the House of Commons. True to its master, the House voted its thanks to His Majesty, and North moved that North Briton No. 45 was "a false, scandalous, and seditious libel." In the debate that followed, Pitt carried the burden of opposition leadership and was most strongly opposed by Charles Yorke. In the final division the minority stood firm at 111; the majority, certain of the eventual outcome, allowed its numbers to drop to 273. At North's instigation the House ordered that the paper should be burned and, as the hour was late, adjourned until the next day. Wilkes had been allowed to express his readiness to waive privilege and trust to the mercies of a jury, but his cause was lost. The opposition had rallied every vote at its command and had come up painfully short.[11]

In the House of Lords the day was no less eventful. According to plan, Sandwich broached the subject of privilege and the use of Warburton's name in the *Essay on Woman*. To prove his point he read the *Essay* aloud—doubtless as much for his own amusement as their Lordships' edification. Lyttelton made a futile attempt to stop this performance, but Sandwich, quite at home in such an element, was allowed to proceed. Without a division the Lords resolved that the *Essay* was a breach of privilege and "a most scandalous, obscene, and impious libel." The ministry then undertook to prove Wilkes the author. One of Wilkes's printers was introduced, and the methods used to secure the *Essay* began to come to light. Only Earl Temple rose to defend his friend, speaking repeatedly against the manner in which evidence had been secured, and declaring that the liberty of the press was involved in the case. Grafton specifically disowned any sympathy for the author of such a production, and Mansfield silenced Temple's legal arguments. Bishop Warburton, true to his promise to Sandwich, spoke warmly—though not in his own cause, he declared—against this threat to religion, society, and decency. Waxing eloquent, Warburton declaimed that "there is so foul a mixture of bestiality interlarding [Wilkes's] fearful blasphemies, that the hardiest inhabitant of hell would *blush* as well as *tremble* to hear repeated." Their Lordships, being no less sensitive than the right reverend bishop, agreed on November 17 to order an address presented to his Majesty for the prosecution of the author of "the said scandalous and impious Libel." The king graciously acceded to their request, and the Lords resolved that John Wilkes appeared to be the author. "This bomb was certainly well conducted," said Horace Walpole. "The management is worthy of Lord Sandwich, and like him."[12]

The parliamentary attack upon Wilkes had begun successfully, but the public formed its own judgment. The Earl of Sandwich was nicknamed "Jemmy Twitcher" in commemoration of his attack upon a former friend, and Wilkes, who fell seriously wounded in a duel with Samuel Martin, a back-bencher of strangely sensitive honor, remained the darling of the people. He was defended in the papers, and many political writers recognized, as did Wilkes, that the *North Briton,* not the *Essay on Woman,* was the true source of his calamities.[13] When the Reverend Mr. Kidgell published *A Genuine and Succinct Narrative* of the events leading up to November 15 and dedicated it to religion, he was promptly submerged by pamphlets abusing and condemning him for the low part he had played.* The *Essay on Woman* was the hero of the opening session of parliament; at least four fraudulent versions were offered to the public within a month. The printers made no secret of where their wares might be purchased, but only one master of a circulating library was haled into court for publicly aping Wilkes's private action, and he was merely ordered to return the purchase money to a dissatisfied customer.[14]

The Grenville ministry, having won the initial round and being no longer embarrassed by Wilkes's presence in the House of Commons, might proceed more leisurely. On November 23 the House determined, by a vote of 243 to 166, to continue discussion of the question of privilege, but it refused to hear Wilkes's complaint. A motion was offered that "Privilege of Parliament does not extend to the case of writing, publishing, seditious libels." The hopes of the opposition were momentarily raised when Charles Yorke opposed the continuation of debate, but they quickly fell when the former attorney-general reverted to his original position on the question of privilege. Pitt again stood foremost in debate on November 24, but his incisive personal condemnation of Wilkes was of more value to the government than Yorke's labored two-hour oration. Pitt readily agreed that No. 45 was a libel; "he condemned the whole series of North Britons; he called them illiberal, unmanly, and detestable. . . . The author . . . was the blasphemer of his God, and the libeller of his King. He had no connection with him:

---

*The reaction of the printing trade to the course of action against Wilkes is demonstrated by the fate of the printers who betrayed him. Michael Curry was unable to find employment in London; he fled to Norwich and then to Bristol, where he met a like reception. He died by his own hand in 1788. Faden and Hassall lost heavily in trade, friends, and reputation—and failed to collect a farthing from the ministry. Kidgell finally retired to the Continent, where the ministry left him to starve.

he had no connection with any such writer." The Great Commoner boasted of his friendship with Temple but declared that he was "totally unacquainted" with the writer of libels.* The motion passed, 258 to 133, and Wilkes was left to the mercy of the law. No. 45 was ordered to be burned by the common hangman, and the Lords were asked to concur in the action of the lower house, which they did on the first day of December.[15]

The opposition Lords were no more powerful than their friends in the Commons, but they were able to express their disapprobation of events in a somewhat more formal manner. On November 29, seventeen Lords signed a protest against the surrender of parliamentary privilege as tending to amplify an inferior jurisdiction at the expense of an ancient and superior jurisdiction. Such a step, they held, gave up the liberty of the subject and placed too great powers in the hands of the government. Furthermore, if one privilege were surrendered, all might be lost; "every lord of parliament, then . . . lies at the mercy of that enemy to learning and liberty, the messenger of the press." The signatory Lords were few—Temple, Grafton, Devonshire, and fourteen others. Here, as in the House of Commons, subsurface tensions found expression. Newcastle and Rockingham declined to join in the protest out of deference to Hardwicke's opinion that the minority were in error, and the Earl of Shelburne, who had adopted Pitt's line of conduct in the Wilkes affair, similarly refused.[16]

By the end of the month it was felt that "Mr. Wilkes is universally given up; and if the ministers themselves do not wantonly raise difficulties . . . they will meet with none." Rents in the fabric of opposition were only too apparent. Devonshire, almost the sole link between Pitt and Newcastle, found the former so impractical in his views that he thought of retiring. Charles Yorke enjoyed delusions of having bested Pitt in debate, though few agreed with him. Weak from his wound and despairing of success, John Wilkes left England for the more friendly shores of France as the year dragged to an end. Walpole sagely observed, "Both sides pretend joy at his being gone; and for once I can believe both." "It is a great mercy," wrote Chesterfield,

> that Mr. Wilkes, the intrepid defender of our rights and liberties
> . . . may live to fight and write again . . . and it is no less a mercy,
> that God has raised up the Earl of Sandwich to vindicate and pro-

*One calculating friend of the government declared that Pitt's diatribe against Wilkes was worth £50,000 to the ministers! H.M.C., *Lothian MSS*, p. 248.

mote true religion and morality. These two blessings will justly make an epoch in the annals of this country.[17]

The City of London took all of this to heart and expressed its sentiments forcefully on December 3, when the *North Briton* was to be burned. A sheriff attended the hangman to the scene of execution and found the mob in control of the situation. The constabulary was powerless; the sheriff's coach was torn to pieces and the *North Briton* nearly rescued from the hands of the hangman as he attempted to carry out his orders.* The mob was evidently organized and directed by Wilkes's political friends, but they managed to remain in the background, offering encouragement from the balconies of shops overlooking the Royal Exchange. Although both houses of parliament expressed their thanks to the sheriffs for their diligence, the London Common Council refused to concur, the Lord Mayor being of opinion that "he should look upon it as prejudging Wilkes's cause."[18]

Members of the ministry were astounded by such a display of independence; Grenville was speechless with rage, the king "disturbed and exasperated." Bedford wished to demonstrate official resentment by exemplary action against the City, but both the king and Lord Mansfield urged moderation. It was doubly aggravating to the two Georges—minister and monarch—that the mob was reported as having said, "We have nothing to fear, the Duke of Cumberland and Lord Temple are with us." London burned a jackboot and a petticoat in defiance of Bute and the Princess Dowager, and the cry was "Wilkes and Liberty." But Wilkes was gone, and when the ministers recovered their temper they proceeded to the final stage of this struggle in which "the right hand of Nonsense armed the King, and her left defended the subject."[19]

Throughout the year 1763 the division of opinion between Charles Yorke and William Pitt had kept the opposition divided in spite of Newcastle's best efforts. The ministry had wisely prolonged both parliamentary and legal prosecution as a means of keeping that schism alive, but on January 19, 1764, the House of Commons finally considered the facts of the case. Wilkes was absent and his excuses unacceptable; by a division of 275 to 70, he was found guilty of contempt of the House's order for his attendance. The younger and more violent

---

*Among the many stories connected with this episode, perhaps the most expressive of public opinion is that related by Lord Bath, that the hangman, unwilling to burn the paper, declared "he had much rather hang twenty North Britons [i.e., Scots] than burn one." Blunt, *Mrs. Montagu*, I, 77.

members attempted Wilkes's defense as the ministry brought forward witnesses and documents to prove his authorship of No. 45. Pitt was ill and absent, and Temple, who quite irregularly stood by and prompted the opposition, was a poor substitute. The Commons obediently resolved: "That it appears to this House, that . . . *John Wilkes* Esquire is guilty of writing and publishing '*The North Briton,* No. 45,'" and "That the said *John Wilkes* Esquire be, for his said offence, expelled this House." "The whole was very triumphant," wrote Grenville; it gave the king "great satisfaction," and it opened the ground for the attack upon the general warrant wherein Pitt, Yorke, and all the leaders of opposition stood united.[20]

Wilkes was expelled the House in the early morning hours of January 20. Before the day was over the opposition had pressed successfully for the consideration of his complaint of breach of privilege under cover of a general warrant. The ministry agreed, and on February 3, Sir William Meredith unveiled the point of the opposition attack by moving for copies of the warrants whereby Wilkes was arrested. Defeated by an adjournment, Meredith repeated his motion on the sixth, only to find that while the opposition had doubled its numbers, the ministers had trebled theirs. A week later the great debate began. Newcastle held high hopes that "we shall have the Yorkes," and Walpole described the ministers as so frightened by the slim majority of thirteen on Meredith's first motion that "Heaven, Earth, and the Treasury were moved to recover their ground." On Monday, February 13, evidence was heard against Wood and Webb for their proceedings against Wilkes. About midnight, Grenville offered a motion to adjourn, but upon Pitt's challenge that members should neither eat nor sleep until the great point had been decided, 379 members voted to continue debate, against 31 for adjournment. "And then," Walpole commented drily, "—half the House went away."[21]

The next day, February 14, the collection of evidence was resumed. Carrington, the senior messenger, "pleased with recounting his achievements, yet perfectly guarded and betraying nothing," underwent seven hours of questioning. It was not until one o'clock that Meredith rose to offer his motion that "a general warrant for apprehending and seizing the authors, printers, and publishers of a seditious libel, together with their papers, is not warranted by law." The ministers found themselves on the defensive, and Grenville defeated an amendment on a motion to adjourn by a scant 207 to 197. It was a quarter after four when the division took place, and more was yet to come. "Crestfallen, the ministers then proposed simply to discharge the complaint; but the plumes which they had dropped, Pitt soon placed in his beaver. He broke out on liberty." Pitt spoke twice at great length and with such effect that Grenville knew he must defend himself— which he did "very finely, very pathetically, very animated." As Grenville confessed to the king, neither he nor Pitt were "confined to the question, but went upon the general measures and state of the Government." At seven o'clock the opposition again called for adjournment, but failing to carry their motion, 184 to 208, they withdrew, leaving "the ministers to satisfy Wood, Webb, and themselves as well as they could." Within thirty minutes the complaints against the government's agents were discharged.[22]

The majority of ten which Grenville had maintained on Tuesday night seemed portentous. When he reported to the king on Wednesday, he found George "angry but not alarmed." The king was aware that "the Opposition might . . . carry the question upon the warrants on Friday . . . but that would make no change in him in regard to this present Administration, which he meant to support to the utmost." His Majesty's "firmness and steadiness" probably weighed more with Grenville than Sandwich's light optimism; other members of the court party were less certain of victory. Their antagonists were jubilant. Walpole swore that hereafter ministers "may pick pockets, but they will pick no more locks," and Temple had faggots gathered for two giant bonfires to celebrate the forthcoming event. Both sides recruited their strength for the crucial division, calling up the sick and afflicted so that when Friday rolled around, the floor of the House, in Walpole's words, looked "like the pool of Bethesda."[23]

After the high hopes and fears raised by the debates of February 13–14, those of the seventeenth and eighteenth seemed anticlimactic; Grenville informed the king that "the debate in general was but an indifferent one." The first few hours were spent maneuvering for position, and Meredith's motion was amended in such a manner as to justify the action of the ministers in Wilkes's case.* This step was an

---

*To the original motion "That a general warrant . . . is not warranted by law" was added, "although such warrant hath been issued according to the usage of office; and both have been frequently produced to, and, so far as appears to this House, the validity thereof hath never been debated in the Court of King's Bench; but the parties thereupon have been frequently bailed by the said Court."

obvious effort to secure the good will of Charles Yorke and was achieved not without some petty but offensive altercations between the former attorney-general and Pitt. The Great Commoner did not rise to his full stature during this debate, but in spite of illness, exhaustion, and interminable dull speeches he was still able to brand the ministers and their followers as "the disgrace of the present age, and the reproach of posterity; who, after sacrificing their own privileges, had abandoned the liberty of the subject."

The ministerial defense line having been erected, Sir Fletcher Norton rose to move an adjournment of the question for four months. Brazenly recognizing the possibility of defeat and the adoption of Meredith's motion, Norton declared that in such a contingency "he should regard a resolution of the members of the House of Commons, no more than the oaths of so many drunken porters in Covent Garden." Such a statement from the principal law officer of the crown (legally sound though it might be) was a challenge which the opposition could not ignore, and the hearts of men who had followed Newcastle into the wilderness swelled with joy and pride as Charles Yorke answered his former colleague "in the most masterly manner possible." All differences were now forgotten, all jealousies put aside. When Yorke sat down the House echoed his praise. "Nothing ever met with such applause," wrote Newcastle's informant. "Pitt is in love with him and so are we all. God be praised. I think now we shall, as Mr. Pitt said, crush our domestic enemies as we have our foreign ones."

Charles Townshend also won some oratorical laurels, but when Pitt rose at three o'clock he was exhausted, "very faint and languid," and spoke poorly. Grenville's reply shone in contrast. At five o'clock on February 18, the House divided on the question of adjournment. The minority numbered 220, but 234 members voted to end debate. The opposition was defeated but not broken; its leaders retained sufficient pride to reject a ministerial offer to declare general warrants conditionally illegal. At thirty minutes past seven Saturday morning, George Grenville seated himself in Downing Street to inform his Majesty that his government stood firm.[24]

The critical issue of general warrants tried the spirit of both parties. The successful efforts of government and opposition to raise their numbers indicates their relative strength, and an analysis of the division suggests the location of public opinion on the issue. The minority drew its support from the counties and large urban constituencies whose members voted decisively against the government. The smaller borough members favored the ministry, but it was the Welsh and Scottish members who saved the day for Grenville. The eighteenth-century electoral system assured the government of a powerful influence in Scotland, but in this division in which Wilkes figured so prominently (if indirectly) a stronger influence was at work. The Scots voted against Wilkes rather than in support of the government, and "it was not so much the condition of the English franchise which defeated the Opposition on this occasion as the conflict between the two kingdoms."[25] Another explanation of their defeat was offered by the minority leaders, however. Charles Townshend, upon entering the House, said to Pitt that they should be in the majority that night. He later qualified himself by saying "he was confident they went *into* the House a majority; but that Lloyd [Grenville's secretary], who had the Minister's private pocket book, made converts before the division."[26] It is unfair to attempt any explanation of the division of February 18, however, without noticing the role played by Grenville. The minister was his own organizer of victory, as the king recognized when he promised Grenville his portrait and added, "I know the difference between you and the rest of my servants; they have many purposes to serve, you have none but my service, and that of the public."[27]

The legal proceedings against John Wilkes had long been held in abeyance. No reason or excuse for delay remained after the debates on general warrants. Between February 18 and 20, crown counsel, with Lord Mansfield's assistance, secured an alteration in the record of Wilkes's case, a change of a technical nature and of doubtful significance, though Wilkes would make much of it later. An attempt was made to pack the jury by sending out false notices of adjournment, and the trial came on February 21. The best efforts of Glynn and Dunning prevailed not at all with Mansfield and the Court of King's Bench. Perhaps more effective were the "inflammatory papers" which Attorney-General Norton observed had been circulated among the jury. The chief justice condemned the action and offered to punish the offenders if they could be found. The foreman of the jury acknowledged receiving Wilkite material, but crown counsel's hopes were deflated when another juryman produced an equally violent paper supporting the prosecution. Inevitably John Wilkes was found guilty of republishing *North Briton* No. 45 and of publishing the *Essay on Woman*, both libels, and sentence was ordered to be given the first day of the next term. As he refused to appear to receive sentence, Wilkes was declared an outlaw, and all legal actions in which he had a part were suspended.[28]

The temptation to reprint the *North Briton* involved two other publishers in the toils of the law. John Williams, whose publications in 1763 closely followed (if they did not pirate) those of Wilkes's press, published a three-volume edition of the *North Briton*, complete with the libelous final issue. George Kearsley was the original publisher of No. 45, and equally subject to legal action. Richard Balfe, the printer of Wilkes's paper escaped prosecution. The ministry watched Balfe closely and having "no reason to believe he is more under Mr. Wilkes's influence than he originally was," granted him a free pardon.[29]

The case of Rex *v.* Williams was heard at nine o'clock, July 26, 1764, before Chief Justice Mansfield at the Guildhall. The case is of particular interest because the counsel for the defense, John Glynn, boldly raised the question of the powers of the jury in cases of libel. This question was to arise in every press case to reach the courts during the first half of the reign, and within six years it would become a most important political and legal issue. Addressing his remarks to the jury, Glynn said, "That in the matter of libel, they were the proper judges of the law as well as the fact; that they had the full right to determine, whether the defendant had published the North Briton with the intent as laid in the Attorney-general's information." Such a declaration cut at the very root of government's power to restrict criticism, for it was commonly accepted that the law officers' ex officio statement that a paper was libelous, when supported by the presiding justice, provided complete legal establishment of the actionable character of the paper. The terms false, malicious, scandalous, or seditious were not held subject to proof but were the customary and necessary descriptions of a libel. Mansfield consequently broke in upon Glynn's remarks and "declared in a very strong and menacing manner, 'That if Serjeant Glynn asserted that doctrine again, he . . . would take the opinion of the twelve judges upon it.'" The worthy serjeant saw the snare; if Mansfield secured the confirmation of the full bench that the jury should concern itself only with the fact of publishing, the ideas which he upheld, and upon which a new concept of freedom of the press would be based, might be crushed in their infancy. His argument had been expressed; Glynn bowed to the obvious displeasure of the court and awaited a more propitious moment in which to renew the strife.

Mansfield, however, had not finished. His charge to the jury consisted of a reply to Glynn's argument and was "grounded upon and enforced by the most infernal principles which ever disgraced any nominal free country." The opinion which so horrified John Almon was a precise and accurate statement of the law as Mansfield and his predecessors interpreted it; the jury were judges of the fact only, and if they believed the evidence that Williams sold the *North Briton,* they must find him guilty of the fact or be perjured.

The jury was out for two hours, and Almon reported to Earl Temple that the foreman and one other juror were strongly favorable toward Williams,

> but one Page, a tool of, and personally known to Lord Bute, was obstinately and resolutely bent on finding the defendant *guilty.*
>
> In this struggle he brought over nine of the jury, urging . . . that as the Minority had left Mr. Wilkes, they certainly looked upon that paper as a libel, &c.
>
> Still the foreman and the other man stood out; at length they capitulated and consented to meet each other halfway, and brought in a verdict in these words, *Guilty of publishing the North Briton, No. 45.*

A fellow printer might declare that this was "no verdict at all," but it sufficed for the purposes of the chief justice; Williams was guilty. Kearsley's trial came on immediately, and he suffered a similar fate at the hands of Mansfield and a pliable jury.

The conclusion of their trials marked the beginnings of their difficulties for Williams and Kearsley. The Court of King's Bench delayed the delivery of its sentence until November. On the twenty-fourth, after frequently attending at the bar during the preceding months, Williams was called up only to be ordered to the King's Bench prison, there to remain until the next term, and then to receive sentence. Four days later Kearsley was dealt with in similar fashion.

The original publisher of the *North Briton* was already paying the penalty of his boldness. About August, 1764, George Kearsley took bankruptcy; broken by the expense of his legal proceedings, he fled to France to avoid imprisonment for debt. His creditors were lenient, however, and when Kearsley return to England (about November 24), they allowed him to retain the £130 which remained to him, as they felt his effects would satisfy their expectations. Toward the end of December they met to consider the possibility of recovering their losses, and at this gathering the celebrated actor Samuel Foote is said to have done Kearsley good service by exclaiming, "Gentlemen, it is a very common case for a bookseller to be seen among the creditors of an author; but for once! strange to tell! you see an author among the creditors of a bookseller." Encouraged by this reception Kearsley appeared before the Court of King's Bench, January 23, 1765, and delivered up an affidavit stating that Halifax had offered him immunity from prosecution if he would name the author of the *North Briton*. Mansfield recommended that the attorney-general advise the crown of this development and submit Kearsley's case to the royal pleasure. At the same time the publisher withdrew certain actions which he had begun earlier against the king's messengers for the seizure of his papers under the general warrant. Consequently Kearsley's application was graciously received, and on January 25, 1765, he was discharged. His creditors, meeting at the Sun Tavern, February 19, unanimously agreed to re-establish him in his former premises, and Kearsley returned to his profession at almost the same moment John Williams was illustrating the lengths to which vindictive law would go.[30]

On the first day of the term, January 23, 1765, Williams came before the Court of King's Bench. In Mansfield's absence, Justice John Eardley Wilmot delivered sentence upon the printer. Wilmot spoke at large upon "the licentiousness of this age" and in particular concerning the libel before him which aimed at "destroying that confidence in [the king's] Government, which is the most solid foundation of the allegiance of his people." "Liberty," declared Wilmot, "can exist only under an empire of laws, made with the concurrence of the people; and therefore cannot be more dangerously wounded than by the resistance encouraged and applauded in this Paper." The defense had rested its case upon the degree of guilt in a republisher and the widespread circulation of the *North Briton* which made sale in the ordinary course of trade almost requisite. On this point Wilmot observed,

> Your case, as the case of a publisher in general, is a very unfavourable one, because publishers give an activity and operation to the poison which is mixed up in private, and would lie in a quiescent state, if no persons could be found to disperse it; and as the prevention of crime is the end and aim of all criminal jurisdiction, there are no means so likely to attain that end, as the spirited exertion of that jurisdiction against printers and publishers.

The demands of trade Wilmot denied. The libel was sold, not in response to the requests of customers, but rather upon the initiative and with the premeditation of the accused. This "repels any presumption of your ignorance of the indignation of Government at this Paper," Williams was told, though the court realized that he "might be deluded by bad example to err with the multitude in this lucrative but dangerous commerce." No more damaging opinion could have been leveled against the printing trade. Its entire social and economic basis was denied by Wilmot in words far more didactic than any Mansfield ever uttered.

Williams' sentence was severe. A fine of £100 was assessed against him, and he was to be imprisoned for six months. At the end of that time he was to find security for his good behavior for seven years, himself in £500 and two others in £250 each. Furthermore, he was to remain in custody until the fine was paid and the sureties found. One other punishment Wilmot decreed: the prisoner was to stand in the pillory in New Palace Yard for one hour between twelve noon and two o'clock. Williams was thereupon remanded to the King's Bench prison.

The pillorying of John Williams took place on February 17, 1765. His case had attracted much attention, and the London mob, ever ready for public entertainment of this sort, began to gather early in the day. About eleven o'clock Williams was brought to New Palace Yard, Westminster, in a hackney coach which bore the magic number *45* on its side. As the crowd of nearly ten thousand people showed no destructive tendencies, Williams mounted the pillory a few minutes after noon. He was greeted with cheers and applause, and opposite the pillory there shortly arose a scaffolding of four ladders between which were suspended a jackboot, a bonnet bearing the label "Scotch bonnet," and an axe. Before the hour passed these emblems of Bute and the Princess Dowager were cut down, the top of the boot chopped off, and all consigned to a fire. More tangible proof of the feelings of the populace appeared in the form of a collection undertaken by supporters of Wilkes for the alleviation of Williams' expenses. An orange-trimmed blue purse, emblematic of the Glorious Revolution, was filled with guineas as well as pennies, and it was estimated that the printer garnered above £200. Williams returned to his prison as he had come, and thoughtful men wondered at a mob which expended its money as well as its breath. " 'Tis poor amends to national honour," observed Walpole, "to know, that if a printer is set in the pillory, his country wished it was my Lord This, or Mr. That."

The public was soon less seriously entertained. Satirical prints portrayed the scene vividly, carefully representing the cries of the mob, "Wilkes, Williams, and Liberty," "Liberty of the Press for ever and No. 45." A young clergyman named John Horne satirized the punishment by petitioning "the right honourable, truly noble, and truly Scottish lords, Mortimer [Bute] and Jefferies [Mansfield]" that he also might receive the new Order of Merit, the "Croix de St. Pillory." Horne was clever enough—and gross enough—to escape prosecution and enjoy Wilkes's company in Paris shortly after. A writer in the *London Magazine* animadverted upon the number *45*, noticing the fate of No. 45 and its author, the pillorying of the printer on the forty-fifth day of the year, and remembering, of course, the rebellion of '45. The authority of government and law were maintained in the case of John Williams. He was discharged from prison July 10, 1765, but Englishmen had begun to think that either the government or the law was in need of change.[31]

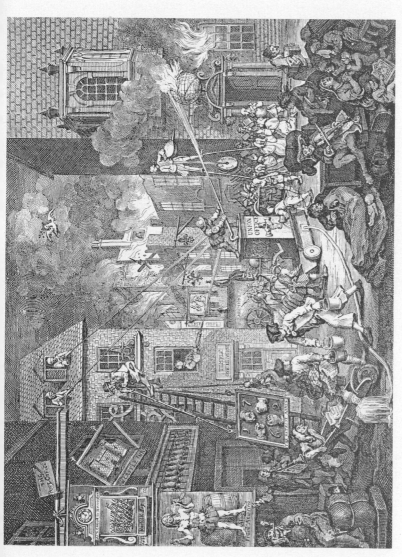

"THE TIMES. PLATE I"

Hogarth's great commentary upon politics incorporates nearly every issue: Newcastle's Inn is tumbling down while the inhabitants of Temple's Coffee House seek to disrupt the Scots and the military who would fight the fire which consumes the Dutch, Austrian, and French establishments across the street. Pitt (on stilts) blows on a world in flames even though he is burdened by a pension—the millstone around his neck. September 7, 1762

"THE TIMES. PLATE II"

Hogarth depicts Bute manning the pump that waters the fruits of the young king's reign; Wilkes stands in the pillory; the Opposition (Pitt in flannels) shoot in vain at the dove of peace.

"THE COFFEE-HOUSE POLITICIANS"

The better class of citizens discussed the news at their favorite coffee-houses, where the latest newspapers were available. April 1, 1772

"THE HUNGRY MOB OF SCRIBLERS AND ETCHERS"

Bute dispenses largess to his supporters. Samuel Johnson, William Hogarth, and Philip Francis, Sr., may be identified. May 26, 1762

"WILKES AND LIBERTY"

Bute raises his dagger to pierce the naked breast of Liberty swooning in the arms of Pitt, while Temple, with raised sword, interposes a shield marked *North Briton.* Wilkes and Churchill (in canonicals) chase off a pair of Scots and trample a fallen foeman whose escutcheon suggests that he is Smollett of the *Briton.* April 23, 1763

"THE FISHERMEN"

On the far side of the Waters of Sedition, Arthur Murphy (left) and Tobias Smollett (right) of the *Auditor* and *Briton* bemoan their poor catch while in the foreground Charles Churchill (left) and Arthur Beardmore (right) of the *North Briton* and *Monitor* pull in a full net. August, 1762

"JOHN WILKES ESQ."

William Hogarth's famous portrait of the leering, squinting Wilkes is a magnificent triumph of satiric art. May 16, 1763

THE BURNING OF *NORTH BRITON* NO. 45

In the background of this representation, Wilkes falls before Samuel Martin's dueling pistol.

"THE DEVILS TRIUMPHANT OR THE MESSENGERS IN THE SUDS"

Wilkes, Camden, and Glynn (center) congratulate one another on the outcome of the first press cases. The printers celebrate their windfall (right) while fiends seize the messengers (left). Norton and Mansfield hide their faces. July 5, 1763

"THE PILLORY TRIUMPHANT"

A representation of the pillorying of John Williams, who wears a "Scotch Yoke." Patriots pummel an unfortunate Scot and prepare to burn a boot and bonnet representing the Earl of Bute. February 14, 1765

"THE BRITISH BULL BAITED BY MUNGRELS"

A pastoral satire on the troubled career of John Wilkes, who is represented by the British bull. The dogs include Mansfield, Norton, Halifax, and Egremont (who lies dead at the left). 1769

"ROUND ABOUT THE CAULDRON GO"

Attorney general De Grey (in gown) leads the dance around a cauldron, into which are tossed the names of Junius' printers—Woodfall, Almon, and Say. Magna Charta lies in shreds before the throne. June 13, 1770

"THE ROYAL CHACE"

The king and Lord Mansfield pursue their quarry, John Almon, publisher of Junius'
"Letter to the King." January, 1770

"THE MORNING NEWS"

A graphic portrayal of those termed by gentlemen "the rabble." December 10, 1772

"THE PRINTERS BEFORE A COMMITTEE OF THE ROBINHOOD SOCIETY"

Samuel Bladon of the *General Evening Post* and Henry Baldwin of the *St. James's Chronicle* before the Bar of the House, Speaker Fletcher Norton presiding, for publishing the Commons' debates. June 1, 1771

"THE VICAR PURIFI'D BY THE SHADOW OF JUNIUS"

The Reverend John Horne literally has the devil scared out of him by the shadow of
Junius, who supported Wilkes in City politics in July, 1771. August 7, 1771

CHAPTER VI

The Late Minority and the Pamphleteers

THE DIVISIONS in the House of Commons leading up to the night of February 17, 1764, seemed to portend a powerful, united, and ultimately victorious opposition:

> Such a minority, with such a leader, composed of gentlemen of the greatest and most independent fortunes in the kingdom, against the majority of fourteen only, influenced by power and force, and fetched from all the corners of the kingdom, must have its weight, and produce the most happy consequences to the public.

So felt the Duke of Newcastle, who congratulated Pitt upon "your great and glorious minority." Nonetheless, it was a minority and soon to be referred to as "the late minority." Many of its members met in a club known as the Coterie, where political differences gave way to convivial friendship. Pitt expressed himself as very satisfied with Charles Yorke and insisted strongly that their differences must not be renewed by any future proposals. With a spirit of remarkably complete harmony prevailing, the minority hopefully waited out the end of the session in utter impotence, and the government leisurely took its revenge upon those of its members who yet retained appointive offices.[1]

The debility of this powerful minority amazed contemporary observers. "At first they seemed to expect that the ministers would come and lay their places at their feet," remarked Walpole, but "the dream itself was over before an effort was made to realise it."[2] Burke, seeking to explain why the Grenville ministry instead of sickening rather seemed to thrive upon its weakness, reached much the same conclusion. The minority was united but it spoke with many tongues poorly attuned to one another; the popular elements and the parliamentary elements of opposition lacked a common bond of sympathy—the populace was more interested in bread than constitutional principles, and those concerned by the latter stirred neither tongue nor pen in favor of the former.[3] "A supineness unparalleled!" cried Walpole, "to be accounted for from the composition of that minority."[4] Pitt, having risen to the crisis, soon retired into his own counsel. Ill and uneasy, he would not countenance the closed ranks of Newcastle's followers; his language became "extremely temperate; . . . he disclaimed the Opposition, and talked as if he wished to act in office with the Government." When Newcastle wished to consult with him on matters of policy, Pitt replied haughtily, "As for *my single self,* I purpose to continue acting through my life upon the best convictions I am able to form, and under the obligation of principles, not by the force of particular bargains." Thus would he go to the House *"free from stipulations."*

> Continuing, then unalterable . . . I could much have wished your Grace had not done me the great honour to ask my advice . . . and I humbly and earnestly entreat, that, for the future, the consideration of me may not weigh at all, in any answer your Grace may have to make to propositions of a political nature.[5]

After such a reply there was little hope of success in the hearts of the late minority. They went their separate paths and George Grenville, when he fell, was rather the victim of the king than of his political opponents.

Despite the parting of ways that divided the heads of faction throughout 1764, there existed a strong popular basis upon which opposition might be built. Walpole felt that out-of-doors all hearts were eager to second the efforts of the minority "with clamour and applause." But "not a pamphlet was written, not a meeting was held, to concert farther measures."[6] Burke struck directly at the problem: there was no man to point the issue, to raise the crisis. "The writer best qualified for that task, by a lucky knack of seasoning his compositions to the palate of the unthinking vulgar, both great and small, was fled."[7] John Wilkes was gone, and his parliamentary supporters were scattered. Temple grieved at the opportunity now lost, feeling that had Wilkes's case been properly managed, "it would have infallibly broken the neck of the Administration."[8] Himself "the soul of faction," the lord of Stowe was now powerless, "detested by the whole party, except his own small connection."[9] Yet to this faction and its leader, Burke paid tribute as he analyzed the failure of the minority in 1764:

> Personal satire might have been of great service . . . to divert the multitude, such is the pleasing nature of scandal, . . . but the late parliamentary resolutions against seditious libels; the judicial

animadversions upon them . . . and the doubts concerning what might be thought seditious . . . kept all the party-writers quiet . . . except one, whose too openly espousing the cause of Mr. W[ilkes] . . . added to the flaws . . . in his own character, took greatly from the weight of anything he could say.[10]

That both Burke and Walpole should agree that one of the great weaknesses of the minority was its inability to communicate with the masses and utilize their support is of more than passing interest. Each of these men knew the power of the press and turned that force to his own purpose upon occasion. Other men—usually young men—were no less aware of the minority's need for adequate mass communication and the support of popular action.[11] The City of London demonstrated an early willingness to lend its weight to opposition when, on February 21, 1764, the Common Council presented a vote of thanks to the City members for "their zealous and spirited endeavours to maintain the rights and liberties of the subject" in the case of general warrants. Further, they voted Charles Pratt the freedom of the City in a gold box.[12] Outspoken Wilkites, politically minded merchants, and economically dissatisfied dockworkers and weavers needed little encouragement to become an active as well as a powerful political force.

The necessity of utilizing this potential was clearly recognized by Charles Townshend. Active in the attack against general warrants, Townshend pressed upon the leaders of the opposition the danger of their lassitude. To Newcastle he represented the political situation at the end of April as "impossible"; popular sentiment was slipping away from the Whig lords, both in the City and in the counties. He urged that the press be rallied now as it had been at an earlier date by Wilkes and Temple. Newcastle turned an unsympathetic ear toward the younger man's proposals. The duke admitted that the political situation was not in every respect what might be wished, and that "it wants a great deal of spirit, care and attention to rectify it," but, he added, "I do not think the spirit in the nation is altered." Newcastle had no hope of beginning a press campaign. "The impression which the Court has made upon the liberty of the press is too certain, and much to be lamented. An exhorbitant fine upon a poor printer . . . will have more effect upon the Press than even any act of Parliament to restrain it."[13]

Townshend insisted upon the desperation of the situation. "Recollect, my Lord, the ingratitude . . . the desertion of the Majority of the

Whiggs . . . upon the frivolous distinction of supporting the Person of the King: the successful attack made upon the freedom of the Press." He wished to see the framework of opposition strengthened by an extension of alliances, "by the reconciling Lord Temple and Mr. Pitt with Mr. Grenville," and within this encompassing structure he would draw the populace by means of the press. "To gain upon the Minds of the People a Daily Paper, upon the Plan of one of the present Prints, should be set up, and circulated, diligently, but quietly; and two good Pens should be employed to write from Materials, suggested by Men of Knowledge, and subject to their inspection."[14]

Nothing seems to have come of Townshend's suggestion; the older members of the party, though increasingly aware of the power of the press, hesitated to use it to free the emotions of the populace. Horace Walpole provides an interesting illustration of this point. Disposed "to widen any breach that might happen," Walpole was not yet ready to face results. He inserted a paragraph in the newspapers pointing out that the unpopular abolition of vails, or gifts, to servants, begun by the Duke of Bedford, a political opponent, had not been followed by the Duke of Devonshire and the Cavendish family. Shortly thereafter, some footmen rioted and roughly handled a number of gentlemen who had been active in this reformation. "I was apprehensive," wrote Walpole, "lest any personal mischief should happen to the Duke of Bedford, and forebore to spirit up that contest." Walpole accepted the incident as evidence of "what I could have done, but, thank God! I was not so culpable as to embrace it." The dilettante stated the problem nicely, "My nature shuddered at the thoughts of blood . . . *there is nothing so difficult as to make the people go far enough, and prevent their going too far.*"[15]

This attitude, prevalent among the great houses, did not extend to those more closely affiliated with the people. John Wilkes, while he soon lost sight of his political goal in the pursuit of boudoir pleasures, clearly retained the propagandist's sensitivity. Writing to a friend in January, 1764, he added to a number of obviously good reasons for not returning to England, "If I stay at Paris, I will not be forgot . . . for I will feed the papers, from time to time, with gall and vinegar against the administration."[16]

Temple also continued the struggle through the press. Having lost Wilkes, the earl turned to others less brilliant but more malleable to his touch. Chief among these was John Almon, the young printer now turned bookseller and publisher. Toward the end of 1763, Almon set himself up in a private establishment opposite Burlington House in Picadilly. The lower floor was converted into a book and pamphlet shop, and Almon's soon became the publishing center for Temple's faction. The list of his clients was catholic, ranging from Temple to Charles Townshend, Horace Walpole, and many others, hacks and literateurs. Almon's success was guaranteed when, at Temple's suggestion, the opposition club at Wildman's officially designated him bookseller and stationer.[17] This union of patron and publisher was so successful that within a few years "Vamp and his Patron" were honored by an anonymous author's hilarious satirical preface, *A Curious Dialogue between a Certain Rt. Hon. Author and His Bookseller*.[18]

The desirability of a regular party publisher became obvious in August, 1764, after the condemnation of Kearsley and Williams. The government's ability to secure convictions from London juries "struck such a panic into the printers," wrote Almon, "that I am afraid I now stand alone in the resolution to publish with spirit." Almon was not uniquely courageous, but he stood foremost among political publishers obnoxious to the administration and had reason to add

> I hope that in case of persecution (which I hear is threatened me, with the addition of the heaviest vengeance of the Administration), I shall have the assistance and support of all those who call themselves friends to the liberties of their country; at least, I will endeavour to deserve it, by acting with that prudence, firmness, and fidelity, which can never injure a good cause, nor hurt them who shall choose to be my friends.

Assessing the condition of opinion in the City, Temple's bookseller advised him that the populace abhorred the ministry and liked the minority "as well as one body of men could another; but they would like them better if they would take more pains to instruct them."[19]

No better illustration of the relationship between press and politics may be found. The union of interest between the publisher and the head of faction was many-sided. Tracts and papers were the bread and butter of the publisher, the lifeblood of the politician. Without them both would fade into oblivion or suffer heavily in purse and popularity. The same press which made Earl Temple a factor to be reckoned with in politics enabled John Almon to become a country gentleman.

Politically the great magnate and the humble businessman were bound together by very real ties. The threat of prosecution stirred the anger of the printer because it threatened his personal and financial security. At the same time it provided the politician, who found himself in the minority, with a cause and a slogan—the liberty of the press—which was capable of endless expansion and certain to attract an audience.

Into this close alliance thrust the shadow of the general warrant, which might touch both parties equally if the publisher's papers were seized and his possibly anonymous but usually identifiable correspondent were run to earth. The ramifications of such a development were shown in the case of *North Briton* No. 45, and although the ministry learned the better part of valor in a relatively short time, the threat remained. After that form of inquisition was condemned, the power of the crown's law officers to file an information ex officio against the publisher of whatever they termed a libel, joined to the legal controls exercised by a Mansfield over the jury which considered the facts of the case, created in effect an even more formidable tool with which the government might strike at its enemies.

The cases of John Wilkes and John Williams outlined the major aspects of the problem early in the reign of George III. The union of press and politics displayed in the relationship between John Almon and Earl Temple was the force which defied the power of authority to repress that which it could not censor. Out of this mutual effort at sustained criticism the English press derived experience and a justifiable sense of pride in its obligation to society. Man being a political animal, the press never completely emancipated itself from politics, nor, as long as freedom of inquiry is considered requisite to free society does it seem desirable that the press should sever its human and political ties. But without the redefinition of the liberty of the press for which men like Temple, Almon, and Glynn fought—interested and narrow though their reasons might be—the reinterpretation of the English constitution without the bloodshed and revolution which Burke and Walpole feared might never have been accomplished.

The avowed party newspaper did not flourish in the first years of the reign. Moderate or timid publishers sought to protect themselves by a show of impartiality, but prolific or impressive contributors to any paper might give it a distinct political bias. This was certainly true of the *London Evening Post,* published by John Meres. By the later months of 1764, it was recognized as a communications medium for the Temple faction. John Almon zealously called his own contributions to the paper to Temple's attention, saying, "I hope the *London Evening* pleases; it has been very spirited lately. I have contributed as much as possible to the public cause, in order to keep up a proper spirit."[20] To Wilkes, the bookseller described the *London Evening Post* as "generally pretty severe and sometimes excellent."

Almon was anxious that the outlawed and exiled patriot should exert his powers in the periodical press. He urged Wilkes to write up his case for the public because he deserved so much from them, and "nothing is more easy than to make them think so." In October, 1764, a plan was on foot to establish a new Wilkite "weekly political paper." Humphrey Cotes seems to have fostered the scheme, and Almon, doubtless the publisher-designate, pressed Wilkes to give his support. "It would turn out not only very highly to your advantage but would effectually unhinge the administration in a very few months." Added to the political possibilities of such a scheme, Almon held out to Wilkes the thought that it might add to his slender means as much as £200 a year. It was poorly disguised flattery for Almon to add, "I am convinced nobody is capable of writing out the administration but you," but past events and future developments showed that his judgment was remarkably accurate.[21]

About the middle of November, Almon reported to Temple upon the failure of the most promising scheme to bolster the lines of the opposition press. The principals in this negotiation for a party paper were William Fitzherbert and Sir William Baker. As both men were connected with Newcastle, and Horace Walpole was consulted upon the project, it appears that this was to have been a medium of communication representing the united minority and supported by all factions. Fitzherbert informed Almon "that if six papers were wrote, the publication should not be delayed one moment; but although one Member of Parliament . . . has wrote two papers . . . yet there is such a backwardness, or rather shyness, in the others who can write, that nothing has been done."

Despite such an unpromising beginning, Almon, urged by "four or five who were most anxious for it," called upon Horace Walpole. The master of Strawberry Hill had tried his hand at pamphleteering that summer, and Almon hoped "he would contribute a paper or two" for the proposed political journal. Walpole approved the scheme and said it was "absolutely necessary." But, he added, "the leaders who are to be benefited by it will disapprove of it, and what can we do without them; upon the very first scrape you get into," he warned Almon, "the leaders will immediately disavow it." Walpole's reasoning, backed by the example of Wilkes's fate, was "too convincing to be resisted." He was admittedly disheartened by the languor of those who occupied the seats of leadership and wished that "certain people"—most especially Pitt—"had the same spirit, and the same hearty desire of going forward as Lord T[emple]. . . . Good God!" Walpole reiterated, "Did ever anybody see an Opposition acting on the *defensive* before?"

Like many others, Horace Walpole felt that if attacked with vigor, "the Ministry would be entirely defeated in a fortnight." The charge was never sounded, however, and Almon told Temple plainly that "the Ministry take advantage of this supineness, and are indefatigable in spreading reports that the Opposition is all a farce, dead, dispersed, broken-hearted, &c." The ministry was very nearly correct.[22]

John Almon summarized the political pamphleteering of 1764, for his friend Wilkes, in a few words: "The Minority are undone for want of proper advocates. Those who can write will not: & those who cannot by attempting it do nothing but play the fool. The Ministry therefore naturally triumph."[23] Such a conclusion is rather harsh upon the many noble and right honorable gentlemen—and their hacks—who took up the pen against George Grenville.

One of the major issues rising from the parliamentary session of 1763-1764 concerned the dismissal of General Henry Seymour Conway from his command because of his consistent support of the opposition throughout the winter. Grenville took this step against his better judgment and because of the king's insistence, and it was not announced until after parliament rose in April. As Conway's was not the only case of this sort, recriminations quickly appeared against a government which judged military ability by political affiliation. To his defense Grenville called William Guthrie, long a pensioner, and within a short time Conway was attacked by *An Address to the Public, on the Late Dismission of a General Officer.* Horace Walpole, to whom Conway's political career gave great vicarious pleasure, rushed to his friend's defense. He felt that the government pamphlet "must have been directed by Grenville himself—and it was tedious enough to have been written by him too." Forgetting his fears of bloodshed he rallied his courage and produced *A Counter Address,* which was praised by his friends and answered by Guthrie in *A Reply to the Counter Address.*[24]

By midsummer Conway's dismissal was debated in all the papers but most freely in those which seemed to Conway himself "to come out more immediately under the protection of Government." He complained of this to Welbore Ellis, Grenville's secretary at war, asking that if any charges could be brought against him they be brought openly. To prove his point and illustrate the damage to his honor, Conway enclosed an anonymous pamphlet, *The Wallet*. He received little sympathy from Ellis: "I know not that any papers are under the more immediate protection of Government, except the Gazette; as to that anonymous pamphlet, the *Wallet*. . . . I have some good reasons to believe that it is neither avowed, approved, or protected by Government." Furthermore, remarked the secretary at war, "I should think that I formed a hard judgment if I supposed that the gross misrepresentations and scurrility which I frequently see . . . against the Government had the approbation and protection of any gentleman . . . who differs with the Administration." Ellis scored a direct hit when he concluded, "I cannot but be sorry that you seem to attribute more authenticity to scribblers on one side than I think just to allow them on the other."[25]

The Conway case failed to create any great revolution in politics in spite of the hopes of the general's political friends; Pitt told Rockingham that the question "touched too near upon prerogative," and Walpole's associates were forced to wait until they were ministers to rectify the situation.[26] A more ready whip with which to chastise George Grenville was found in his fiscal measures. In March, 1764, Grenville "opened his statement" concerning national finance in the House of Commons. The minister's speech, or the substance of it, was published in the March 20 newspapers. Here was a candid effort on the part of administration to secure public support for its measures. The opposition could not let it pass unchallenged. The retributive pen was that of David Hartley, and he voiced the opinion of the followers of Newcastle and Rockingham. Hartley had already written at least one political pamphlet, but it was his detailed and spirited attack, *The Budget; Inscribed to the Man Who Thinks Himself Minister*, which appeared in April, 1764, that established his position among party writers.

The importance and popularity of *The Budget* was quickly demonstrated. The life of the transient pamphlet was usually brief, but in August, Almon (Hartley's publisher) advised Temple that "The *Budget* still keeps going off, and it is amazing how it has opened the eyes of the public."[27] The pamphlet continued to "go off"; by 1766 it had reached the eleventh edition and was again being reprinted, presumably still effective and still profitable to its publisher. It had by that date attracted to itself a host of replies and counter-replies which placed before the public all the arguments that had been utilized in the House of Commons by opposition spokesmen. Grenville castigated the public discussion roused by *The Budget*. He "inveighed bitterly in the House of Commons against such liberties, and protested he had never been concerned in any libels." To Horace Walpole the scene seemed worth recording:

> I sat and heard these solemn falsehoods;—having . . . seen Mrs. Grenville take out of her bureau and deliver to the author in my presence a rancorous pamphlet, written against Lord Temple and Mr. Pitt, corrected by Mr. Grenville's own hand, and published immediately afterwards.[28]

Whether Walpole was himself guilty of a "solemn falsehood" or not, there is no doubt that Grenville took an active and personal interest in the public defense of his policy. In July, 1764, he and his private secretary, Charles Lloyd, were engaged in planning the publication of a new pamphlet by Bute's penman John Campbell in answer to Hartley's *Budget*. Lloyd informed the ubiquitous Jenkinson that "we have had a good deal of discourse about the manner of announcing the birth of this literary production to the world, the advertising circulating extracting from it." Campbell's work was evidently prepared from materials furnished by Jenkinson, and prepared with Jenkinson's cooperation, for to him Campbell wrote announcing his intentions of calling to submit his manuscript, in order that "you may be better able to alter, add, or leave out, as shall be necessary."[29]

Lloyd's note to Jenkinson illustrates the problems of the government press. Grenville's secretary pointed out that "the denomination of *An Answer to the Budget* has been already forestalled by a meer catchpenny published evidently by an enemy." He complained of the delay with which "our auxiliaries" put themselves in motion, and added, "They put me in mind . . . of the Russian army, who it is said are the most expensive body in Europe to get into the field. For my own part to carry on the allusion, I should be for trying whether a scarcity of forage might not force them to scour about."[30] John Campbell's provender was the position of royal agent for the province of Georgia, which he secured in March, 1765, shortly before the end of Grenville's ministry.

The pamphlet to which Lloyd referred was apparently not *An Answer to the Budget. Inscribed to the Coterie,* a pro-government pamphlet possibly written by Israel Mauduit. This *Answer,* however, did its best to counteract Hartley's pamphlet. *The Budget* was described as "absurd and ill-written," but it was admitted that "in almost every Company the first Question is—*Have you seen the* Budget?" The anonymous pamphleteer defended the dismissal of Conway as open and spirited: "The Writers for the present Administration . . . publicly and honestly acknowledge, that the Dismission . . . was for his Opposition to the Ministry." The interests of ministers may well have been expressed in the complaint that criticism of the government was universal and that "unless some Method is taken that shall effectually put a Stop to this increasing licentious Practice, it will be next to impossible to carry on the public Business."

More to the point was the series of pamphlets written by Thomas Whately during the two years following *The Budget's* appearance. The first of these was entitled *Remarks on the Budget; or, A Candid Examination of the Facts and Arguments Offered to the Public in That Pamphlet,* published in 1765. Nor did Hartley let the official confutation of his figures pass unnoticed. Before the middle of the year he had written *The State of the Nation, with a Preliminary Defense of the Budget.* The *Critical Review* said of this pamphlet that it was obviously a party publication, were there no other evidence than "the very modest price it bears."[31] The series was continued in 1766, by Whately's detailed analysis of Grenville's economic policy, *Considerations on the Trade and Finance of This Kingdom, and the Measures of Administration with Respect to Those Great National Objects since the Conclusion of the Peace.* Once more external and internal fiscal policy was meticulously studied, income and taxes estimated, and conclusions drawn along party lines. The whole series of pamphlets shows considerable spirit mixed with a keen interest in facts and figures—an appeal to that portion of the merchant class to whom governmental economy represented industrial prosperity.

The significance of statistical criticism of the type Hartley wrote is shown by the abortive plans to submit pamphlet and author to the tender mercies of the law. *The Budget* was offered to the law officers for their opinion and pronounced a libel. However, opinion differed among Grenville's political associates. It was currently believed that Sir George Savile, a prominent Yorkshireman high in the counsels of the opposition, had written *The Budget,* and the weight of reason lay against legal proceedings: "It was not judged prudent to commence a prosecution against a character of such eminence and respectability," especially when he was a member of the House of Commons and while the privilege of that house in cases of libel was so freshly surrendered.[32]

This incident was in many ways typical of the Grenville press policy—a policy of cautious repression (after the Wilkes case) thoroughly carried out with due regard to all possible ramifications and supplemented by an active and authoritative government press. It is unfair to judge Grenville's relationship to the press from the *North Briton* episode alone. A survey of the activities of the ministry from 1763 to 1765 reveals a thoroughly consistent policy, moderate and in keeping with the character of the chief minister.

From the first days of July, 1763, the periodical press was carefully scrutinized, and official contributions were forthcoming upon occasion. As the *North Briton* failed to disappear with the end of Wilkes's tenure, ministers kept a close watch on it. Halifax instructed Edward Weston to counteract a story in the *North Briton* concerning a pension charged on the Irish establishment with "a short Letter which I desire may be put tomorrow in the London, Whitehall, St. James's, and other Evening Posts, and . . . in the Publick Advertizer, and the Daily Gazetteer of Wednesday morning." The *North Briton* again came under surveillance in August and November because of several scandalous articles reflecting upon the late Earl of Egremont.[33]

One friend of the government, less concerned in affairs of state, took physical action against the paper. In September the *North Briton* had reflected upon Scottish colonial governors, and the recent appointee to West Florida, George Johnstone, proceeded to vent his wrath on the editor, Brookes, who wrote as "John Caesar Wilkes." After the governor had used fist, stick, and sword upon the hapless editor, Brookes applied to the law for redress and, through Arthur Beardmore, instigated a fruitless prosecution for assault.[34]

Such activities were more embarrassing than advantageous to the government, and the *North Briton* was allowed to go its way unmolested until "a most furious" article appeared on June 23, 1764. The attorney-general was "desired to give his Opinion whether it may not be prosecuted as a Libel by Information"; he reported August 3, that the paper was actionable, but doubts arising as to the expediency of prosecuting at this time, nothing was done in the secretary of state's office.[35]

During October the *St. James's Chronicle* was also under observation as a result of having given "much offence" by two letters signed "Civicus" and "X." The attorney-general and solicitor-general reported the next month that the articles were derogatory to the honor of the crown and parliament and legally subject to prosecution. They were of the opinion, however, that prosecutions could not be carried on successfully, and their views seem to have been accepted.[36] In each of these cases a regular pattern of observation, consultation, and decision was followed. The under-secretaries assumed responsibility for all but the final decisions which were taken by cabinet ministers.

The limitation of political propaganda by court action having been reduced to a minimum, other means were employed. Personal suggestions or hints sufficed to cool the ardor of many publishers. The *Gazetteer* of January 7, 1764, carried the announcement that due to ministerial observation of the papers, the publisher was called upon to request that "all who honour this paper with their favours will have a regard for the safety of the printer." A similar announcement appeared in the *London Evening Post* the same month. Such methods sufficed to curtail criticism, but not to eliminate it.[37]

Ministerial contributors were prepared to fill space denied to opposition writers. Almon declared that "the Ministry . . . are indefatigable in their productions both in newspapers and pamphlets," and the "Father of Candor" spoke of "the little scraps of politics and intelligence, which one now and then finds in the *Daily Gazetteer,* and which the common reader . . . attributes to Jemmy Twitcher [Sandwich], (or his second, Dr. Shebbeare)."[38] Horace Walpole was not alone in accusing Grenville of fathering his own propaganda. The anonymous author of *A Letter to the Rt. Hon. George Grenville* accused him of being the inspiration, if not the author of "that laborious and contemptible ministerial paper, called the *Plain Dealer.*"[39]

The Earl of Sandwich, usually a difficult colleague for Grenville, contributed his part to the propaganda efforts of the ministry. After demonstrating his talents in the Wilkes affair, Sandwich next interested himself in the Cambridge University election. Thomas Gray noticed that "L[or]d Sandwich & his friends do what they can to keep up an interest & a bustle. here [at Cambridge] is a poor Scribbler, that he hires to write a weekly paper called the *Scrutator,* who by abuse of characters does all in his power to provoke people: but can not so much as get himself answer'd." Gray admitted that the paper was quite insignificant, but added that in view of the situation, little more was needed.[40]

The contribution made by Sandwich's penman, Dr. James Scott, was of greater importance. About 1764, Scott became intimate with Sandwich, Halifax, and other members of Grenville's ministry, and under their patronage he wrote the series of letters signed "Anti-Sejanus," which appeared in the *Public Advertiser.* Scott possessed more than moderate ability, and Anti-Sejanus was one of the most popular writers of short articles between Wilkes and Junius. He hewed to the party line, attacked "the favorite" as well as the Rockingham Whigs, and maintained a high regard for George Grenville. It has been said that Scott's letters were so popular that the sale of the *Public Advertiser* was increased from 1,500 to 3,000 daily. Scott's Anti-Sejanus letters drew replies from "An Occasional Writer" for the Rockingham ministry in 1765, and John Almon believed that Edmund Burke, among others, wrote several replies to Scott. Grenville's use of "every coffee-house and every news-paper" to sway opinion enabled Scott to retire in 1771, unbowed and undefeated.[41]

The Grenville ministry retained the most valuable of the men Bute had employed, and dismissed the hangers-on. Edward Richardson had worked for Bute in the City in 1762–1763, but with the change of ministry he was promptly dropped, on the pretext that he overrated his merits and emoluments. Nonetheless Richardson remained a friend to the ministers, and in December, 1763, offered Jenkinson sound advice: "If the Ministry imagine themselves able to bring over the citizens to the Court by the merit of their own administration, depend upon it, they are deceived." He urged that the friends of the government "have hitherto . . . but too much contemned popularity, which . . . in this free country has ever been the scaffolding to ministerial buildings. We have seen a fair lay'd foundation but shall never behold its progress without the aid of your citizens poles, scurvy as they are to raise it."

Among the many applicants to the Treasury for pecuniary aid came Joseph Cawthorne, who reminded Jenkinson "of the great expence I had been at by writing and causing others to write in support of the just cause of my Lord Bute." It seems doubtful if Grenville allowed him anything on that claim after the autumnal negotiations in which the earl played so conspicuous a part. Jonathan Scott, the former printer of the *Monitor,* also laid his grievances before Jenkinson. "My imprisonment and sufferings have been without an equal, and the more surprizing still the suffering in behalf of the Government." Scott was ready to return to the fray—with Jenkinson's assistance—and doubted not "the getting the better of [my enemies] . . . in my turn."

Even William Guthrie came to Jenkinson complaining, "I have been able to get only one letter into the Gazeteer, and that too, under pretext of rendering it more decent, was robbed by the printer of all its virility." Like his adversaries in opposition, Guthrie realized the need for a party paper. "I cannot help repeating," he wrote, "that if the Government had a weekly paper of its own, it would be attended by many public advantages. The success of the late trials [which the crown had lost in Common Pleas] have made unfavourable impressions, but they are not uneffaceable after the people begin to cool."[42]

One of the few writers of an earlier period to prosper under Grenville's administration was John Shebbeare. His rise from pillory to pension was completed in 1764. After an unhappy experience with the law during Pitt's ministry, Shebbeare sought Bute's support, only to fail because he had once been a "most notorious Scotch baiter." Grenville was less sensitive concerning his northern neighbors. On February 29, 1764, a memorial was presented to the minister setting forth Shebbeare's contributions to the unofficial government press since 1761 and requesting Grenville to secure him "an annual pension . . . that he may be enabled to pursue that laudable inclination which he has of manifesting his zeal for the service of His Majesty and his Government." The "constant malevolent publications of the enemies of the Government" persuaded fourteen gentlemen to sign this memorial. The appended list of pamphlets indicates that most of Shebbeare's activity came in the relatively brief period following Bute's retirement and also suggests why he waited until Grenville seemed settled in office and at odds with the Scot before submitting his application. The memorial was accepted, and Grenville added Shebbeare's name to the pension list for £200 yearly.[43]

Dr. Shebbeare may have been implicated in the amusing episode of the *Moderator,* a projected weekly paper of November 19, 1763. The first number was published by John Wilkie and, according to Walpole, "was so scurrilous against the Chief Justice of the Common Pleas, that his court took up the printer." The writers of the *Moderator* were promptly discovered to be John Shebbeare and Philip C. Webb. Philip Francis noted on his copy of that paper that "the second number was never published, the author being threatened with a prosecution." The court was as moderate as the paper was prudent, and the rule to show cause why an attachment should not be granted was never made absolute.[44]

That catalog of ignoble authors—the pension list—currently carried the names of Guthrie, Campbell, Johnson, the Reverend Philip Lloyd (the brother of Grenville's secretary), and Philip Francis, as well as Shebbeare. Little is known of Philip Lloyd's activities. Walpole believed he was employed in counteracting the influence of Hartley's *Budget*.[45] His work, whatever it might have been, sufficed to secure him a £200 pension.

The career and emoluments of the Reverend Philip Francis did not suffer by the change of ministry. To the £600 which he enjoyed annually as a result of Bute's generosity, Francis added another £300 in January, 1764. No wonder he could exclaim to Grenville that he felt "an honest indignation against those who, either for interest or ambition, would betray or destroy" the constitution. The means by which this additional pension was secured are not clear. Francis' son declared that when Henry Fox, Lord Holland, left England for Italy in 1763, he bequeathed the elder Francis to Bute, who in turn transferred him to Grenville, and "Thro' this Recommendation, he afterwards obtained a Pension." There seems to be no doubt that the Reverend Francis was displeased by the offhand treatment he had received from Holland. According to Walpole, Francis sent to Charles Churchill certain papers which might be used against Holland to prove him "a still greater villain than the world believed him." These were discovered after Churchill's death in November, 1764, and, Walpole added, "To silence that wretch [Francis], Lord Holland sent him £500." The story may have some elements of truth in it, but it is at best suspect. Francis' indebtedness to Bute is more readily illustrated by his unsolicited offer to Charles Jenkinson in December, 1764, to defend the earl from the attacks of the opposition. Francis was ready to take up this task "if it be thought proper to answer . . . without injuring the gratitude which I hope I shall ever preserve to Mr. Grenville." Jenkinson, himself close to Bute as well as Grenville, felt "much obliged . . . for this instance of your attention to those who have contributed to be of service to you." The decision lay with "the principal person," however, not with the Treasury secretary, and the project was shortly halted upon Bute's direct orders. It is difficult to say where Francis' loyalties lay, though he was certainly always true to his own best interests.[46]

In view of the multitude of pamphlets, letters, and papers describing the dangers to the liberty of the press in 1763 and 1764, one case of repression by act of parliament stands out in mock-relief during the administration of George Grenville. This was the affair of Timothy Brecknock's *Droit le Roi*. The pamphlet appeared early in 1764, at a time when general warrants, privilege, and the other issues bound up in the Wilkes case were at white heat. Into this scene came "this pestilential treatise . . . a collection from old statutes and obsolete customs of the darkest and most arbitrary ages of whatever tended . . . to show and uphold the prerogative of the Crown." "Such a code," declared Walpole, "spoke for itself. It was incense laid on an altar erected to power on which human sacrifices had already been offered."[47]

The attention of the House of Lords was directed toward *Droit le Roi* by Lord Lyttelton on February 21, and it was severely castigated by him as a reflection upon all things sacred to the memory of liberty and the Revolution. Lord Dartmouth supported Lyttelton and went even further in his condemnation. The ministry, unable to defend the pamphlet had they been willing, could do little but concur. Halifax's censure was elaborate, but he found occasion to complain that Lyttelton had not informed him of his intentions. Marchmont "proposed to tack a compliment to the King on his love of liberty," to the resolution that *Droit le Roi* was "a false, malicious, and traitorous libel." Without a division the book was condemned to be burned, the House of Commons was asked to join the Lords's resolution, and the printer, William Griffin of Fetter Lane, was ordered to attend at the bar of the House. On the twenty-third, Griffin appeared and named Timothy Brecknock, "a retainer of the law, and a hackney writer," as the author. The printer was discharged and Brecknock ordered into the keeping of the Gentleman Usher. The House of Commons concurred with the Lords the next day, and on Saturday, February 25, the common hangman burned the pamphlet at the gate of Westminster Hall. The ceremony was repeated on Monday before the Royal Exchange. As for Brecknock, wrote Walpole, "the latter part of the sentence nobody took any pains to execute." The author of *Droit le Roi* ended upon an Irish gallows, hanged for murder.[48]

This episode was unimportant in itself. It served to embarrass the ministry slightly and allowed the old Whigs to congratulate themselves on saving the constitution. No effort was made to discover if Brecknock wrote at ministerial instigation, although Walpole felt that there was some significance in his later attachment to the Earl of Northumberland. He seems to have been simply a controversial pamphleteer who hoped, by displaying a smattering of learning, to garner a few shillings. More significantly, the case of *Droit le Roi* is an illustration of the readiness of parliament to intervene actively as the guardian of public reading—an attitude independent of party and of consequent importance when parliament and the press clashed a few years later.

In addition to semi-official papers and articles, sober correspondents and impecunious hacks contributed to swell the pamphlet literature of 1763–1765 in support of ministers. Quite typical was Owen Ruffhead's *Considerations on the Present Dangerous Crisis,* which was written during the summer of 1763. The pamphlet attacked all ministers preceding Grenville, and struck at factional use of popular opinion and the press by men like Temple—"a noble Lord, who should degrade his quality by appearing publickly . . . to give countenance to such an offender [as Wilkes], as if, by his presence, he meant to encourage and uphold sedition, in open defiance of his country's laws." Ruffhead struck hard at the current declamation upon the dangers to liberty by men like Wilkes. "Such writers, together with their patrons and adherents, under the specious mask of being friends, are in truth the most dangerous foes, to freedom. By their boundless licentiousness, they afford the only plausible pretext for restraining the most valuable of all rights—the liberty of the press." Against the appeal to public opinion—"to the passions of the multitude"—Ruffhead threw the charge "unconstitutional." The lawful and right course for friends to their country lay in unified support of the crown and the "young and virtuous monarch." A reply was forthcoming, according to John Almon, from the pen of Horace Walpole.[49] *The Opposition to the Late Minister Vindicated* was well written, moderate, most friendly to the Newcastle-Devonshire Whigs, and attracted little attention.

Illustrative of another class of writers and their pamphlets was John Brown's *Thoughts on Civil Liberty, on Licentiousness, and Faction.* A typical "church and crown" pamphlet, Brown's work was filled with righteous platitudes. Faction and civil liberty were declared to be incompatible, and the author bewailed the prevalent immorality of the highest and lowest classes. He acutely remarked, however, that "the people of this kingdom" were not "the populace of the capital" despite the efforts of faction to confound them by styling "the clamour of the populace [as] the voice of the people." The dissemination of political rumor and personal calumny by "enemies of virtue and freedom" was condemned. "He would by no Means discourage the *Freedom of the Press:* Yet, sure, its *Licentiousness* might seem an Object of the Magistrate's Regard." Such an attitude, cautious and conservative as it was, and antagonistic to changes which were taking place, was shared by many an Englishman who, like William Strahan, felt that "as to the liberty of the Press, I never thought it in any Danger, but from it's too great Licentiousness."[50]

One final aspect of press politics during these years deserves to be mentioned. The anti-Scotticism of Wilkes and his fellows naturally aroused a reaction north of the Tweed. Scottish constituents voted laudatory resolutions to their representatives in open defiance of English sentiment. The publication of these resolutions was begun during the summer of 1763, but was halted upon warning from the managers of Scottish politics. Stuart Mackenzie, for one, cautioned his friends against the "immense impropriety" of stirring up greater national friction "at *such* a time." These expressions of official public opinion were consequently ended, and the defense of Scotland's honor left to the ready pens, tongues, and votes of North Britons in London.[51]

George Grenville may not have been a statesman of the visionary, dynamic school of Pitt, but he was a competent and efficient administrator. At the conclusion of the session in 1764, Barrington felt that "George Grenville has done admirably, indeed triumphantly, in the House of Commons." The ministry had proved its strength and secured "in favour of its stability the publick opinion."[52] The *Critical Review* passed its biased approval by stating that "this is the first reign ever known in the British annals, in which wit, learning, reasoning, and literary accomplishments of every kind, were almost entirely on the side of government." "The anti-ministerial writers suffer themselves to be shot at like so many hares in their seats," continued the *Review*. "This silence might be ascribed to the very worst of all causes, had we not seen . . . the most virulent libels that ever were aimed at an administration pass unprosecuted, uncensured, and unpunished."[53] For another year Grenville held his position against the attacks of faction and the efforts of his own master to force him from office. When he fell, neither parliamentary nor popular opposition was the victor, but the one man in England to whom public opinion meant nothing, George the Third.

CHAPTER VII

The Case for the Press in Pamphlets and Parliament

THE FAILURE of the minority in the House of Commons to condemn the use of a general warrant against the press forced discussion of the question out-of-doors. In papers and pamphlets the arguments were placed before the reading public, usually in the form of a defense of the ministry or of the opposition. On the part of the government, an effort was made to demonstrate by a compendium of warrants issued since the Restoration that nothing contrary to custom and usage had been done in Wilkes's case, and that the majority in February, 1764, had simply upheld an ancient and honored practice. The opposition pamphleteers sought to disprove Dr. Johnson's dictum that a general warrant is ". . . a matter about which the people care so very little, that were a man to be sent over Britain to offer them an exemption from it at a halfpenny a piece, very few would purchase it."[1]

The task of stating the case for the opposition fell upon Charles Townshend. During the summer of 1764, he employed his time in writing, and early in August, John Almon published his *Defence of the Minority in the House of Commons, on the Question Relating to General Warrants.* Townshend's pamphlet was a reply to the numerous governmental publications which he accused of misrepresenting the attitude of the minority toward general warrants. They were, said Townshend, opposed only to the use of general warrants when issued against seditious libels, a case in which not only the liberty of the press was concerned, but also the rights of individuals and society in general. He strongly denied any connection between the late minority and John Wilkes—they were not "the factious Suite of any Man." The pamphlet was well written, but it owed its fame and success (it quickly went through five editions) more to its source than its content.

The Defence of the Minority came off Almon's press on August 13. The publisher forwarded an advance copy to Stowe, and on the fourteenth, Townshend also sent Earl Temple a copy, bespeaking "your candour or partiality in reading it." In his letter, the author reminded Temple that "I designed it as a remonstrance, not as a pamphlet, and thought it most prudent, in so great and good a cause, to assume the temper and deportment of a serious and impartial man, writing from principle, and arguing from facts." Townshend's attempt at "brevity, simplicity, and the general strength of composition" was fairly successful, although the "amplification, brilliancy, or inflammatory passages" which he sought to avoid were closest to his natural style. "They tell me," Townshend wrote, "the representation already begins to have effect, and I am called upon to second the blow; but I should hope others will contribute to maintain whatever advantage ground this fair and full state of this important matter may give us in the public judgment." He begged for Temple's candid opinion in order "that I may take your better taste for my future guide."[2]

Friends of the ministry described the pamphlet as "one of the best that has yet made its appearance," and according to Almon, Grenville, "observing the impression it made upon the public, expressed his wish to see it answered." The minority, however, were less pleased. Within two weeks Walpole commented, "It is well written, but does not sell much, as a notion prevails that it has been much altered and softened." John Wilkes's reception of the pamphlet was stated more bluntly, "I do not like the Defence of the Minority. It gives too ample room for cavil. Talking is Charles's talent, and he should have kept at it." Although written with the bitterness of defeat dripping from his pen, Horace Walpole's notice of Townshend's *Defence* in his *Memoirs* is probably an accurate evaluation of the reception and influence of the pamphlet. In spite of declarations that

> 'Mr. Pitt says it has had prodigious effect, and turned many. Grenville says it is serious, of great weight, and very hostile.' . . . I happened to know that Mr. Pitt declared he would not read it; and having afterwards read it, said he found it very inaccurate. There was the same want of truth in affirming that Grenville called it *very hostile*. Townshend was afraid his friends should perceive how far it was from being offensive.[3]

The minister's own opinion is perhaps best reflected in the action taken by his secretary, Charles Lloyd, who immediately took up the task of answering Townshend. Lloyd's *Defence of the Majority* thoroughly crushed its rival. "The writer," said Gilly Williams, "has proved that Charles has gone altogether on false facts, which you know is uncommon, and has gone through the whole with such spirit, that it is much the best performance that has ever appeared on our side."[4] Lloyd admitted that "The Defence of the Minority is writ with a Spirit and Eloquence of Stile which sufficiently distinguishes it from the vulgar or ordinary Productions of Party writers." He then proceeded to dissect Townshend's effort in a dispassionate and meticulous manner. As a parting shot he suggested that "*Liberty, Constitution, Magna Charta,* the *Habeas Corpus,* and the *Revolution,* are Words which, if they were less frequently sounded, would probably be more strongly felt, and more duly revered, by Men of all Descriptions."

Like any good pamphlet, *A Defence of the Majority* called out the skirmishers of the opposition, the anonymous pamphleteers and letter writers. Especially was this true when "the friends of the Ministry were at no pains to conceal the mint from whence [their *Defence*] issued."[5] Sir William Meredith wrote *A Reply to the Defence of the Majority,* in November, which Almon also published, and which supported Townshend's pamphlet in detail. "We [ought] not to be out of love with that *vital Part* of Liberty, which we term the liberty of the Press; nor continue the existence of a Power over it, that is incompatible with its Freedom," wrote Meredith. "It is unhappily blended with the Nature of Liberty, to degenerate often into Licentiousness; but, 'tis so impossible to draw the Line between Them, that if you resort to more than legal power to *Suppress* the *One,* you will soon *destroy* the *Other.*"

The same principles had been set forth by the anonymous writer of *The Hugonot* earlier in the year, who cried out that "an English oligarchy, under the banners of a Scotch faction, has undermined juries into court panders!—Spies and informers spread over the face of the land. . . . The Liberty of the Press stolen away by grains! O Shame! O Distraction!" The threat to the liberty of the press by curtailment of the rights of juries also formed the basis of *An Enquiry into the Question Whether Juries Are, or Are Not, Judges of Law, as well as of Fact,* by Joseph Towers, which was as short as it was dull.

Ministerialists were not behind-hand in answering the efforts of the opposition press. The anonymous author of *The Conduct of the Administration in the Prosecution of Mr. Wilkes* took a high line of attack against Chief Justice Pratt, defended the parliamentary surrender of privilege in cases of libel as "generous" and "disinterested," and spoke of George III as a "patriot King" who had need of "a patriot people" and the power to restrain those who would excite sedition against his government. He also made a strong and timely bid to separate the moderate members of the opposition from the Wilkites. By the beginning of 1765, this pamphlet exchange had reached the point at which postscripts to postscripts in answer to pamphlets in reply to other pamphlets were commonplace.[6] The shops of John Wilkie, who published most of the ministerial pamphlets, and John Almon, the opposition's bookseller, were constantly bringing out new material, or rather they were repetitiously revising the old timeworn phrases and setting them under new titles, for it cannot be said that this flood of propaganda contributed greatly to the discussion of the question of the press in politics and before the law.

Out of the flurry of pamphleteering and newspaper correspondence emerged one name that deserves to be ranked among those of the great Georgian pamphleteers. At the end of July, the *Public Advertiser*, issued by Henry Sampson Woodfall of Paternoster Row, printed a letter signed CRITO which attempted to justify government prosecutions of the reprinters of *North Briton* No. 45. In the next issue of the paper, August 2, CRITO was answered vigorously by the pseudonymous correspondent Candor. So forceful was Candor's letter that Woodfall censored a part and in his August 7 paper announced that

> If our Correspondent C[andor]. will make himself known to us, we shall be induced to comply with his request [for space]; but if he is unwilling *to step forth and avow himself the author, or indemnify us* for any charge whenever we are called upon by *authority,* the printer does not chuse to run the risk of an expensive prosecution and perhaps a *personal* trouble into the bargain.[7]

Woodfall had stated his case clearly. Candor's remarks lay too near debatable ground, and the printer's close association with many good friends of government made him rather anxious to please authority and avoid "a *personal* trouble."

When his first publisher refused his offering, Candor turned elsewhere. He sought out a man who "has hitherto published nothing but what is in opposition to the present Ministry" and sent him a manuscript originally intended for Woodfall's paper. On September 22, John Almon published *A Letter from Candor to the Public Advertiser.* Candor denounced Mansfield's recent charges to the juries in the cases of the printers of No. 45 and compared him to the infamous Judge Jeffreys in sentiment and expression. He satirized the ex officio power of the attorney-general to file informations as "really an excellent device for keeping the scribbling race from meddling with political questions, at least from ever drawing their pens a second time upon such subjects." Of greater significance was Candor's recognition of newspaper ridicule and lampoonery as an accepted form of political criticism which the people no longer considered libelous.

Having found a bold publisher, Candor wrote again, and on October 19, Almon advertised a second *Letter from Candor to the Public Advertiser.*[8] The correspondent turned pamphleteer proved an instantaneous success. Temple was informed by his bookseller, November 12, "I have received another pamphlet from *Candor,* which is very long, very severe, and very good; it is upon juries, libels, warrants, &c."[9] The manuscript bore the date October 17, 1764, and Almon worked rapidly that the delay in publication might not be extended. Before it was off the press this new pamphlet was advertised as *The Power of Juries, Shewing They Are Judges of Law as well as Fact,* but the *Public Advertiser* of November 28, noticed that "Tomorrow will be published *An Enquiry into the Doctrine Lately Propagated Concerning Libels &c. &c.* The pamphlet lately advertized under the *Power of Juries* is *included in this performance.*" The inescapable "Letter" was this time addressed to Mr. Almon, and perhaps as an added note of mystery and with an eye to greater sales, the pseudonym was changed to the Father of Candor. Thus was born the pamphlet which most exactly and vigorously set forth the case for a free and untrammeled press in the early years of the reign of George III.[10] Within three months it ran through as many editions; two more, supplemented by postscripts and additions, were added during 1765, and in 1771, a seventh edition with an appendix was printed. By the time of the second or third edition the title was changed to *A Letter Concerning Libels,* a more sonorous description and one which its doting publisher further contracted to *A Letter on Libels* as it swept him into fame, fortune, and the Court of King's Bench.[11]

The author of the pamphlet set forth his views boldly and with clear purpose. "The Liberty of exposing and opposing a bad Administration by the pen, is among the necessary privileges of a free people, and is perhaps the greatest benefit that can be derived from the liberty of the press." In the attorney-general's power to file informations ex officio he saw an "odious prerogative [that] has been, and may most certainly be again, the means of great persecution. . . . Many an useful publication has been nipped in the bud by an information *ex officio* (that great suppressor of truth) and by the gripe of its executioner, (that enemy to light) the messenger of the press." *A Letter Concerning Libels* pointed out that the practice of granting informations in the Court of King's Bench in effect established the existence of libel without reference to a jury. It became consequently necessary for the jury to retain in itself the power of determining both questions of law and fact—especially so since their representatives had declared that parliamentary privilege did not extend to libel, and "prosecutions for libels generally arise from, and are pursued with a spirit of party revenge."

"When men find themselves aggrieved by the violence or misconduct of . . . the Ministry," wrote the Father of Candor, "it is natural for them to complain . . . and to remonstrate in print against the public proceedings." To attempt to suppress or control this expression by general warrant, close confinement, the seizure of papers, and the requirement of exorbitant sureties for good behavior was all part of

> a doctrine injurious to the freedom of every subject, derogatory from the old constitution, and a violent attack, if not an absolute breach, of the liberty of the press. . . . I will venture to prophesy, that if the reigning notions concerning libels be pushed a little farther, no man will dare to open his mouth, much less to use his pen, against the worst Administration that can take place. . . . In short, I do not see what can be the issue of such a law, but an universal acquiescence . . . a downright passive obedience.

Looking forward to the coming session of parliament, the author reminded members that "most people are of opinion, when a power, dangerous at any time to be exercised, is made use of . . . unnecessarily, the parliament should immediately brand so violent and irregular a step." Candor's parent, who considered Pitt "the Great Dictator," was not, however, buoyed up with optimism: "There is of late such a lack of . . . public men, that I am persuaded there are many gentlemen who would deem Locke on government a libel, were it now published for the first time."

Such there may have been, but many agreed with Walpole that this pamphlet was "the finest piece that I think has been written for liberty since Lord Somers." It was, he added, "the only tract that ever made me understand law." Thomas Gray, to whom Walpole recommended the work, advised his friend, "Your cannonical book I have been reading with great satisfaction. . . . If Englishmen have any feeling left,

methinks they must feel now; and if the ministry have any feeling
(whom nobody will suspect of insensibility) they must cut off the
author's ears, for it is in all the forms a most wicked libel." The magazines literally reprinted the pamphlet, and only Wilkes among the
more liberal politicians seems to have been displeased—and that because " 'coarse worthless fellow,' I am called twice."[12]

The arguments brought forward by the Father of Candor were
devastating. His publisher described the pamphlet as irrefutable and
declared that "the ministry did not attempt to answer this work. It
was invincible."[13] Measured by success, the *Letter Concerning Libels*
stood unanswered, but replies were soon offered. Charles Lloyd added
a postscript to his *Defence of the Majority* and remarked, "Let these
Gentlemen . . . set their Minds at rest: their own Productions sufficiently evince the Liberty of the Press still existing in full Force."
Grenville's secretary refused to meet Candor's arguments, however. On
the salient question of the right of a jury to determine law as well as
fact, he excused himself on the grounds that "it is a Question of too
much Delicacy and Importance for me to decide."[14] A more detailed
refutation was attempted in the anonymous *Considerations on the
Legality of General Warrants,* whose author defended the ministry
and the King's Bench in their respective administrative and juridical
activities. "The danger to the subject," he added, "is a mere phantom
of Imagination."

The identity of the Father of Candor was no less ghostly, but his
sentiments led many to speculate with assurance that John Dunning
wrote the *Letter Concerning Libels* with the aid of Lord Camden.
Almon, the publisher, declared of the author, "He was a noble peer,"
but also that "the real author was a late master in chancery; he had
much assistance from Lord Camden." The two statements are not
entirely conflicting and it has been suggested that Almon's "late master
in chancery" was Robert Pratt, the Chief Justice's half-brother.[15] The
question is academic; either Dunning or Camden might have fathered
Candor. It is most pleasant to imagine Dunning in the role, for to him
fell the defense of the pamphlet and its publisher as the Court of
King's Bench unleashed the "dogs of the law" upon John Almon.

The *Letter Concerning Libels* struck most harshly at the legal problems of the press in politics and animadverted directly upon the recent
stand taken by Mansfield and his fellow jurists in the cases of Williams
and Kearsley. Such criticism was not to be tolerated by the gentlemen

in the full-bottomed wigs. Attorney-General Sir Fletcher Norton moved the court for a writ of attachment against the publisher for contempt of court. A copy of the offending pamphlet had been purchased from a saleswoman in Almon's shop on January 17, 1765, and six days later, the motion for a writ was made. On the strength of the deposition of John Bell, a messenger of the press, that he had secured the pamphlet from the publisher, Almon was given until January 25 to show cause why a writ should not then be issued against him.[16]

When the defendant's counsel appeared on the twenty-fifth, but one judge sat on the King's Bench, Sir John Eardley Wilmot. Almon and his friends felt that Mansfield's delicacy kept him from being party to a cause in which he had such a personal interest; the other justices were unavoidably absent. Despite the plea of the defendant's counsel that an immediate hearing or a dismissal might be granted, Wilmot declared the case worthy of a full bench and "too much to take upon himself." Upon the attorney-general's motion, he bound Almon over until the next term, when a full court might convene.[17]

In the meantime parliament met, and the opposition took up the struggle for the press. The question of general warrants was reopened by Sir William Meredith, and "the great Trial of the Opposition" was held on January 29, when Meredith offered an unqualified motion condemning the use of a general warrant against authors, printers, or publishers as "not warranted by law, and . . . an high violation of the liberty of the subject." The minority did their best, but Pitt was absent and Yorke lukewarm. All the old arguments were brought forth once more, but the ministry rested their defense upon the fact that the question was still *sub judice* in Westminster Hall. Debate was maintained until six o'clock the next morning. By that time a qualifying amendment had shown the strength of the two parties to be 224 and 185. The decisive element was that middle party "which felt the courts needed no stimulus in this matter. They had amended it into oblivion in the preceeding session; now they did so again," and the main question was negated.[18]

As winter passed into spring and the opposition remained leaderless and impotent, one further attempt was made to alleviate the plight of the press. On March 4, Nicholson Calvert moved that "leave be given to bring in a Bill for relief of his Majesty's subjects, touching Informations in the King's-bench, by and in the name of his Majesty's Attorney-General." Though well-meaning, the motion was ill-planned and poorly directed. It was aimed against the person of Attorney-General Norton, and as an attack upon the legal profession it was coldly received by the lawyers in the House. Even friends like Conway, "having observed that those popular questions only terminated in confirming the power that was abused, had vainly laboured to prevent the motion."

Calvert was seconded by Serjeant Hewitt, "but in so cold a manner, that the motion . . . received no material support from his speech." Calvert had argued that the method of proceeding by information allowed punishment without conviction because of the heavy costs borne by the accused. "Thus bad ministers have it in their power to harass any of the best-designing men with frivolous and vexatious prosecutions." Both he and Hewitt admitted, however, that no abuse of the power existed; they insisted "only that it might be an instrument of oppression in bad times." Norton took advantage of his openings, saying, "He had the satisfaction to know that he had never filed an information upon which the party had not afterwards been convicted." "He could not," he added, "consent to strip the Crown of its just prerogative." The opposition factions were fairly well united this day as followers of Newcastle, Pitt, and Temple supported the motion, but Charles Yorke came out flatly against it. He particularly noticed "the many libels which had been published, and the lenity of the Government with regard to them." The Father of Candor had not treated the House of Yorke with kindness, and Charles had his vengeance.

> He observed what strange doctrines of law had been propagated, and amongst others, that of the jury being judges of the law as well as the fact, which would deprive the subject of the benefit of moving in arrest of judgment, and of having the opinion of the Judges in point of law, as well as of the jury in matter of fact, before he could be condemned.

As the supporters of the motion could show no excessive use of the power, their argument of possible abuse was easily refuted by the declaration that there was then no reason to limit it. The House sat until between seven and eight o'clock, and then, by a division of 204–78, rejected the motion.[19]

It is an interesting commentary upon the late eighteenth-century constitution that the opposition which could muster but seventy-eight votes on a popular issue in March, within three months, during which it underwent schism rather than conjunction, should replace Grenville's victorious ministry. George III was determined to change his servants; his cabinet had not been stormed and he might expect compliance to his wishes among a chastened and ineffective minority. He reckoned without his host, however, for Cumberland's negotiations in May stumbled on the block of Pitt and his brother Temple. The king found himself at the mercy of ministers who had no cause to love him, and they extorted a bitter revenge. By forcing George to break his word in dismissing Stuart Mackenzie from office as Lord Privy Seal of Scotland, Grenville and his colleagues freed the king of any vestige of compunction in dealing with the minority.

A new negotiation with Pitt was opened in June. The Great Commoner was given a free hand to construct a ministry to his own tastes. These designated Temple as first lord of the treasury, but the earl refused to come in despite every effort on the part of Pitt and the king and certain knowledge that Pitt would not go on without him. But one avenue lay open to the king, recourse to the great Whig lords, and there he turned in July, welcoming back those men he had driven from place and power in the first years of his reign.[20]

The ministerial change of 1765 had a considerable effect upon the press. The accession of the party which had fought for the liberties of the political press since 1763 bespoke a tolerant attitude toward its own representatives who had suffered for their activities and also toward those who might follow the late ministers into the wilderness of opposition.

John Almon watched the course of negotiations with care and interest. As Temple's personal publisher he expected, had the earl gone to the Treasury, to secure "a situation" from his patron. In this Almon was disappointed, as were most of Temple's friends. A second opportunity for advancement appeared momentarily when Charles Townshend accepted the office of paymaster. Wilkes was informed that Townshend "has given Almon, the serving the Pay Office with stationary wares." Such may have been the new paymaster's original or seeming intent, though it may well have been no more than a humorous jibe at Grenville, "the present nominal minister," who was even then prosecuting Almon. The publisher took Townshend's remarks seriously, and was considerably hurt when they failed to materialize.[21]

In his legal tribulations the publisher of the Letter Concerning Libels had reason to be grateful for the change of ministers in July. Almon's case was resumed before Justices Wilmot, Yates, and Aston, on

Wednesday, May 1, and counsel were heard for both parties. Against Norton and Solicitor-General William De Grey, Almon had secured the services of Serjeant Glynn and John Dunning. The defense seized the initiative and branded the court's procedure as a breach of "the inherent, the native, the peculiar privilege and glory of Englishmen"— trial by jury. Glynn sought to deprecate personal antagonisms by denying that the pamphlet reflected upon "the portrait of an original [Mansfield], it deviated so far from the likeness of any chief justice, particularly the present one of the court of King's bench."

Attorney-General Norton dwelt at length on the dastardly form of Almon's offense. He suggested that had Almon made his submission to the court in January, the case would have been dropped. To the contrary, this rascally printer had rather circulated his pamphlet more widely. From nine o'clock until one-thirty that afternoon Glynn and Dunning attempted to discredit the case against their client. At the end of four and a half hours, Wilmot announced that the strength of the arguments and the importance of the case merited careful deliberation on the part of the judges; the court would notify counsel when ready to deliver their opinion.[22]

Judicial scrutiny of the case brought to light an amazing discovery. The original process upon which action was taken read *the King against John Wilkes* rather than *John Almon!* The clerical error, heretofore unnoticed, completely negated the proceedings against the publisher of *A Letter Concerning Libels*. The court was not prepared, however, to admit defeat and allow Almon to escape upon a technical (if material) error. As early as June 10, Almon met with Glynn and Dunning and warned them that he had received "undoubted information of an intention in the Court to shift the ground of charge." Both men replied, "It could not be, . . . they could never believe the Court would do such a thing and not allow, nor give them notice to make a defence against it." This error in judgment nearly cost Almon his case.

Between one and two o'clock, the afternoon of June 14, Justice Wilmot called for Almon's counsel to appear before the bar immediately. The day's transactions were concluded, and it was mere chance that Dunning was present at this critical juncture. He was able to recall Glynn to the court just as the latter was stepping into his coach, and together they heard Wilmot ask for their consent to amend the writ from *Wilkes* to *Almon* and enlarge the grounds of complaint. Glynn firmly refused to accede to such a demand. Wilmot persevered, though admitting the peculiarity of his request, and "for near an hour, coaxed and bullied them by turns." Tempers rose as an audience of two hundred people gathered in the hall to join Aston's good-natured laughter at his colleague's difficulties. In desperation Wilmot turned to Glynn, with whom he was personally friendly, and asked him, upon his honor, to consent to the proposed alteration like a gentleman. His ire fully roused, the serjeant curtly retorted that, "upon his honour," he would *not* consent.

Yates and Aston now intervened to avoid personal recrimination between Glynn and Wilmot. Yates supported his brother judge and said that the error had only come to their attention the previous evening and "he thought the proposed alteration right and necessary." Aston trimmed, confessing that what was asked "was not altogether the practice." Almon's counsel were not intimidated. Glynn moved to discharge the rule, but the court refused his request. Attorney-General Norton agreed to consent to the original rule being discharged if the error were cited in the motion, but Dunning opposed this as opening a breach for further action against his client. Rebuffed, the court demanded of the defendant's counsel a rule to show why it should not correct the erroneous process on its own authority. The charge fell upon John Dunning, who was defending a pamphlet he may have written and which held that

> The law is the sole sovereign of England, and that law is known and settled, on the firm basis of immemorable usage, innumerable precedents . . . and upon the statutes of kings, lords, and commons. And it is this circumstance which makes the security, the independence, and the preeminent felicity of Englishmen.

Nearly speechless with wrath, he refused to comply and, with Glynn at his side, retired from the hall.[23]

Undeterred by their initial failure, Almon's persecutors took prompt action to recover their position. The Court of King's Bench discharged the original process on June 18; Treasury solicitor Webb at once introduced a new accusation of contempt, and Norton moved for a new writ of attachment against the publisher. Almon hurried to Glynn's residence, and his counsel, now believing the bookseller's secret information that the court intended to commit him until the November term, earnestly advised him to leave London immediately. The only means by which a long imprisonment might be avoided was to insure that the messengers could not serve the rule in person.

Almon followed Glynn's advice. Evading the shadowing messengers, he slipped out of the city that evening. His problems were not thereby solved, for as he wrote to Temple shortly after, "To increase my misfortune, my wife was next day taken in labour, and all my affairs thrown into confusion. . . . my house has been constantly beset with Webb's and Carrington's gangs." The ministerial agents, unable to find their man, moved the court that "leaving a copy of this rule with, and showing the original to any of the family of the said John Almon, shall be deemed good service of this rule." Dunning was able to secure a delay on this process, however, as the intent of court and crown was only too obvious and the case too important.[24]

At this point the ministerial change interposed to rescue Almon from his legal entanglement. The Rockingham ministry replaced Norton with Charles Yorke. The new attorney-general had little sympathy for libelers and publishers, however, and none for the publisher of the *Letter Concerning Libels*. He was willing to continue the prosecution but was overruled when Almon secured the good offices of William Fitzherbert to plead his case with Rockingham. The marquis intervened to prevent further action, although Almon's publications had already begun to veer to a new line of politics which was established by the reconciliation of Temple and his brother George Grenville.[25] There is no doubt that political developments alone saved John Almon, for Wilmot drew up an opinion (which was not delivered) in favor of granting the second attachment. Wilmot held that if the authority of judges "is to be trampled on by pamphleteers and newswriters, and the people are to be told that the power given to the Judges for their protection, is prostituted to their destruction, the Court . . . will instantly lose all its authority. . . . A greater scandal could not be published." A later jurist described this opinion as "the hasty and warm ebullition of a mind fraught with arbitrary notions, . . . the very reverse of . . . a considered, digested, ulterior opinion!" It was nonetheless representative of the legal attitude toward press criticism.[26]

The Rockingham ministry of 1765–1766 was able to express its lenient attitude toward the press in the cases of the various printers. The origins of these difficulties—John Wilkes and the general warrant— were another matter, though neither problem arose until the last days of this short-lived administration. On April 22, 1766, the question of general warrants was reviewed; the initiative now lay in the hands of the administration, and the motions of Sir George Savile and William Meredith bore belated fruit. It was declared that "a general warrant to apprehend the author, printer, or publisher, of a libel, is illegal; and, if executed on the person of a member of this House, is also a breach of privilege of this House." The question was carried by a division of 173–71. Seizure of papers was similarly condemned with the support of nearly all parties.

Just as the House was rising, a disturbing element appeared. Pitt, who had remained a free agent throughout the past year, stood to announce that he should move for a declaration that all general warrants were illegal. He was supported by none other than George Grenville, now the leader of the largest opposition faction. Meredith replied for the ministers, abusing Grenville and claiming (not without reason) that credit was due rather to himself who had first introduced this measure than to those who followed after. Pitt haughtily denied any debt to Meredith and joined with Grenville in a bout of mutual admiration and justification in which Temple was included.

The ministers were taken aback. On the twenty-fifth, Pitt moved his resolution that "a general warrant . . . being illegal, except in cases provided for by act of Parliament, is, if executed upon a member . . . a breach of the privilege of this House." This attempt to condemn all general warrants was warmly adopted by Charles Yorke but opposed by Fletcher Norton and Solicitor-General William De Grey. Grenville gave halfhearted support, Sir George Savile wholehearted, and of Pitt, it was said, "No man ever rode upon a better dressed horse, or brought him up to the object which made him snort, with more address than that rider did upon that occasion." The lawyers (excluding Yorke) were not convinced, but the resolution was adopted.[27]

That all questions might be resolved, leave was given to Grenville and Pitt to bring in "a bill to restrain the issuing of any warrant, for seizing papers, except in the cases of treason or felony." The ministry refused, however, to entertain a similar bill against a general warrant for seizing persons. The draft proposed was read by Grenville on May 2, got a second reading on the sixth, and survived an attempt on May 9 to delay action for two months. After a weekend in committee, the bill was read for the third time May 14, and sent up to the Lords as "a bill to prevent the inconveniences and dangers to the subject from searching for and seizing papers."

Their Lordships received the bill on May 26, and granted a first reading two days later. Friday, May 30, the judges were ordered to attend the second reading, and after some debate the House of Lords resolved to commit the bill for two months. As parliament was prorogued the following week, no further action was taken and the bill disappeared.[28]

The Rockingham ministry was tottering on the brink of dismissal at the time they took up the problem of general warrants, and both Pitt and Grenville seriously embarrassed their efforts. Edmund Burke summarized their services by simply noting that

> The personal liberty of the subject was confirmed, by the resolution against general warrants.
>
> The lawful secrets of business and friendship were rendered inviolable, by the resolution for condemning the seizure of papers.

It was, after all, a "short administration."[29]

To John Wilkes who proclaimed himself "still devoted to 'the good old cause,'" the Rockingham ministry showed only the coldest politeness. After a period of high hopes in the early autumn of 1765, the exiled patriot came to realize that he could expect little from the party which had most unwillingly supported him at an earlier date and had only recovered its strength after he fled. Wilkes was not easily disheartened. In May, 1766, he returned to London intent upon realizing something from the Rockingham ministry and placing his claims sufficiently high that he might gracefully accept less than he asked. Wilkes was quite frankly advised that Rockingham "had not the least intention" of serving him; Burke and Fitzherbert made it clear that the ministers felt no obligation toward him and would not protect him from the law. After two weeks he returned to France a sadder but scarcely a wiser man. The ministry had placed £1,000 at his disposal out of personal kindness, and Fitzherbert loaned him £100, but John Wilkes was still a homeless outlaw.[30] And as political upheaval swept the English scene once more, political journalism sank to the depths of factional squabbling, inconsiderate and inconsiderable.

CHAPTER VIII

The Press in Action, 1765–1768

THE COLLAPSE of George Grenville's ministry and the return of the great Whig lords to office marks a new phase in the journalistic warfare of the period. The positions of the Grenvillian and Rockingham propagandists were reversed, but a disruptive element was added by the anomalous position of Pitt and Temple. In short, during the period 1765–1768 English politics labored under the worst handicaps of a factionalism which very nearly deserved the epithets used by contemporaries in describing its evils.

The press reflected the political scene with a fair degree of accuracy. Factionally speaking, newspapers and pamphlets represented the attitude of the Rockingham government and the Grenvillian opposition. Then in 1766, after a second change of ministers, the governmental effort almost disappeared before the onslaught of writers belonging to Grenville, Temple, and Rockingham. The Chatham-Grafton ministry, politically the weakest of George III's early ministries, was also the least well equipped to wage psychological warfare. Whereas at an earlier date it had been said that government writers had all the best of it, after 1766, factional writers on the other side (which scarcely deserved the name "opposition") held the field after every engagement.

When Grenville left the king's services he took with him his best political writer, Charles Lloyd. No sooner had the new ministry kissed hands than there appeared a pamphlet which set forth *An Honest Man's Reasons for Declining to Take Part in the New Administration.* Rockingham's ministry was described as "composed of the extravagancies of youth, and the infirmities of age." Grenvillian hatred of Bute was apparent as the "honest man" accused the new ministers of being the tools of the Favorite and at the same time predicted that they would fall if they dared oppose him.

A reply to the Grenvillian attack was published within a few days. *A Candid Answer* to Lloyd's pamphlet was written by Grey Cooper, a young lawyer in search of a government place. He described the new ministry as a return to the old system which had prevailed before the rise of Bute and accurately set forth Rockingham's attitude toward Pitt "with whom a speedy reunion is most sincerely desired" and whose support was expected, "whether as a minister, or as a private man." Similar sentiments were expressed in *A Pair of Spectacles for Short-sighted Politicians.* When Lloyd acknowledged Cooper's activity in *A Critical Review of the New Administration,* he was promptly answered by *The Merits of the New Administration Fairly Stated.* This last pamphlet sufficed to recommend Cooper for a place. Apparently no firm believer in the stability of the men whose permanency he had been arguing, Cooper held out for a pension as well, and when that was arranged he accepted appointment as secretary of the treasury.[1]

The charge leveled against Rockingham—of being Bute's tool—was a dangerous weapon, for governmental writers could easily turn it upon the late ministers. One accusation, however, seems to have pricked the sensitivity of the new administration most deeply. Edmund Burke, Rockingham's secretary, complained that "they charged the M[arquis] of R[ockingham] with a jockeyship." Poor loyal Burke then spent the better part of a column in the *Annual Register* refuting the dastardly implication![2]

Chesterfield rejoiced that "the paper war is carried on with much fury and scurrility on all sides, to the great entertainment of such lazy and impartial people as myself." The *Daily Advertiser* and the *Public Advertiser* printed "all the political letters" and amused the old earl "for an hour or two every morning." The substance of ministerial propaganda was summarized by Sandwich with sarcastic accuracy: "the late ministers are rogues, rascals, and idiots . . . they sold employments, and were governed by Lord Bute; . . . the present people are extremely popular, and likely to be able ministers, if their unkind and cruel adversaries will but give them time to learn their trade."[3]

Among the ranks of Grenville's writers now appeared William Knox, an Irishman of considerable talent who defended the late minister's colonial policy. Knox wrote in support of Grenville's government in 1764, but did not declare himself openly until November, 1765. The Earl of Sandwich's penman, Scott, writing as "Anti-Sejanus," also provided his "daily libel" to the press, switching his attentions to fit his master's whim. No one was impressed in January, 1766, when Grenville "talk'd much" in Commons "of Newspaper Writers & Falsehoods they had propagated." Even the king remarked that "Ye. few squibs on ye.

Address would have appear'd to me as plan'd by a late Sec. of State [Sandwich] even if He had not been a Speaker yt. day; from yt. quarter I make no doubt but every Art will be us'd to hamper Adm[inistratio]n."[4]

Probably the most significant factional statement issued during the Rockingham administration was *The History of the Late Minority,* written and published by John Almon. The *Late Minority* portrayed events of the past half-decade as they appeared to a propagandist closely associated with Temple. In virulent and bitter terms he attacked Bute and his ministry; in laudatory phrases he set forth the merits of Pitt and Temple. A first edition of twelve copies, designed for private entertainment, demonstrated the writer's talents, and early in June, 1766, a second impression allowed for wider circulation. By the middle of the month Almon published a third printing, and in time *The History of the Late Minority* was translated "in Holland, France, and other foreign nations."

The line adopted by Temple's publishers produced violent reactions in many quarters. When John Wilkes read the pamphlet's criticism of his activities during the summer of 1763, he complained, "I am very ill treated. . . . Everything is offered up to the shrine of Stowe." And he threatened to "contradict the gross falsehoods respecting me in that history." Wilkes was assured that Temple was in no way responsible for the pamphlet (and so Almon himself claimed many years later), but the patriot could not help wondering "after all, how the author . . . got at some secrets."[5]

The History of the Late Minority also proved embarrassing to George Grenville. At the moment the pamphlet appeared, Temple and Grenville were firmly united, and through the younger brother a tentative approach was being made toward some of Bute's closest adherents. Leicester House and the Scots took immediate offense; Bute "was himself hurt and and surprised that such a publication should be made at this time." Grenville was asked on June 10 to authorize a declaration that the *Late Minority* did not enjoy Temple's sanction, and the next day, after talking with the lord of Stowe, he informed the Scots that his brother "has neither advised nor encouraged the writing or publishing of any political paper whatever, and more particularly not this pamphlet." Despite prompt denial of Temple's connection with the *Late Minority,* Grenville continued to be discomfited by Almon's publication. Publisher and patron and brother were too closely associated to be easily separated, and not until June 25 was Bute satisfied with the proffered explanation.[6]

The delicacy of political negotiations in June, 1766, forced Grenville to retrench, even among his own writers. Philip Lloyd, who was engaged in preparing a pamphlet on American affairs for Grenville, was ordered to avoid being concerned in any publications and promptly dropped the work he had in hand. Thomas Whately, who seems to have acted as a press supervisor for Grenville during this period, immediately complained that his chief's actions threatened to expose their whole system, for if Lloyd attempted to withdraw his pamphlet from the printer's hands "he might probably meet with a refusal, and certainly would exasperate the printer to tell all he knows, and to trace the pamphlet when he sees it published by another." Whately himself "would not on any account appear," so he urged Grenville to let the pamphlet run its course. A good example of Whately's activities may be found in a letter addressed to Grenville in September, in which Whately wrote, "I have endeavoured to trace the author of that paper which you thought so well done, but can only find that it is not any of the persons we guessed."[7]

As spring passed into summer, George III prepared once more to change his ministry. The Rockingham administration had never been strong, and despite the latent ideas of party which its leaders may have entertained, it was far from homogeneous. Royal influence was as strong as ever, and Pitt felt that "no solid system for giving . . . any tolerable degree of safety can be possible under his Grace's [the Duke of Newcastle's] auspices . . . his influence colours and warps the whole."[8] The death of Cumberland and the alienation of Pitt, the open opposition of placemen who looked to the king for instruction, and the dilatory resignation of Grafton removed every buttress of the ministry. It lacked the confidence of the nation, despite Burke's claims, and early in July the king opened negotiations with Pitt.

The Great Commoner was willing enough to form a ministry. He sent for Temple and offered him the Treasury. On July 15 the brothers-in-law met, and friends of Temple predicted they would kiss hands the next day, Pitt as secretary of state, Temple as first lord of the treasury. Once more, however, the earl declined to join Pitt in government; the ministry was to be Pitt's and he refused to share his power. Temple therefore declined the honor of standing as "a capital cypher, surrounded with cyphers . . . the whole under the guidance of that great Luminary, the great Commoner."[9]

The "cyphers" who made up the new ministry included Grafton, Shelburne, Camden, Charles Townshend, and Henry Conway. Grafton was given the Treasury, Conway the leadership of the Commons, and Pitt, reserving for himself the Privy Seal, was created Earl of Chatham and entered the House of Lords. There was more than politeness in the king's letter informing the new earl that his patent was signed: "I know the Earl of Chatham will zealously give his aid towards destroying all party distinctions, and restoring that subordination to Government, which can alone preserve . . . Liberty, from degenerating into Licentiousness."[10] No political leader agreed more closely with George's attitude toward political organization; none detested party or faction more wholeheartedly than the Earl of Chatham. But the Earl of Chatham was not Mr. Pitt.

While the nation recoiled before the realization that Pitt's voice would be heard no more in the House of Commons, the outgoing ministers took steps to retain their claim to popular sympathy. The Earl of Hardwicke advised his brother, Charles Yorke, to see to the public announcement of his resignation himself, while Newcastle and his friends looked with favor upon the avidity with which rumors of Temple's estrangement from Pitt were taken up by the newspapers.[11] The primary effort of the displaced ministers came from Edmund Burke, who in a few hours, drew up a party manifesto which was published as *A Short Account of a Late Short Administration*. This brief four-page epitaph praised the Rockingham ministry for its support of "the liberty and commerce of their country" in opposition to "placemen and pensioners." "They were in office long enough to accomplish many plans of public utility," wrote Burke, "and by their perseverence and resolution, rendered the way smooth and easy to their successors; having left their king and their country in a much better condition than they found them." Whether or not "the nation felt and allowed their merit," it was Burke's facile pen, his ability as a propagandist that made him valuable to Rockingham. Burke's pamphlet set off a series of recriminations from the Grenvillian camp, chief among which was Charles Lloyd's *A True History of a Late Short Administration*, but Walpole rightly observed that "the glory with which the late ministers retired was half of it plucked from the laurels of the new Earl of Chatham."[12]

The breach between Temple and Chatham was at once obvious, and the results were immediate and violent. As one of Shelburne's friends wrote, Temple "played a foolisher part than before. He . . . set himself up as the head of a party in opposition to William Pitt in conjunction with the most unpopular man in England, his brother. The Pigmies are in arms against the Giants." This description of the situation was correct except in one detail; Bute, not George Grenville, was "the most unpopular man in England," and Temple's propagandists knew well how to use that ammunition in the general melee which ensued. Chesterfield had prognosticated on July 11 that Pitt would head a new ministry and had suggested that he would have to accept Bute's assistance in doing so. "When that shall come to be known," he added, "as known it certainly will soon be, he may bid adieu to his popularity." Temple's friends firmly believed that "our full blown flattering hopes are blasted by that damned Northern wind . . . P[itt] has joined with the Thane." With such an attitude prevailing among those most capable of influencing public opinion, it mattered little whether Bute's influence was imaginary or whether he was the new minister's ally. "Can it be possible such oyl and vinegar could incorporate?" asked one lady. "Tis said and by Pamphlets prov'd, Bute and Pitt are so."[13]

The furor roused by Pitt's pension in 1761 was as nothing compared to the turmoil of the press in July and August, 1766. In the first instance the Great Commoner had had Temple at his side; the Earl of Chatham faced no more bitter opponent than the lord of Stowe, whose press connections had been refined by five years of opposition pamphleteering. Two weeks after Lord Chatham appeared, an unfriendly commentator remarked: "The fury of the people against the Apostate Commoner is beyond all description, and it is really difficult to say, whether his former friends . . . or enemies load him most with execrations, in short his popularity is annihilated."[14]

The press attack upon Chatham was inspired by Temple and carried out by his pamphleteers and publishers. Walpole informed Lord Holland that Temple, at the close of his negotiations with Pitt, had "recollected Almon and Humphrey Cotes; not for Lords of the Treasury; but as responsible to them."[15] The accuracy of Walpole's statement must be doubted, but the tenor is certainly clear. The men whose hopes rested upon Temple's accession to office led the attack upon the man responsible for their disappointment.

Early in August a pamphlet entitled *An Enquiry into the Conduct of a Great Commoner* was advertised. Even before it was published it was recognized as Temple's challenge to Chatham. Newcastle was aware that Humphrey Cotes had the manuscript on August 3 and that Almon was to be the publisher. He was further informed that "it was *authentick*." Charles Lloyd learned on the fourth that "Almon . . . (who says that he had authority for the particulars of what he intended to publish), had received orders not to publish it," but on August 5, Lloyd informed George Grenville that Almon planned to publish his pamphlet the next day. Temple's feelings in the matter are not clear. There is no doubt that Cotes, who was the principal author of the pamphlet, received his detailed information from Lord Temple. Almon says, however, that Cotes "without Lord *Temple's* participation, caused them to be published." Almon would certainly not have gone ahead with his plans against Temple's wishes, and it seems most likely that the *Enquiry into the Conduct of a Late Right Honourable Commoner*, which he subsequently published, was the offspring of Temple's easily heated passions, which were already beginning to cool. By August 24, Temple was begging Cotes "not to proceed further in anything of this sort" and describing himself as "very miserable" because of the vilification showered upon his brother-in-law.[16]

An Enquiry into the Conduct of the late Great Commoner was a bitter scrutiny of Chatham's career from 1760 to the formation of his new ministry. The close connection between Pitt and Bute was emphasized, and the resignation of 1761 was described as owing solely to the "truly patriotic resentment" of Earl Temple. Pitt was castigated for his failure to support Wilkes fully, and Temple was praised for disrupting the proposed "Butal and Ducal" negotiations of the previous year. The recent negotiations were discussed with details which only Temple could have provided; Pitt was declared to have "sacrificed his noble friend and relation, and all the ties of affection, gratitude, honour, faith, and . . . his domestic peace" for a union with Bute. Beyond libeling Chatham in every way possible, the pamphlet also issued an invitation to political alliance from Temple "to the Gentlemen *out*. . . . You are now the only men from whom the Public hope for . . . security. . . . And being possessed of great and real property in the kingdom, you are most naturally and nearly interested in the public welfare, and may truly be stiled the . . . guardians of the people." Overthrow this "*Faction* formed by an unnatural connection between the Deserter of the people and the Favourite of the Court. . . . In this great, this truly patriotic work, . . . you will have the assistance and support of all good men, all real well-wishers to their country."

The pamphlet created quite a sensation. Temple chastened the author on his "*many* mistakes." Bute complained to the king that "unapprised of what has happened [I] am again by Humphry Coates declared the cause of Temple's conduct." Lady Sarah Osborn, who reveled like most letter writers in a plenitude of scandal, declared that there was "more witt flying about than for some years past." Nor was Cotes's by any means the only pen leveled against Chatham.

> Every day brings forth some new production from Stowe, endeavouring to prove Lord Temple the wisest, honestest, greatest, and most disinterested patriot of the age, and Lord Chatham the most contemptible, avaritious man that ever lived, the lowest and most servile flatterer of Lord Bute, and the wretch who to serve his own ends has basely betrayed the interest of his country.

The family reunion of Temple and Grenville brought Charles Lloyd into the fray with *An Examination of the Principles and Boasted Disinterest of a Late Right Hon. Gentleman* vindicating Temple and condemning Chatham. Temple's old friend Lyttelton added his bit to the blast, and countless unidentifiable journalistic insects swarmed hungrily about this open political wound.[17]

The late Mr. Pitt was not defenseless. Despise printers and papers he might, but by the middle of August, Chesterfield believed he had found "an article that expresses such extreme contempt of Lord Temple, and in so pretty a manner, that I suspect it of being Mr. Pitt's own."[18] This was probably the anonymous *Short View of the Political Life and Transactions of a Late Right Honourable Commoner*. The author set out "to remind the public that the Earl of Chatham has acted in no manner derogatory to . . . Mr. Pitt." He recognized the significance of the press attack in unflattering if accurate terms: the "conductors of the press" have "basely deserted" Pitt "for the important consideration of raising their respective papers an additional half quire, and gaining a new set of readers." In refuting the *Enquiry's* description of the recent Pitt-Temple negotiation, the *Short View* revealed that its author did not write under Chatham's direction; his facts were wrong. It was his treatment of Temple that made Chesterfield envision Chatham's touch. Of "the illustrious earl" now squirting his "impotent invectives" he said, "Had he not fastened himself into Mr. Pitt's train . . . he might have crept out of life with as little notice as he crept in, and gone off with no other degree of credit than that of adding a single unit to the bills of mortality."*

Every device was used to blacken the Chatham peerage. One pamphlet took the form of *A Letter from William, Earl of Bath, in the Shades, to William, Earl of Chatham at Court*—a reminder of that other "great commoner," Pulteney, who had retired into noble oblivion. Another, *The E[ar]l of Ch[atha]m's Apology, a Poem,* reminded its readers that Pitt's meager fortune was in part the gift of one who had admired his determination at an earlier date to remain in the House of Commons. A very bitter *Letter to Will Chat-em, Esq; of Turn-about-Hall, from His Sister* called to the new earl's attention his own criticism of Anne Pitt, who had once asked in vain for a pension.

Virtue is less interesting than vice. The writers who defended Chatham demonstrated an almost uniform dullness. *A Vindication of the Conduct of the Late Great C[ommone]r* did no more than its title promised; *Seasonable Reflections on the Present State of Affairs* did no better than to note that the panegyric on Temple in Cotes's *Enquiry* "is such, as to make every well-wisher to his country, glad that the personage whose hand is so conspicuous in several parts of it, is not in the present ministry." Some slight interest attaches to the eulogy of Chatham, apparently drafted for foreign consumption, in the *Supplément au ministère de Mr. Pitt*—although no Englishman would have read it through.

The most interesting of the Chathamite pamphlets, because of its recognition of the importance of the press in forming public opinion, was *A Letter to the Right Honourable the E[arl] T[emple]*. To his unpretentious text, the anonymous author prefixed *A Curious Dialogue between a Certain Rt. Hon. Author and His Bookseller*. The

---

*Internal evidence suggests that Charles Townshend was in some degree responsible for *A Short View*. He is described (for no very good reason) as "this great man [who] spoke with a force of eloquence that was actually amazing, and a fund of information that seemed to be unlimited." The suggestion is strengthened by the author's dictum: "No man should attach himself blindly to a party." So Townshend —a member of the Grenville, Rockingham, and Chatham administrations. At the very moment this pamphlet appeared, Townshend was trying to woo Almon from Temple's camp; he had been one of the chief proponents of a vigorous press policy, and he was one of the few men in Chatham's party who appreciated the power of the press.

lengthy dialogue presents a highly amusing satirical description of Temple and Almon preparing a new pamphlet against Chatham. Little Vamp, the bookseller, boasts of his abilities, and his patron is made to remark, "Egad the fellow's mad; the sale of the History of the Minority has turn'd his brain—another such hit would entitle him to a place in Bedlam." Vamp regains favor, however, by a touch of judicious praise and a readiness to prepare a harmless *Answer* to his patron's own pamphlet. The noble author is flattered and assures Vamp, "—you'll be an alderman in two years,—and then may make every motion I want in the city."

The joint activities of Almon and Temple were perhaps not very honorable to either, but evidence of their effectiveness was forthcoming. Charles Townshend approached the publisher about the middle of August and apparently tendered some remunerative token on behalf of the ministry in an effort to silence his press. Fully cognizant of the bookseller's loyalty to Temple, the new chancellor of the exchequer suggested that Almon first secure his patron's approval. Almon lamented the fact that his best friends now differed politically, but he flatly refused to broach the subject to Temple. "You know his lordship's temper; he is warm and decided; particularly at the present moment." The risk of alienating a sure support, in hope of favor from a ministry in which no one believed, had little appeal for a London merchant whose trade was steadily increasing. Almon refused to transfer his allegiance.[19] By winter the personal rivalry between Chatham and Temple had ceased to attract readers. "The newspapers themselves have done with politics," wrote Walpole. "Lord Temple just crawls about Almon's window in the shape of an autumnal fly, that a child could crush."[20]

It is difficult to assess the results of the press campaign which was conducted under Temple's auspices during the late summer and fall, but it was certainly effective in bringing about the collapse of the new minister's popularity. As for Chatham's own reaction—he was a proud man, easily wounded in his weakest parts, and Jenkinson's correspondent may have spoken authoritatively when he wrote, "Lord Chatham is supposed not to be insensible of the abuse that is bestowed upon him. They have indeed bespattered his Lordship very sufficiently."[21]

The career of the new ministry was as erratic as that of its leader. Constructed on the basis of "men, not measures," the Chatham ministry soon demonstrated its lack of cohesion. The first parliamentary skirmish engaged Chatham and Camden on the side of prerogative against Mansfield's defense of liberty—to the great glee of the Grenvillians who led the opposition. The adherents of Rockingham, who had remained in a position of friendly neutrality, were alienated almost immediately thereafter, and resigned en masse, excepting only Conway. Chatham was creating his own opposition, and when he failed to secure the support of Bedford's followers, he had no recourse but the "King's friends." Then, at the close of the year, his health failed. Leadership was suddenly thrust upon the Duke of Grafton, who became "a plaything in the hands of fate and Charles Townshend." Chatham's illness was certainly not political, as his enemies (and some friends) insinuated, but Grafton can hardly be blamed for despairing when he read his chief's declaration that "his fixed purpose has always been, and is, not to be a proposer of plans, but as far as a seat in one House enables, an unbiassed judge of them."[22] Three days after this statement of political abdication, the government was defeated in the House of Commons on the proposed land tax.

Defeated on a money measure, his chancellor of the exchequer in open rebellion and aided by his Commons spokesman, Chatham made a final effort. The king assured him, "As for losing questions, that did not intimidate his Majesty: he would stand his ground and be the last to yield, although he stood single." But Chatham was a broken man, broken in body and spirit, and after a feeble effort to regain control, he relapsed into complete inactivity. Grafton attempted to hold the ministry together—a noble, futile, courageous, and stupid example of loyalty to men, not measures, that won him universal contempt. George III was more astute. "What would my own steadiness avail," he asked, "unless the minister is equally resolved to carry on my business? It is ever in the power of an administration to lay me upon my back." Realistic, politic, the king set to work. His success is measured by the tenure of the Grafton ministry and the fact that North's ministry survived its birth pangs. The opposition was powerful, but, remarked John Almon, "I wish I could not add venal too."[23]

The political press of 1767 was feverishly active but, like the leaders from whom its cue was taken, confused, contradictory, and above all factious. Early in the year the former chancellor of the exchequer, William Dowdeswell, prepared a pamphlet for Rockingham which the Marquis liked "most exceedingly; and wish the public was in possession of." He cautioned the author, however, against allowing his identity to appear. This unidentified pamphlet foreshadowed the great Rockingham manifesto of 1770, for like the *Thoughts on the Cause of the Present Discontents,* Dowdeswell's opus circulated among the party leaders. Burke saw it; Rockingham kept it for some time and did not hesitate to suggest changes to the author.[24]

George Grenville's writers continued active; Whately kept Grenville informed of various journalistic projects, and Lloyd was busy writing in close association with his chief. When superimposed upon the efforts of Temple's penmen, the Grenvillian press was relatively impressive. It was sufficient to draw from Horace Walpole a snort of anger when, in November, Grenville complained in the House of Commons of being "much misrepresented in libels." "Nothing could be less justly founded," wrote Walpole. Grenville "himself wrote one . . . in which Lord Rockingham and Conway were treated with contempt and bitterness. His friend, the Dean of Norwich [Philip Lloyd], Thomas Pitt, and Rigby, not to mention his brother Lord Temple, dabbled continually in that way." Augustus Hervey was another frequent writer in Grenville's camp, although he seems to have acted upon his own volition. He frequently contributed to the *Gazetteer* as "A Briton."[25]

The activities of the government toward creating a favorable press are less clear. About this time the Scottish bard, James Macpherson, foster father of Ossian, took up the work of press supervision which he continued under Lord North. In 1767 he was "specially engaged to act as the Treasury editor," and the £200 salary he had secured from Bute was continued in remuneration of such services. A system of news control was in operation at this time, as is evidenced by the complaint of George Grenville that a colonial letter he wished to see published had been "refused [by the papers] under the influence of those who have bought those channels of public intelligence, that the people of Great Britain may be continued in ignorance." It was perhaps at this period that James Scott made his futile attempt to secure the services of Oliver Goldsmith for the political press. The political parson later reminisced, "I told him my authority; I told him that I was empowered to pay most liberally for his exertions," but Goldsmith would not stoop to such a menial task. One member of the administration used the press as an outlet for his good spirits and disgust with his colleagues. George Townshend, elder brother of the chancellor of the exchequer, and Lord-Lieutenant of Ireland delighted in caricaturing himself "with his hands tied behind himself and his mouth open.[26]

As at an earlier date, however, it was that group of publishers and writers connected with Temple who delivered the most telling blows. Chief among these was John Almon. In replying to Grenville's complaint of abuse in November, 1767, Conway, who spoke for the government in the House of Commons, replied that "he himself was abused by . . . Almon once a month. . . . He always bought the pamphlet,—the only hurt he did to the printer." "Everybody must live by their trade," he added, "abuse was Almon's trade."[27] The "pamphlet" to which Conway referred was in reality a monthly magazine, the *Political Register,* and while it appears to have been instituted on the sole responsibility of its publisher, Almon, it was recognized as the official organ of Temple and his faction.

Almon had toyed with the idea of a political periodical in 1764, but not until the spring of 1767 did his plans come to fruition. The prospect of securing contributions from John Wilkes was influential in the establishment of the journal. Almon knew the power of Wilkes's pen, and he urged the exile to put it to paper once more. "What comes from your pen must be good: and to me it is a matter of astonishment the public have not been favored with something long ago since no man is so capable of affording them entertainment." On April 14, 1767, Almon announced the imminent publication of the *Political Register* and openly asked Wilkes to write for him. Before the end of the month, the initial advertisements were published, boasting of the contributions of many "men of the first rate talents."[28]

The new magazine appeared in May. Its "chief design" was set forth in the preface: "To direct the people . . . in the study of Politics, and to explain to them the conduct, the views, and principles of those who undertake the government of the state." The *Political Register* differed little from the pattern of its many contemporaries. Politics, book reviews, letters, and fugitive papers made up its bulk. Each issue was accompanied by a handsome black-and-white plate satirizing a timely political issue. Bute, Chatham, Fox, all figured prominently as dupes or villains, and a desecrated Britannia was the standard victim of their follies. Indecent satire and ribald verse were but the necessary trimming demanded by eighteenth-century readers.

Almon's editorial boldness won him a wide circulation. His repeated requests for material from Wilkes were eventually gratified, and as the fifth number of the magazine was being offered to the public, Almon wrote to Wilkes, "The Political Register succeeds beyond my most sanguine expectations. It is become the fashionable publication of the times. All parties buy it, and the public approve it."[29] The public was not, however, "all parties."

The *Political Register* enjoyed the distinction of being the second periodical within the decade which looked to Temple for support and created serious political difficulties for its noble patron. Long before Almon's magazine appeared, Temple's attitude toward the press had been an irritant between the earl and the Marquis of Rockingham. In January, Lord Lyttelton had attempted to negotiate a union of the opposition factions and had been told "fairly and fully" by Rockingham, "In regard to Lord Temple, . . . his conduct in the matter of libels and in his public *conversations,* had been such, that I believed, amongst our friends he was not a man to be talked upon."[30] Worse was yet to come.

By July 17, the ministry, leaderless and torn by dissentient opinion, had tried every means but one of securing new allies and a new lease on its political existence. On that date the king commanded Rockingham to draw up a plan for a comprehensive administration which would exclude no one. He was asked in effect to do the impossible. Both Grafton and his master fully anticipated the results: "it may disunite parties freshly and loosely cemented, and . . . some one among them may find it for their interest . . . to fall in honourably with the present Administration. If resentment comes in aid . . . this event may still be the more likely."[31]

On the evening of July 20, the opposition factions held their council at Newcastle House. The chiefs were present—Rockingham, Newcastle, Bedford, and their satellites—excepting Temple and Grenville, who were represented by Richard Rigby. Inauspiciously the conference opened with the presentation of Grenville's *sine qua non,* a firm colonial policy and places for his friends; neither he nor Temple asked to be included in the cabinet. No agreement was reached on the first point, nor on the second. Then Rockingham outlined his demands, which included the retention of Conway as leader in the Commons. To this Bedford and Rigby objected, and after hours of jockeying, the meeting broke up. The following day agreement was reached upon one point; each faction was now free to seek its own ends. The king's victory was complete. No matter how weak his ministers, their opponents were more feeble. Death removed Townshend in September, and the ministry was strengthened by the acquisition of Lord North. The opposition factions were at each others' throats when parliament convened, November 24, and in less than a month places had been found for Bedford's followers. As they quickly proceeded to fortify their position it was apparent to all that George III was the unshaken master of English politics.[32]

The negotiations of July 20–21 left the factions in opposition separated but not alienated. Tempers had been high on all sides, but apologies for hasty words were promptly made. A seed of resentment and suspicion had been sown, however, by the Grenvilles' demand for a formal declaration upon colonial affairs. Why, asked Rockingham, should such a request be made unless they "would lay it before the public with whatever coloring they thought proper, so as to throw a construction upon our conduct to our disadvantage."[33] Unknown to the marquis, the entire negotiation was about to be laid bare in John Almon's *Political Register.*

Rockingham had scarcely retired to his estates after the negotiation failed than Temple's publisher learned every detail of the July 20 meeting "from the mouth of one of the persons present" at Newcastle House. Almon's informant was undoubtedly Richard Rigby, Grenvillian spokesman and no stranger to the political materials which Almon published monthly. The account was detailed and accurate, but so laden with political explosives that Almon was at a loss as to the course he should take. "One party advises me to publish the narrative as my copy is perfect . . . ," he wrote to Wilkes, "the other party are strongly against it, so that I am at my wits ends what to do. But affairs must soon take a turn one way or other and then I believe I shall put it into the Political Register." Almon's hesitancy was probably due to the rumor that "another negotiation is . . . on the tapis with Mr. G[renville]."[34] When this failed to materialize, no major obstacle stood between the manuscript account and its publication.

It seems likely that several copies of the proposed article were drawn up and submitted to the heads of faction for their approval during the first week of August. In some manner one of these reached the hands of the Marquis of Rockingham, and he quickly realized the worst of his fears. Here was "a capital performance in regard to insidious perversion and misrepresentation of facts . . . equally indecent and injurious." By the middle of the month Rockingham had begun to outline his tactics. His own copy he sent to Dartmouth, and other leaders in the faction were soon supplied with the text. The Earl of

Albemarle assured Rockingham on the twenty-seventh that the account *"will be in print,"* and that it would appear in the *Political Register.* Albemarle attributed the report to either Temple or Grenville and suggested, "If any of our friends know of it, I wish they would suppress their feelings till it has made its appearance in print, as I then think Lord Temple's retreat from it will be difficult."[35]

The marquis immediately wrote to Edmund Burke, informing him of the course of events and asking that he discuss further action with Albemarle and the Keppels. Rockingham believed the account came from Temple and that "it will raise many of our friends' indignation." This consideration, he told Burke, made it desirable that nothing be said about the sketch before it was published, "lest the hearing that *we* were warm, might occasion the author . . . to suppress or lower the venom." It was Rockingham's hope that publication of the account would alienate the Duke of Bedford from the Grenvilles and that the former "would even agree with me . . . in thinking and declaring, that the publication is a most infamous and scandalous proceeding."[36]

In due time the fourth number of the *Political Register* was published. The leading article was "An Impartial Account of a Late Interesting Conference." To all intents and purposes it was accurate inasmuch as the ultimate point of disagreement was described as Rockingham's insistence upon Conway in opposition to Bedford. The effect of Grenville's colonial demands was, however, misrepresented, and they were described as having been passed over very easily. Rockingham was portrayed in a harsh but honest light, while Bedford was allowed every advantage of friendly interpretation.

The article created quite a sensation. The newspapers promptly copied it in their columns, and it was accepted by the public as authoritative. The effect of the *Political Register*'s story was not what Rockingham had expected, however. While he exulted that his own faction was growing farther apart from that of Grenville and explained it simply that "George Grenville's and Lord Temple's conduct made it impossible to proceed to any good end," he failed to realize that he had not separated Grenville and Bedford. In vain did Newcastle, knowing that hope lay only in union, plead with his young successors to abandon Conway. In vain did the duke point out the undeniable veracity of the *Political Register*'s account of the negotiation. Newcastle was ready, Rockingham noted with concern, "to palliate, or, indeed, to justify Lord Temple and George Grenville's conduct" in order to secure "a solid junction with the Duke of Bedford."[37] Newcastle was right. The "one great use" which Rockingham had hoped to make of the published Grenvillian account, "shewing the Duke of Bedford that my ideas in regard to Lord Temple and that school have been now fully justified," failed utterly. When parliament met, Grenville, knowing he was proscribed by Rockingham, delivered a searing attack upon the marquis and his followers. Bedford's spokesman sat silent; the duke held Rockingham accountable for the schism; effective opposition was at an end.

In December, Bedford's friends entered the ministry. "Having thrown over Rockingham for the sake of Grenville, they now threw over Grenville for the sake of office."[38] This final result of the July conference was duly noted in the *Political Register* by "A Word at Parting to His Grace the D[uke] of B[edford]." Avowedly Grenvillian, these "parting words" condemned Bedford for the step he had taken. Almon's publication gave "great offence," and Temple was once more held responsible for the painful accusations hurled from the press. Grenville assured Bedford's friends that neither he nor his brother were concerned in the matter; so also did Temple. But the belief persisted, and at Christmas, Grenville instructed Whately to take every opportunity to insist upon Temple's innocence: "he had nothing to do, either directly or indirectly [with "A Word at Parting"], being an absolute stranger to it till he saw it in print." There can be little doubt that this was a politically expedient lie. John Almon attributed the article to Charles Lloyd; the editor of the *Grenville Papers* ascribed it to Temple himself. In any case Grenville's denial is worthless evidence—Temple rightly harvested the fruit of his own vindictiveness. Whately, however, assiduously carried out his instructions,[39] and it was not until the *Political Register* struck at higher titles that its close connection with Temple was brought to an end.

In the fourteenth issue of his magazine Almon printed a secret plan for augmenting the military forces in Ireland. As the proposal had been formulated in the privacy of the royal household, his Majesty saw fit to inquire how Almon had secured it.[40] The publisher declined to betray his informant, but in July, 1768, the publication of the *Political Register* was placed in the hands of Henry Beevor in Little Britain. The ostensible connection between the magazine and the Grenvilles was thus broken, but the *Political Register* continued to reflect their interests. In August, 1768, William Knox, then George

Grenville's most active writer, utilized the magazine for political purposes, and apparently with Grenville's blessing.[41]

Throughout the year 1768, the ideas and aims of the House of Grenville were made available to the public in a series of publications which bore their stamp of approval. Thomas Pownall's fourth edition of *The Administration of the Colonies* was dedicated to Grenville with his permission, and William Knox drew heavily upon his patron for material while he was completing his major work, *The State of the Nation*. This pamphlet was almost as much Grenville's as Knox's, as it was completed only after lengthy correspondence between the two men.[42]

Almon remained the chief Grenvillian publisher. When Knox sent an early copy of his pamphlet to Grenville on October 4, he described the activities of a party publisher about to bring forth a new work:

> Almon has general orders from a great number of Members of Parliament to send them whatever comes out in the recess, and he intends taking the opportunity of the intervening fortnight, between the meetings at Newmarket, to convey this pamphlet to them. He thinks of sending one elegantly done up to the King, as he has done with some other such matters. He is an excellent fellow at circulating a work, and understands all the mystery of raising its character, and exciting purchasers.[43]

This was a time when a competent publisher and bookseller might reasonably expect to enjoy prosperity at the hands of an eager clientele. New pamphlets were anticipated and snatched up as soon as they were published, particularly if they bore the political brand of publication by some one like the Piccadilly bookseller. Young Lieutenant John MacMurray, about to establish one of the great modern English publishing houses, remarked most cannily, "Many Blockheads in the Trade are making fortunes; and did we not succeed as well as they, I think it must be imputed only to ourselves."[44]

Pamphlet and publisher rose and fell together. A semi-official bookseller like Almon, with a party platform such as *The State of the Nation* in his shop, was assured of sales. When the public decided that George Grenville was the author, custom increased. Within a month three editions were printed, and Knox, flattered by his success, preferred not to "discountenance the supposition" that Grenville was responsible. "Mr. Lloyd has," he observed, "published an advertisement disavowing your [i.e., Grenville's] part in it, but it is not credited." The impression that *The State of the Nation* appeared "by authority" and the presumption of Grenville's authorship brought a rival upon the scene with dispatch. "*Observations* . . . have been advertised these three weeks," wrote Knox, "but have not appeared . . . and I fancy they are kept back until there will not be time to answer them between their publication and the meeting of Parliament."[45]

The reply came from none other than Edmund Burke, whose *Observations on a Late State of the Nation* was published the next year. Knox's pamphlet had left the Rockingham faction "a little hurt," and Burke wrote in the belief that he was answering his archenemy George Grenville.[46] The *Observations*, Walpole remarked, "did more honour to his talents as a writer than as a politician."[47] Knox's facts and figures were skillfully refuted, but when he launched into the general picture of politics, Burke was less brilliant. He disliked the present ministry as much as did Grenville, and yet he could not condemn individuals in it. "The present ministry is . . . at once indolent and distracted," but their vices were as virtues compared to those of Grenville's party. The *Observations* concluded with a dirge upon political divisions which culminated in the promise that one upright group stood ready to save the nation when called upon—the followers of the Marquis of Rockingham. As Walpole realized, the pamphlet lost sight of its immediate objective, "made no court to the King, left the Cabal equally offended, and yet scarce marked out to the people any objects of unpopularity."[48]

Burke had complained bitterly of the Grenvillian press: "they turn round in a perpetual circle of their own reasonings and pretences; they hand you over from one of their own pamphlets to another." Had he known the inner workings of that press, he would have been even more outraged. Grenville, Knox, Whately, and Almon formed a publishing team complete with specialist, writer, field scout, editor, and distributor. It was a competent organization which drew upon outside talent when occasion arose but protected its more sensitive contributors from the dangers of public recognition. Almon, "a thorough judge of times and seasons for publication," worked in close cooperation with Knox. That gentleman, between pamphlets, busied himself sending Grenvillian propaganda to Ireland for reprinting and supplying "every American ship that sails" with the latest product of Almon's press.[49]

The respectable party pamphleteer occupied a foremost place in the political literature of 1768, but already signs of change were noticeable. The rising virulence of the anonymous newspaper correspondent was ominous, and as Grenville's informant Whately warned, "It is to be expected from those who are guilty of the present confusions . . . that they should endeavour to divert the attention of the public to any other subject than themselves."[50] Unfortunately for the Duke of Grafton and his colleagues, the initiative was not left to them. In February, 1768, John Wilkes returned to England. The master propagandist was not slow in mobilizing the press in his cause, and within a year he was joined by that master of invective, Junius. Together, though seldom in conjunction, they created a popular press which was neither respectable nor representative of any accepted parliamentary faction. It was a new force representing new men, and it had no place in the constitutional structure of eighteenth-century England. Inevitably it came into conflict with that most ancient and respectable of bodies, the high court of parliament.

CHAPTER IX

The Causes of the Present Discontents

> Notwithstanding the great utility of the liberty of the press it is
> certainly liable to manifold injurious abuses, sometimes pregnant
> with great mischiefs. . . . Every considerate and sincere friend to
> the freedom of writing laments these abuses perpetrated by the vari-
> ous enemies of the public weal. *Libertas non est licentia.*[1]

IN THE reign of George III, England enjoyed a free press—a press unre-
stricted by prior censorship. Few men would have denied the necessity
of regulation, however; church, crown, revolutionary settlement, parliament, all were essential and deserving of defense. After the expira-
tion of the licensing act the controls which were deemed desirable
consisted of the economic check of the stamp tax, the legal rein applied
by the courts and law officers of the crown, and the right of both houses
of parliament to regulate their own affairs. By 1760 the economic
restrictions of the stamp duties had ceased to be effective. The courts
of law, in which the attorney-general exercised his right to file informations against offending publications, provided the most active brake
upon the liberty of the press. The high court of parliament, on the
other hand, was the most exalted seat of authority, capable of compulsion, jealous of its rights and privileges, and it united in its corporate
entity powers of legislation and adjudication which were not clearly
defined. Those aspects of parliamentary privilege and control which
directly concerned the press were twofold: the right of members to
freedom from criticism elsewhere than in their own chamber and the
right of both houses to regulate the flow of information disclosed in
debate. Essentially, the problem was one of privilege—the privilege of
members to express themselves freely without fear of a vengeful executive. It was a healthy privilege and necessary to freedom of discussion
in parliament, but it was based upon the assumption of a difference of
interest between the crown and the two houses. In the eighteenth century there was no fundamental variance between those factors which
constituted parliament, and the received doctrine of parliamentary
supremacy was a distorted survivor of an earlier age.

The idea of supremacy implies a subjugated element. By the reign of George III, there could be but one such body in British politics—the people. Inasmuch as these same people (or at least a part of them) elected a portion of the all-powerful trinity, a significant contradiction of terms existed. The problem confused and confounded politicians and theorists alike during the first years of the reign. Parliament was supreme, but in order to express supremacy either the crown or the people had to be excluded. Inasmuch as the historic limitations imposed upon the crown had made it an integral part of the parliamentary function, there remained but the one possibility which forced "Whig" and "Tory" alike into an intellectual impasse: parliament was supreme over the people. This negation of rationalism in an age of reason led to the differentiation between "the people" and "the mob" in the eighteenth century. This fallacious application of terms led the early historians of the reign of George III to create the myth of royal encroachment upon the rights of Englishmen. This was the great issue of the era, and the reinterpretation of the British constitution, the redefinition of terms in the years 1760–1832, must rank beside the Civil War and the Glorious Revolution as a measure of the progress of modern constitutionalism.

The relationship between the press and parliament in the first decade and a half of the reign was of the utmost significance because the press offered the only means other than physical violence by which the excluded element in British politics could express its sentiments on affairs of state. Such a service justified an exercise of the liberty of the press which closely approximated license.

Opening as it did in a brief aura of union and harmony, the reign of George III witnessed no difficulties between press and parliament until 1762. By that date the course of politics had been well outlined and the great factional struggles had begun. On January 20, complaint was made in the House of Commons that John Wilkie had, in the *London Chronicle* of December 22–23, 1761, printed an account of the proceedings of the House in open breach of the ancient privileges of that body. Wilkie was ordered to attend on the following Monday. He appeared on the twenty-fifth and explained that the offensive report had been inserted in his paper without his knowledge. Nevertheless, Wilkie was found guilty of breach of privilege and ordered into the custody of the serjeant-at-arms. The next day the culprit's petition for release was read. He declared himself "sensible of the greatness of his said offence, . . . extremely sorry for the same, and will never be guilty of the like for the future." More cogent was his argument that "confinement is of the utmost detriment to . . . his business." A compassionate House ordered Wilkie discharged. He knelt before the bar to receive his reprimand on January 27 and was released upon paying his fees.[2]

Such were the terrors of the House of Commons. One printer had been deprived of three working days and was several shillings out of pocket in fees and gratuities to sundry doorkeepers and petty officials. Was the liberty of the press thereby endangered? Hardly more than the honor of the House of Commons was threatened by the printer's inadvertent error. No single case, considered alone, can explain why the simple extension of this recognized authority led in less than ten years to a political crisis in which the vested as well as the popular forces of the city of London combined to effectively destroy that power in the House of Commons.

The germ of elucidation is to be found in the action taken by the House on March 3, when numerous complaints were made that "the publishers of newspapers had of late taken upon them to give accounts of the proceedings . . . and of the debates pretended to have been had thereupon." To clarify its position upon the subject, the House of Commons, following the precedent of decades, resolved that it was "a high indignity to, and a notorious breach of, the privilege of this House" to print any report of its activities.[3] In effect, the deliberations of the sovereign legislative body were not the concern of the nation. Here was a statement of parliamentary supremacy—not over the crown, whose placemen and supporters sat in privileged sanctity—but over the people of England, the sole political factor which could be described as outside the walls of parliament. The challenge, as expressed in 1762, was based upon long precedent and usage and was in no way new or unique. Yet the printers and publishers of London rose to champion the cause of the people, for in acting against the press, parliament exerted its authority against a minority whose primary interest lay in satisfying the desires of that very people in whose name the battle was fought.

For over thirty years the proceedings of parliament had found their way to readers of periodicals and magazines. The *Gentleman's Magazine* had been a pioneer in the practice, and even Samuel Johnson had done a stint as a parliamentary reporter.[4] These early reports were far from satisfactory, for they were printed only after a session's end and were highly inaccurate and incomplete in most instances, and they were often crudely disguised with regard to place, date, and the speakers' names. The increase in the reading public and its interest in political affairs created a situation in which it was mandatory that the press improve its methods of acquainting the public with parliamentary events. The reaction of the House of Commons was shown in Wilkie's case, that of the House of Lords appeared in the more famous affair of John Meres.

Early in 1764, when the political press was under fire in parliament, John Wilkes, an exile in Paris, sent to his friend Almon a letter which insinuated against the Earl of Hertford, the English ambassador whose secretary was the eminent Scottish philosopher David Hume. Almon sent the letter to the *London Evening Post,* in which he was interested, and it was published on March 15. The next day the rival *Gazetteer* reprinted it. Henry Seymour Conway, resenting the reflection upon his brother Hertford, asked the Duke of Somerset to complain in the House of Lords of misuse of a peer's name. "His Grace's bashfulness made him choose rather to second the complaint," wrote Walpole, "but he desired Lord Marchmont to make it, who liked the office."

On March 16, Marchmont submitted a complaint naming John Meres and J. Gretton as the offending vendors of the *London Evening Post,* and Charles Say of the *Gazetteer.* They were ordered to attend the House on Monday, at which time Gretton excused himself from further action on the grounds that he only sold the paper for Meres, the printer. John Meres sought to extenuate his error by explaining that the letter appeared "through Inadvertency and Hurry of Business." It had been "flung over the Hatch-door of his House," and he was unfamiliar with the handwriting of the manuscript. Charles Say, identified as the printer of the *Gazetteer* by fellow pressman George Woodfall, readily admitted copying the paragraph into his own paper from the *Post.*[5]

The Lords quickly resolved that the use of Hertford's name had been of a "false, malicious, and scandalous" nature, "a gross and wanton Breach of the Privilege of this House." Marchmont moved that Meres should be fined £100 and held in Newgate Prison until the fine was paid. Temple led the defense, reminding their lordships that his own and the Duke of Cumberland's name had been much abused in the administration press, and in reply to Bedford's complaint that many peers' names were being printed in full, he declared that the practice had begun when he and Pitt had resigned three years ago. Nonetheless, Marchmont's motion passed, and Charles Say was swiftly awarded similar punishment. Sentence was duly carried out, and Meres's additional miscellaneous costs were estimated at £30 to £40.[6]

For his part in Meres's case, Marchmont won notoriety as the great defender of privilege. "He sedulously examined the newspapers every day, with the ardour that a hawk prowls for prey." Such open abuse of privilege, whether effective or not, was bound to bring recriminations. Serjeant Hewitt is said to have led a movement among the minority in the House of Commons to protest Marchmont's zeal. Action was forestalled, however, when Marchmont, in accordance with Lord Mansfield's advice to curb his enthusiasm, resigned himself to seeing the names of noble lords in print.[7] The policy seems to have been fairly effective, however; Newcastle remarked at the end of the session, "An exhorbitant fine upon a poor printer for abusing *Mr. David Hume* will have more effect upon the Press than even any act of Parliament to restrain it."[8]

"This little circumstance gave birth to the great one, of regularly printing the whole proceedings of both houses." London printers and publishers smarted at the blow to their profession. Resentful of the encroachment of the privileges of parliament upon the profits of the press, they determined to print reports of debates in spite of opposition. Accounts were avidly perused in London coffeehouses, and alert businessmen saw in the reports an opportunity to increase newspaper circulation. Hopes of advantage were not always fulfilled. Almon wrote that "the expense is more than the gain; and if Parliament had taken no notice of this Hydra, it would have killed itself."[9]

In March, 1765, the House of Lords noticed that Lord Byron's name had crept into print in *A Circumstancial and Authentick Account of a Late Unhappy Affair,* about a brawl in which Byron had killed a man. The pamphlet was printed by J. Burd of Fleet Street, and upon hearing evidence that Burd was the publisher, the House ordered the Gentleman Usher of the Black Rod to place him in custody until further notice.[10] More serious was the complaint leveled against the *Public Advertiser's* publisher, Henry Sampson Woodfall, who was ordered to attend the House of Lords, May 21, 1765, for "having had the Insolence to print a false Account of the Proceedings" of the House. Woodfall acknowledged his sin, but insisted it had been committed

"inadvertently and without any Intention to affront their Lordships."
Further, he pointed out, the offending paragraph had simply been
copied from the *St. James's Chronicle*. The penitent received no leniency. He was found guilty of breach of privilege, fined £100, and confined until that sum was paid.

The next day the Lords called for Henry Baldwin, printer of the
St. James's Chronicle, who, taking his cue from Woodfall, introduced
the name of Charles Say as the original printer. Baldwin was given the
same punishment his predecessor had received, but before he could
leave the House, a new complaint was raised, and their Lordships inquired how he might excuse himself a second time. The printer replied,
"Being out of Town when the Paper was printed, he was incapable of
giving any information concerning it," but he had left discretionary
powers with his servants, and on the new complaint the earlier sentence
was repeated.

The publisher of the *Gazetteer* was dealt with on May 24. Say's
defense rested upon the plea that he had hoped, by his article, to be
"instrumental in preventing any future Mob: This was the true Motive." He concluded with an appeal in the name of his "family of Six
Children," but that numerous progeny must have gone on short rations
thereafter, for Say was given the standard sentence—£100 and confinement until paid.[11]

This incident demonstrates the common practice of pirating parliamentary reports from one paper to another and the importance of such
reports in the eyes of the newspaper world. The *Gazetteer, St. James's
Chronicle,* and the *Public Advertiser* were three of the leading papers
of the decade and their publishers' judgment was sound. The reward
of greater sales was worth the risk of punishment by an irate House.

Horace Walpole remarked that "no attempt was made [in Parlia-
ment] to punish the authors and printers but under the administration
of Grenville, Lord Sandwich, and that set."[12] Walpole's statement con-
tains a grain of truth, but only a biased observer could discover any
factional significance in the activity of parliament against the press in
the early years of the reign. Punishment of infringing pressmen was
usually agreed to without dissent. In the case of Meres, friends of the
Grenville administration took an active part, but the motivation came
from that opposition favorite Henry Conway, and the complaint was
made in the name of his brother—close friends and relatives of Horace
Walpole! Support of parliamentary privilege was largely a nonpartisan

matter, and those who had the most crying grievances were often the most lenient toward their persecutors.

After the Rockingham ministry displaced Grenville, the late ministers came in for more than a fair share of abuse, none more so than the Duke of Bedford. The exaggerated complaints of writers and publishers should be read with an eye to the duke's letter to Henry S. Woodfall of the *Public Advertiser*, November 5, 1765:

> The Duke of Bedford has observed for some time past, with surprise, himself marked out in the public newspapers . . . particularly in the 'Public Advertiser,' published by H. S. Woodfall. He has treated this insolence with the indifference and contempt it deserved, whilst it applied only to himself. But seeing . . . the name of a noble lady inserted at full length in the same paragraph with his own, he finds himself obliged to give . . . H. S. Woodfall notice that he must expect to be treated with the utmost severity of the law, for any offence of this kind . . . should the like be ever again repeated.[13]

If Grenville upheld the authority of parliament against the press, Rockingham gave no indication of a different attitude. William Richardson printed a pamphlet relative to a bill pending in the upper chamber and was called to account for his temerity in June, 1766. Both Richardson and his author disclaimed any intent to contravene the privileges of the House and escaped further action when parliament was prorogued.[14]

Charles Say of the *Gazetteer* found himself once more before the House of Lords, January 28, 1767, for comments on the proceedings of the House in his paper. Asked "if he did not know, that it was a Breach of Privilege to print any Thing relative to the Proceedings," Say replied that the material was provided by an unknown person, and that "he published them by Way of Argument; but did not think there was any Harm in so doing." Say shortly learned that there was £100 worth of harm in his action.[15]

The recriminatory power of the press soon came to the persecuted printer's aid. On February 3 the *Public Advertiser* ran a letter from PICTOR declaiming, "The liberty of the press . . . has ever been the scourge, and terror of pride and tyranny. When therefore this sacred right is invaded, we may be sure that the political Lent of forty days tyranny is not far removed." The next day the *Gazetteer* itself undertook a cautious defense. Say printed a letter from SERIOUS which maintained that the liberty of the press "is the beaten path that gradually and gently leads us to destruction." It roots out religion, subverts justice, "provokes malice and causes discontents." The editor appended to this diatribe a note of his own:

> If the liberty of the press ever becomes Licentiousness, there are sufficient laws in being to curb and punish it; but the whole house need not be destroyed because a chimney smokes sometimes;— though indeed it is much to be wished that a proper line was fixed to divide the one from the other, and ascertain what is, and what is not, the legal and constitutional liberty of the press.

With his own recent experiences in mind, Say continued, "For want of this criterion men are frequently drawn into great inconveniences, and have *ignorantly*, nay . . . *innocently*, incurred the displeasure of their superiors, whom they have not had the most distant intention to offend."[16]

The consistency with which the peers defended their privilege had some effect. John Almon, who had begun in 1766 to report speeches for the *London Evening Post*, advised Wilkes in March, 1767, "I am not now concerned in any of the public papers they are so often brought before the House of Lords, and there is so little faith among the printers."[17] Prosecution was assuming a more political air, and George Grenville set out to prove it when he complained of "a libel printed in N[orth] America as a matter of privilege, it containing many reflections on the parliament, and insisted that the house must receive the printed paper at the table without a Question." Grenville raised the issue on November 25, but action was postponed until the twenty-seventh, by which time the government had determined to shelve the issue by an adjournment of six months.[18]

The old parliament indulged in one more orgy of printer-baiting in its last session. The approach of a general election led to widespread canvassing of constituencies, and in the *London Chronicle* of December 29, 1767, and the *Gazetteer* for February 4, 1768, advertisements were printed in behalf of parties interested in buying a seat in the House of Commons. The respective printers, John Wilkie and Charles Say, attended the House upon order February 9, but were unable to identify the offender who openly considered a seat in the Commons to be a commodity on the public market. Wilkie was finally released on February 18, after being reprimanded upon his knees and paying the usual fees. Charles Say appears to have escaped the vengeance of the House for once in his checkered career.[19]

The elections in 1768 produced a parliament which was in every way typical of eighteenth-century deliberative bodies. The price of seats may have risen, the number of new men was high, but parliament's attitude toward its privileges was determined by precedent. The new parliament convened on May 10, 1768, to the sound of gunfire and an angry mob in which cries of "No king! No regal government!" were blended with the old slogan, "Wilkes and Liberty!" The years of 1768–1774 were destined to see stirring events at Westminster. On the opening day of the session George III remarked upon "the paper that was distributed today, recommending the driving the Commons out of their House, which they for their own sakes are bound to take notice of."[20] The Commons seem not to have done so, although they took notice of many other papers in the next six years. The first sign of the attitude of the new House appeared on May 13, when it was ordered "That the serjeant-at-arms . . . do, from time to time, take into his custody any stranger or strangers that he shall see, or be informed of." Here was the final stronghold of privilege—secrecy. Barrington stated the government's view that "strangers should not be allowed to come into the House to hear our debates." He was answered by George Grenville, who declared, "I ever wished to have what is done here well known." Significant of things to come, Lord North brought the discussion to an end by deftly shifting the topic.[21]

Thus the "Unreported Parliament" began its attempt to assure that popular political ignorance which theoretically restricts the people from intelligent participation in government. This parliament succeeded only in winning a name for itself; it miscalculated on at least four important points. Through the private and personal efforts of Sir Henry Cavendish, the "Unreported Parliament" is probably the best reported parliament of the late eighteenth century. Those members who would have excluded strangers erred further in believing that simple expulsion would remove the press from their midst or their actions from the columns of the London papers. The parliament sinned more consciously with regard to John Wilkes, duly elected a member for Middlesex (though never seated), and Wilkes and his followers very nearly demonstrated the fourth error in the parliamentary attitude, the basic error of believing that poorly enforced ignorance incapacitates the people. As North, Barrington, and a new member, Charles James Fox, were to learn—very nearly to their sorrow —the people, if not allowed the privilege of political knowledge and intelligence, still retained one prerogative and one power—the power of a mob to burn, loot, sack, and destroy even to the very doors of the deliberative chambers themselves. In such an atmosphere began the great struggle between the press and parliament, and the great failure of the divided minority to free the press in parliament.

John Wilkes was the man to make the best of an enforced absence from the English political scene, but the delights of Italy could not cool his ardor for his native land. Having been rebuffed by Rocking-ham, he anticipated better treatment from the Chatham-Grafton min-istry. In October, 1766, Wilkes again visited England and submitted to Grafton a touching complimentary letter in which he set forth "the rigours of a long unmerited exile" and his hope to "be allowed to continue in the land, and among the friends, of liberty."[22] Grafton, himself no friend of Wilkes, referred the matter to Chatham, and knowing the earl's sentiments, Wilkes returned to France. Angry and disgruntled by his reception, the patriot employed his sharpest pen to produce a caustic *Letter to the Duke of Grafton*.

Wilkes made no secret of his sentiments toward the new ministry. The Earl of Rochford, visiting Paris in April, 1767, advised Chatham that "Mr. Wilkes . . . intends publishing here a pamphlet . . . the drift of which is to attack your Lordship's administration; and if it is writ-ten conformably to the language . . . he holds, it will be both abusive and violent." Rochford suggested that publication might be prevented by a word to the French government, but he spoke too late.[23] The author sent his pamphlet to John Almon on April 7, and it reached other London presses shortly thereafter. The *Letter to the Duke of Grafton* was no more than a vociferous reminder of the trials and tribulations of John Wilkes, but it had a remarkable effect in stirring up sentiment for its author. The *Letter* appeared in the newspapers without attracting the attention of the government, but when Almon published it as a pamphlet, the House of Commons was stirred to action. Almon reported that the subject was "much talked of" on April 30, and Wilkes's brother Heaton declared that "Administration w[oul]d have taken [Almon] up for it had not Col. Onslow warmly opposed it as he declared to them he w[oul]d personally oppose them in the House."[24]

The incident had little effect upon Almon, whose profits had been great. He encouraged Wilkes to believe that "there is nothing you can print in France which I cannot as readily get done here. There is no difficulty in finding printers. The danger is in the publication." Almon then set before Wilkes the delicate situation of an opposition publisher:

> Give me leave to remark that your spirited letter to the D[uke] of G[rafton] would never have been read by one-fortieth part of the persons who now almost adore it, and you, if it had not been reprinted. And would you have deemed me in my senses if I had reprinted it verbatim et literatim from your copy? Certainly not. And yet castrated even as it was, I was in real danger of a commitment by the Ho[ouse] of Com[mons]—if one word (not a name) more had been inserted, I had not escaped. And where is the party . . . that is worth running a risk for? Sir, there are not five men in the kingdom I would go across the way to serve.[25]

While Wilkes was warming himself to new efforts by attempting to write a *History of England,* he considered a scheme for setting up a newspaper at Calais with which to bombard the opposite shore with Wilkite propaganda. The proposal was immediately scouted by Almon, who thought "the project needless at least for the present; why should you put yourself to so much expence & trouble without a prospect of adequate advantage?"[26]

More vigorous action followed Almon's request to the exile for "a few of your fugitive papers." About the first of April, Wilkes forwarded a copy of the lengthy letter he had written to Temple in 1762 describing his bloodless duel with Talbot. Wilkes intended it for the *Political Register,* but Almon at first declined to print it for reasons which he explained to Heaton Wilkes. Another copy of the letter was sent to Henry Baldwin, publisher of the *St. James's Chronicle,* and appeared on May 16 in that paper. Not to be outdone, Almon promptly inserted the article in the first issue of the *Political Register.*[27] Publication of Wilkes's letter had unexpected repercussions. Lord Talbot, who had recently been coquetting with the minority, took umbrage and challenged Temple to deny that it was published with his approval. Temple acknowledged that the original was addressed to him and that it had been returned to Wilkes. "This authenticated the letter, & made Lord Talbot more angry." He demanded a signed statement that Temple had not authorized publication, and the warm temper of the master of Stowe began to show itself:

Lord Temple replied, 'Not by compulsion.' Lord Talbot then called
out Lord Gower & Lord Harcourt & asked them if his demand was
not reasonable? They said, 'No.' Still he was not satisfied & swore
he would fight Lord Temple: the latter said, 'With all his heart,'
& actually drew his sword. The other lords prevented any thing
further, except Lord Temple's declaring he was ready to fight Lord
Talbot at any time or place.[28]

The affair left an unpleasant taste in the mouths of all parties. Heaton
Wilkes upbraided his brother for his poor judgment; Almon publicly
denied that Wilkes had intended the letter to be printed and privately
advised the author, "Your letter to Lord Temple concerning the Battle
of Bagshot did you incredible harm. Your best friends disapproved."
Temple himself was less than pleased with the outcome and subsequently acted much more coolly toward Wilkes.[29]

Having effectively recalled his name to English memory, the exile
crossed the Channel in February, 1768, arriving in time to participate
in the general elections in March and April. With more audacity than
discernment he stood for a seat in Commons for the City of London.
Failing there, Wilkes recouped his losses in the adjacent county of
Middlesex. "Wilkes and Liberty!" and "Number 45" became passports
to safety in and around the capital as the exultant populace demonstrated its approbation of the newly elected member of parliament.
The threat of his outlawry still remained, however, and after an amusing exchange of excuses Wilkes finally appeared in the Court of King's
Bench, April 20, and Glynn argued the irregularity of his case. The
court agreed that Wilkes was not properly before the bar, and no
action was taken. On the twenty-seventh he was finally brought in on
the proper writ and committed to the prison in St. George's Fields to
await trial.

While Wilkes held court for his friends and admirers, both high
and low, St. George's Fields became the central rallying point of the
London mob, which saw in Wilkes a political victim whose oppression
paralleled its own economic grievances. A jeering, milling crowd, a few
firebrands, a detachment of Scottish soldiers, and on May 10, the
inevitable clash occurred. A volley was fired and a score of citizens fell.
Public indignation soared, and the mob became less pleasant to reflect
upon as well as to hear.

In May, counsel for Wilkes and the crown presented their cases.
Finally on June 8, 1768, Mansfield laid down a lengthy decision which

overwhelmed the lawyers with its erudition but raised many critical
eyebrows in political circles. Speaking freely upon the law and himself,
Mansfield boasted of his own purity of purpose and his lack of fear of
popular recrimination; he sought rather "that popularity which fol-
lows; not that which is run after." Almost incidentally he reversed
Wilkes's outlawry on the grounds of a technical error in the writ.[30]

The mob—so closely packed that "Judges stuffed out with dignity
and lamb-skins . . . not absolute sprites . . . had much ado to glide
through the crowd"—cheered for Wilkes. Mansfield need not have
worried about an accession of popularity. A violent *North Briton* chas-
tised the chief justice in violent terms and even threatened rebellion.
"Prosecutions were ordered against the publishers and vendors," remarked Walpole, "and there, I suppose, it will end."[31]

Serjeant Glynn made a final effort to free his client on June 14,
but four days later John Wilkes received sentence from Justice Yates
for publishing *North Briton* No. 45 and the *Essay on Woman*. Wilkes
was fined £1,000 and sentenced to twenty-two months imprisonment.
In addition he was to find surety for seven years, himself for £1,000 and
two others for £500 each.[32] The sentence was described by Mansfield
as moderate—"a Refinement in Politics, which reduc'd the Scoundrel
the sooner to Obscurity"—but he privately complained to David Hume
that "it was impossible for him to condemn him to the Pillory, because
the Attorney-General did not demand it."[33] Happy oversight! Wilkes
in the pillory might have fired the mob to revolutionary violence;
Wilkes in prison was merely a bird in the hand—still, however, an
unequaled propagandist and once again a member of parliament.

Few men feared Wilkes on the floor of the House of Commons, and
many felt he would have been most safely ensconced there. The ministry, though embittered by Wilkes's popularity, determined to delay
action until the second session of the new parliament, when the law
would have dealt with him and time might have opened new political
doors.[34]

Meanwhile the press was active. Wilkes made fine fodder for pamphlets like *A Comparative View of the Conduct of John Wilkes, Esq.;
as Contrasted with the Opposite Measures during the Last Six Years,*
and the patriot explained his own position in a letter to "the Gentlemen, Clergy, and Freeholders of the County of Middlesex." This
epistle appeared on June 18; two days later Serjeant Nares, acting in
behalf of the attorney-general, moved the Court of King's Bench for an

attachment against the printer because the letter *"tended to inflame the jury"* before which the reopened case of Wilkes *v.* Halifax would be heard. The court refused Nares's request; it had done with Wilkes, if not with printers in general.[35] Under-secretaries were busily perusing newspapers and pamphlets for actionable articles and were quite able to find them, as evidenced by a note to Grafton which accompanied "a paper . . . of so dangerous a nature, that it seems . . . necessary that it should be taken notice of immediately." The messengers of the press were busy, but their results were pitiful.[36]

The most notable outcome of the violence of the press in May, 1768, was the case of William Bingley, continuator of the *North Briton,* whose paper reached the depths of scurrility at this time. On May 28, Bingley published a vicious attack upon Mansfield. The attorney-general moved on June 3 for a writ of attachment against Bingley and two vendors of the paper, Mr. Brett and Mrs. Langford, for contempt of court. The next day an Extraordinary *North Briton,* No. 4, was presented and actions were begun against Staples Steare, the publisher, and John Williams and John Pridden, booksellers. On the seventh, Bingley appeared in court to plead his own case and appealed to the public with *North Briton* No. 51. The various rules were made absolute on the ninth, and a new complaint against No. 51 was confirmed two days later. As it was rumored that he had absconded, Bingley demanded that the writ be served immediately. He refused to give bail and was deposited in Newgate on Sunday evening.

While Bingley languished in jail, his fellow newsmen enjoyed surprising lenity. The motion against Mrs. Langford was discharged; the others gave bail, June 23, to appear in court the first day of the next term. On November 24 they were duly summoned before the King's Bench and received sentence. Steare was committed to prison for three months; Pridden and Brett were fined 6s. 8d., and Williams 13s. 4d. By such petty annoyances the ground was prepared for the greater troubles to come. The Newgate prisoner had meanwhile been parading his woes before the world; the *North Briton* was in no way intimidated by its publisher's imprisonment. Finally on August 22, Bingley was taken to Mansfield's house in Bloomsbury Square and admitted to bail twice in £300 with four sureties of £150 each that he would appear in court next term.

Accordingly, November 7, Bingley surrendered himself, but he refused to enter into a new recognizance to answer interrogatories, on the ground that he might be forced to incriminate himself. No less stubbornly the court refused to hear the process on Bingley's attachment and, after thirty minutes of heated argument, remanded the publisher to the Marshalsea. By the first week in December, Bingley began to think less of martyrdom, and at the discretion of Sir Joseph Yates he was discharged upon entering into two recognizances to appear (but not to answer interrogatories) at the King's Bench the first day of the succeeding term.[37]

By the end of the year 1768, the political changes following the general election had begun to show a definite pattern of development. The resurrection of John Wilkes posed a problem for all parties. The Duke of Richmond expressed no sorrow that "the ministry should see that there is in the people a spirit of liberty . . . it will show the administration that, though they may buy lords and commons . . . yet they are not so much approved of by the nation." Camden, on the other hand, looked askance at the fugitive, "a criminal" whose conduct he considered "audacious beyond description."[38] The summer passed nervously at Newmarket; beyond the island, Corsica fell to France and colonists in America grew more daring. At Hayes, Chatham recovered his senses, both physical and political, and seeing that he could better act outside of a ministry he could no longer control, he resigned on October 12; Shelburne followed him within a week.

These changes were portentous but not immediately effective. Grafton stood his ground, unable to move in any direction. Wilkes, incapable of physical action, could employ the pen. Aware that the ministry's policy of quietly ignoring him could easily be broken, the patriot prepared to act offensively. He commented upon the resignations of Chatham ("King Lear") and Shelburne ("the heir apparent of Loyola and all the College"); he called Grafton a Janus. When the minister offered him political protection in return for political peace, Wilkes declined even an answer.[39] Parliament had scarcely settled to its task when Wilkes's petition for redress of grievances was presented—and allowed to gather dust. Ministers would not raise Wilkes to the floor of the House if they could avoid it—Wilkes would if he could.

The St. James's Chronicle of December 10 printed a letter from Lord Weymouth to Daniel Ponton, chairman of the justices of Southwark, on the use of troops in quelling civil disturbances. The Introduction to the letter condemned the practice in terms which had a familiar ring. On the thirteenth, a complaint was made in the House of Lords, and the printer was ordered to attend. Henry Baldwin appeared the next day, and being informed by the lord chancellor that "if he expects the Lenity of this House, he do inform their Lordships who is the Author of that Paragraph," the printer frankly owned it came from Wilkes. The fact was readily proven on the fifteenth—with Wilkes's approval. Baldwin was discharged on the sixteenth, the Introduction was resolved a libel, and their Lordships stopped to consider what was passing in the other House.[40]

Lord North informed the Commons of the course of events in the upper chamber and asked their concurrence in condemning "an insolent, scandalous, and seditious Libel." "No paper," he declared, "ever deserved the appellations more." Wilkes had no personal friends in the House, but many applauded Sir William Meredith's decision: "if I see the laws and the constitution violated through him, I will support him." Burke, looking beyond the man and seeming to seek a crusading cause, earnestly declared, "All censures of men in public situations have ever been called libels. If that is to be the case, there will not be a shadow of the liberty of the press left." Evidence was ordered to be heard on the nineteenth when Baldwin should attend. The day was not a happy one for the ministry, and although the printer willingly named his author, it could have been but small encouragement to ministers to know that since May, Wilkes had been writing "literary articles for the good of the public, please your honor, and the booksellers." The whole question was consequently laid aside until after the Christmas holidays.[41]

Wilkes was not the only journalist to be noticed; as Constantine Phipps remarked, "Ever since the opening of the session . . . the time of parliament has been taken up . . . in examining horse-waterers and newspaper-jackals."[42] The press, officially excluded from the houses, took prompt revenge. Barrington might declare that "no gentleman . . . can mind what is said of him in the newspapers; can be disturbed by a weed taken out of Mr. Almon's garden"—the nettles remained firmly implanted. When Dixwell, a publisher in St. Martin's Lane, brought out a pamphlet on a case pending in the House of Lords, he was called up along with his author. Their Lordships confiscated Dixwell's stock and discharged him. William Bogle, the author, incriminated Edward and Charles Dilly and John Wilkie, publishers, who were similarly treated, and the whole crew were discharged after being reprimanded upon their knees before the bar.[43]

The House of Commons amused itself pursuing the publishers of a spurious "Speech of Oliver Cromwell at the Dissolution of the Long Parliament." The speech, printed as a broadside, had attracted the attention of Colonel George Onslow, who pointed out that such phrases as "Ye are a factious crew, and enemies to all good government. Ye are a pack of mercenary wretches, and would . . . sell your country for a mess of pottage," struck too close home. The colonel had apprehended two culprits, Denis Shade and Joseph Thornton, a milk-seller, and they were ordered to attend. The implications of the broadside were strong; Onslow, no "enemy to the liberty of the press," "a Whig in principle," was supported vehemently by Wedderburn and North. Shade escaped punishment, but the milk-dealer was committed to Newgate, December 10, for breach of privilege. After such a rigorous defense of the honor of parliament, it is rather surprising to note that Thornton was discharged on his petition just ten days later.[44]

The House of Commons resumed consideration of the Wilkes case on January 23, 1769, after the Christmas holidays. The question of privilege was raised by Joseph Martin, M.P. for Gatton, who moved that "John Wilkes, esq., although he is convicted of publishing a seditious libel, is entitled to Privilege of Parliament." This was a dangerous motion for the administration, and North demonstrated his parliamentary skill by amending it beyond all recognition. Grenville refused to support "any question in favour of Mr. Wilkes, in the present situation of affairs," and Colonel Henry Lawes Luttrell violently attacked the absent member for Middlesex despite the protests of Sir George Savile. Burke was greeted by a groan as he rose to proclaim that the liberty of the press was being destroyed. "The maxims of the Roman law and the spirit of the Star Chamber are the prevailing spirit of the law of England with regard to libels—a law directly contrary to the spirit of the constitution . . . and the very existence of a free country." North carried his amendment 165–71, and the main question was passed in the negative. Insult was added to defeat; by 96 to 52, the House refused Martin the courtesy of entering his original motion in the day's votes. The plea of parliamentary privilege was once more denied to John Wilkes.[45]

Four days later Wilkes's petition for redress of grievances came before the House. Against an attempt to bring about a general discussion of the case North, aided by De Grey, Norton, and Rigby, turned a majority of nearly 150 members. Savile, Dowdeswell, and Burke spoke for the Rockingham faction, the latter remarking that he had several pamphlets in his pocket which libeled the constitution, but such publications "are not complained of; are not punished." Rigby defended governmental inaction on the basis that libels of that nature "were innocent, as they hurt nobody." Isaac Barré immediately turned his guns on Rigby and gave him "a pretty trimming." He further condemned those prosecutions which government had begun only because the defendants had "generally treated of liberty." As for Wilkes, he told the Treasury bench, "If you have a mind perfectly to annihilate him—take him into the administration."[46]

The patriot's grievances were heard on January 31 and February 1, and were dismissed with the comment, "frivolous." Close observers might have noticed, however, that as the official majority rolled up its victories, George Grenville began to take a vigorous part with the opposition; on February 1, he gave unqualified support to a minority heretofore baffled by his insistence upon separating the man Wilkes from the cause he represented.[47]

Thus far, wrote Walpole, it had been "a fair trial between faction and corruption; of two such common whores, the richest will carry it."[48] The Introduction to Weymouth's letter came under discussion on February 2; questioned concerning his authorship, Wilkes said, "I avow it. I think it a meritorious act. . . . Whenever a Secretary of State shall write so bloody a scroll, [I shall] write some prefatory remarks upon it." Burke spoke in Wilkes's defense: "Is not the construction of the law of libel large enough? We ought not to take upon ourselves the office of prompters to the attorney-general." But prompted by the attorney-general the House voted the Introduction "an insolent, scandalous, and seditious libel." Cabinet members had no need to apply to the common courts when they controlled the high court of parliament.[49]

George III, when he received North's report, commented, "Nothing could be more honorable for Government." Though surprised at the late reaction in Wilkes's favor, the king looked forward to "a very proper end of this irksome affair this day."[50] The House of Commons, on February 3, was extremely full, the debate heated. Barrington moved that for his libelous Introduction to Weymouth's letter, his conviction on *North Briton* No. 45, and the "obscene and impious libels" in the *Essay on Woman*, John Wilkes should be "expelled this House." The motion was supported by North, De Grey, and the great legist Blackstone, all of whom castigated Wilkes's character and spoke in adulation of king and church. "As to the liberty of the press," said one member who favored the motion, "the only way to preserve that blessing is to check the abuse of it." Burke, Dowdeswell, Pitt, and Beckford felt otherwise. The opposition saw and remarked the threat to every Englishman inherent in Wilkes's expulsion, but it was George Grenville who carried off the honors of the day. He held no blind sympathy for Wilkes; he was free from prejudice and party. Ministers, he declared, had treated the prisoner leniently enough, but the present motion was "a capital injustice." With studied calm, Grenville pointed out that the motion might allow Wilkes to be unseated, "although three parts in four of those who expel him should have declared against his expulsion upon every one of the articles contained in this charge." Thus would he be condemned by a minority and despite the laws of England, punished repeatedly for a single crime. And then? He will be re-elected, prophesied Grenville: "Is it not more advisable . . . to conciliate the heated minds of men by temper and discretion, than to enflame them by adding fresh fuel to discontent?" For if Wilkes be returned, you must reject him—depriving the electors of representation—or seat a minority candidate. "When the public discontent is founded in truth and reason . . . a storm may then rise which may tear up the constitution by the roots, and shake the palace of the King himself."

Grenville never made a better speech; his cause was just, his logic devastating, his prognostication accurate. As Grenville spoke for the constitution, so Burke upheld the cause of the press. "The late hour— the candles—all put me in mind of . . . the last act of a tragi-comedy, performed by his Majesty's servants, for the benefit of Mr. Wilkes and at the expense of the constitution." "This, Sir," said Burke quietly, "will put the last hand to the liberty of the press." If ever that liberty should expire, it would be in parliament, for by law there was no liberty of the press. Expel Wilkes and "all the counties of England will be libellers. . . . Would to God I had colours dipped in heaven to paint this mischief to you! Let me not be told . . . that this is declamation. I dread the consequences of this violent struggle between the two tides of power and popularity."

"The honourable gentleman," remarked North dryly, "is always terrifying himself where there is no danger, and puts me in mind of the fable of the shepherd's boy who was always crying out that the wolf was coming." The mocking chorus silenced the prophets. About three o'clock on the morning of February 4, the House divided 219 to 137, and John Wilkes was expelled.[51]

Burke was wrong; this was not the final act of the drama, for in the succeeding weeks the electors of Middlesex fulfilled Grenville's promise. Thrice they elected John Wilkes, only to hear the House of Commons declare the return invalid, their representative incapable of election. Finally in April, Henry Luttrell, daring the wrath of the Wilkite populace, garnered nearly 300 votes, and the House, having maneuvered itself into a political maelstrom, cast off its last vestige of integrity and declared that Luttrell "ought to have been returned." He was consequently seated as the representative for Middlesex.[52]

The expulsion of Wilkes, his repeated victories at the polls, and the sophistical logic of the House of Commons which led to the seating of Luttrell occupied the attention of the press for the better part of the year. John Wilkes acted as his own press bureau, writing and editing a constant stream of letters and articles in the papers.[53] Pamphlets originated from every source. For the government, Jeremiah Dyson, a loyal placeman, seconded the legal arguments of William Blackstone, the political innuendoes of Edward Weston in the *Gazette,* and the bluster of Samuel Johnson's *False Alarm.* Replies were soon published by opposition writers, among whom Sir William Meredith was outstanding. Dowdeswell presented the Rockingham point of view, and more radical penmen secured aid from the wealthy republican Thomas Hollis.[54] The government press, though it produced no great spokesman, attracted the attention of the liberal members of parliament by its scurrility. When government propagandists dismissed the populace as a beggarly rabble, Burke warned, "Sir, if party distinction is to be raised up in this country between the gentlemen and those who have been . . . called beggarly—if such a party should ever arise—woe betide the gentlemen!" In vain might Meredith complain that his character was blackened by writers in the *Gazetteer*; his case was merely referred to the committee on privilege for investigation.[55]

The rising tide of public opinion made many realize as never before the necessity of controlling its power. Burke advised Rockingham that the sentiments of the people must be brought before the king's eyes in order to discredit the ministry. "We must strengthen the hands of the minority within Doors by the accession of the publick opinion; strongly declared." Nor did he hesitate to rebuke his chief for laxity in using the press while noting that Temple "took care to transmit immediately to the News paper" any item of political interest.[56]

The Grenvillians were not caught unprepared. Temple was probably a frequent contributor to the papers, and William Knox appears to have attacked the servile parliament with George Grenville's endorsement that "this right is essential in the most limited idea of the liberty of the press, and I imagine will scarcely be questioned at present."[57] The most forceful propaganda for the camp at Wotton was marshaled without Grenville's consent or approval. About October 21, John Almon's busy presses turned out *The Speech of a Right Honourable Gentleman, on the Motion for Expelling Mr. Wilkes.* The pamphlet was compiled from minutes, possibly taken by Cavendish and corrected by Grenville, which were designed for private circulation. Lyttelton received a copy, Temple also, no doubt, and perhaps through that channel it reached the publisher. Grenville had not intended to publish his speech, and was "much surprised" when Knox sent him a printed copy. He immediately asked his correspondent "to apply to Mr. Almon, and endeavour to stop publication, though I am much afraid . . . that it will now be scarcely possible to prevent it."[58]

Knox followed his instructions but found that Almon "had already circulated so many copies, that although it had not been advertised nor generally sold . . . yet it was beyond all probability to call in what were gone forth without supposing that some other printer would get hold of one and republish it." Grenville's protest did move Almon to add to his advertisement the notice that "it is published without the approbation, consent, or knowledge of the Right Honourable Gentleman who made [the speech]." This satisfied Grenville, and he shortly provided a correction sheet with the proviso "You must by no means give my paper to the printer; if you do, it will be said to be corrected *by me.*" Knox had expressed his approval of the publication in an earlier letter; Grenville's hesitancy was now explained—he had no faith that "the publication of the truth is the sure means of stopping lies" and misrepresentation. "I am afraid," he wrote, "that the experience of these times has not corresponded with that observation."[59]

Although the pamphlet was not published until October 30, by November 10 the second edition (corrected by Grenville) had come off Almon's presses. The pamphlet sold well. Knox informed his chief that Baldwin of the *St. James's Chronicle,*

. . . who has hitherto been your sworn enemy . . . and who refused two guineas from me to insert an extract from the American Controversy because it was in defence of your opinions . . . has voluntarily made a large extract from your Speech, and introduced it with a general account highly commendatory of the performance.[60]

The most significant reply to Grenville's *Speech* came from John Wilkes, whose pride suffered before the speaker's unbending legalism. About November 4 Wilkes wrote *A Letter to the Right Honourable George Grenville* in which he described Grenville's statement as "a direct act of hostility . . . as to the vote you gave in parliament against his expulsion, he had not the obligation of that vote to Mr. Grenville . . . he had always detested you as a minister, but despised you as a private man." Wilkes's scorn was similarly lavished upon Grenville's "ingenious friends" Whately, Lloyd, and Knox. He scoffed at "the late Grenvillian family compact" of Grenville, Chatham, and Temple, and though he sought to flatter the lord of Stowe, this pamphlet seems to have resulted in "a total annihilation" of all commerce between Wilkes and Temple.[61] The clash of interest between the parliamentary and the popular opposition leaders would produce serious repercussions in the future.

Antagonism toward the government among the people was expressed in a series of petitions and instructions which originated in the councils of the Wilkites in the City and spread throughout the nation. In the meetings at Mile-End and Exeter Change, the gentlemen of the press made known their grievances. John Horne, doffing clerical garb for a Cap of Liberty, encouraged the freeholders of Middlesex to instruct their representatives "to confirm our old constitutional and only rightful trial—by jury." To this sentiment the Westminster electors added the phrase—"to the general exclusion of proceedings by information and attachment." The City Livery echoed these sentiments at the Guildhall, February 10, and Bristol followed suit the next month with the instruction: "use your utmost endeavours, that all trials for libels . . . be carried on agreeable to the known rules of law, and . . . zealously discourage all proceedings by information and attachment, as contrary thereto."[62]

In May the freeholders of Middlesex, 1,576 strong, signed a petition which listed among its complaints:

> PRINTERS punished by the Ministry in the supreme Court without a Trial by their Equals—without ANY Trial at all.

A Writing determined to be a Libel by a Court where it was not cognizable in the first Instance.

A Person condemned in the said Court as the Author of the supposed Libel unheard, without Defence or Trial—

Perpetual Imprisonment of an Englishman without Trial, Conviction, or Sentence, by . . . ATTACHMENT, wherein the same Person is at once PARTY, ACCUSER, JUDGE, and JURY—

Partial Attacks on the Liberty of the Press: The most daring and pernicious Libels against the CONSTITUTION, and against the Liberty of the Subject, being allowed to pass unnoticed, whilst the slightest Libel against a MINISTER is punished with the utmost Rigour—[63]

William Bingley added fuel to the fire. Returned to the King's Bench prison in January, he published, February 16, a declaration that he would not

at any time, WITHOUT TORTURE, answer to any interrogatory tending to accuse himself, or any other person, of being author, printer or publisher of the North Briton . . . , as a bookseller, should esteem himself infamous, and deserving of no credit, if he betrayed the confidence of any person who should instruct him to publish or conduct any work whatever.[64]

This modest admission of patriotic martyrdom garnered the unhappy prisoner a handsome piece of plate from an anonymous admirer, and Bingley secured James Townsend's agreement to present his petition for redress to parliament. The case was debated on March 30, but the petition was refused because "the Court had proceeded against him agreeable to custom." Dunning, although solicitor-general, spoke against the use of interrogatories, but "all agreed, that . . . while there is any concern for the dignity and authority of our Courts" the practice must be upheld.[65] So Bingley remained in the King's Bench prison despite his efforts (and those of his creditors) to secure his release or his removal to the Fleet. From that sanctuary he continued to edit the North Briton with even less compunction than before. The court could do little more to punish him and defend its tarnished honor than forbid him the benefit of the rules.[66]

Wilkes also turned his cell into an editorial office. Isaac Fell, the patriot's chief publisher at this period, introduced him to Cuthbert Shaw, who edited the Middlesex Journal which Fell printed. Shaw, with an eye for profit, besought Wilkes's pen for his paper.

> if *YOU* & the other *Friends of [Free]dom* will write in its' support,
> it may yet [come] to be the most popular paper extant: Otherwise
> from the mean selfish Principles of Printers [in] general, a Channel
> may shortly be wanting for [the] Conveyance of Public Grievances.

A working agreement was reached which pleased both parties, and the
paper prospered as an organ of radical propaganda. Wilkes remarked
of one item which he wrote that "the St. James's [Chronicle] did not
find the dish courtly enough to be served up at their table: the Middlesex [Journal] find it turtle."[67]

Wilkes had little reason to regret his imprisonment. In May, his
outlawry being reversed, the Court of Common Pleas reopened the
case of Wilkes *v.* Halifax. The case was heard November 10 before
Chief Justice Wilmot. Earl Temple testified in Wilkes's behalf, and
Glynn's attack was conducted in "a very elegant and spirited manner."
The patriot asked £20,000 compensation, but the jury, instructed by
Wilmot to find "liberal but not excessive damages," were not Wilkites.
According to Charles Lloyd, three jurors favored £1,000, four preferred
£3,000, and £5,000 seemed reasonable to the other five. After three divisions they compromised on £4,000 for the plaintiff. The discrepancy
between Wilkes's desires and his reward was so unpopular with the
mob that the jury found it discreet to leave the hall by a rear door.
Knowledge that the crown would stand Halifax's expenses did nothing
to pacify the citizens of London.[68]

The radical periodical press thrived on Wilkes. William Bingley
had begun a triweekly paper, the *Independent Chronicle,* shortly before his imprisonment. With No. 9 it passed to the respectable shop of
George Robinson and Roberts in Paternoster Row. The *Political Register* maintained its position among political magazines, and was seconded by the *Freeholder's Magazine,* which purported to be sponsored
"*By a Patriotic Society.*"[69] With pamphlets and periodicals supple-
menting private correspondence and word of mouth, it seems incredible
that within sixty miles of London the name of Wilkes was almost
unknown, yet the parishioners of the "remarkably loyal and peaceable"
town of Olney

> had just heard his name and that he was in prison; comparing the
> imperfect account they had of him with what they read in their
> Bibles they took it for granted that a person so treated must of
> necessity be a minister of the Gospel and under that character they
> prayed earnestly that he might be supported and enlarged—.

Three thousand miles away Wilkes was the hero of Bostonian radicals, for every ship carried the latest London papers.[70] The power of the press was great, but its influence was dependent upon the whole network of communications. Until that was perfected, the press, Wilkes, and the City was not merely a natural but a necessary combination.

While bloodshed, destruction, and revolution seemed to rise like specters behind the radical press, moderate individuals went quietly about their work. William Strahan paid high tribute to the power of the press when he wrote to his American correspondent:

> The Singularity of our present Situation is this, that while there is actually no National Dissatisfaction existing, our Newspapers are filled with nothing but the most daring and unprecedented Attacks upon the Ministry and the King himself.—And all this is in reality the Work of an Inconsiderable Junto of Men.[71]

Others felt the stirring of the social depths and were alarmed. Sir John Eardley Wilmot feared for "that subordination to law and government, which is the true and only source of the happiness of a people." David Hume's Scottish soul "delighted to see the daily and hourly Progress of Madness and Folly and Wickedness in England. The Consumation of these Qualities are the true Ingredients for making a fine Narrative in History."[72] The Jacobite in Hume might gloat, the philosopher must have wondered, when the 1770 edition of his essay on "The Liberty of the Press" appeared with the conclusion "that the unbounded liberty of the press" is an evil for which "it be difficult, perhaps impossible, to propose a suitable remedy." The essay had formerly declared that any attempt to bound that liberty "will probably be the last efforts of a despotic government. We may conclude, that the liberty of *Britain* is gone for ever when these attempts shall succeed."

Friends of government felt that "the license of our press is intolerable" and that the liberty of the press was threatened thereby, but they were not inactive in maintaining the paper warfare.[73] *A Mirror for the Multitude; or, Wilkes and His Abettors No Patriots* condemned the "licentious mischievous freedom" of the newspapers and accused publishers of fomenting sedition for profit. The *Political Register* placed a ministerial label on *The Political Conduct of the Earl of Chatham* which blackened the names of Chatham, Grenville, Rockingham, Bute, Shelburne, and Townshend with equal asperity. Grenville and Temple were lashed by "Cornelius Scipio" in *An Epistle to Junius Silanus* [i.e., George Grenville].

Government writers included both veterans and novices, as ministers sought to counteract the efforts of the powerful opposition press. Hugh Kelly was pensioned with £200 for corrupting the *Public Ledger* as well as the stage. James Scott contributed his bit of pseudonymous filler to cinch his parish and win immortality as "Twitcher's Advocate." James Macpherson continued his work as a newspaper manager, and Edward Weston, admitting that the reputation of the *Gazette* was "greatly lessened, and consequently the sale greatly diminished," sought to bolster the paper by an increased and exclusive supply of foreign news. An important cog was removed from the Grenvillian propaganda machine in 1770 when William Knox accepted the place of under-secretary of state. Caleb Whitefoord was both active and effective in combating the Wilkites and worked closely with Thomas Bradshaw, secretary of the treasury. Tobias Smollett confided to Whitefoord, "If you had two or three Coadjutors of equal Talents, to play to one another's hands, and keep the Ball of Argument and Ridicule, you would . . . either shame or laugh the people out of their absurd Infatuation."[74]

As presses on both sides poured forth volley after volley, parliamentary action entered a new phase. When the two houses met January 9, 1770, the oratorical barrage laid down by Chatham and his supporters caused the ministry to reel in blind confusion. Camden and Dunning soon rejoined the opposition, and in a final effort to maintain a lost cause, Grafton and the king forced the Great Seal upon Charles Yorke. The results were fatal. Yorke died on January 20, and Grafton threw down his tattered standard two days later. With astounding coolness George III turned his back upon the opposition which had destroyed the ministry and called upon the man whose tactical skill had nonetheless maintained the government's majority in the House of Commons. On the twenty-third, Lord North was formally invited to head the ministry. The king's first written communication advised North, "Whatever You may think do not take any decision . . . without a further conversation with me."[75] It was an auspicious beginning; the history of the next decade was a tribute to the courage and political skill of both men. Throughout the spring session North maneuvered, cajoling recalcitrant members, giving ground when necessary, but never surrendering his control over the majority, always prepared to utilize any sign of dissension in the opposing ranks.

The failure of the opposition to crack North's ostensibly weak defense seemed to whip the press into renewed fury. "Their excess was shocking," wrote Walpole, "and in nothing more condemnable than in the dangers they brought on the liberty of the press." The *Middlesex Journal* passed to publisher John Wheble on Beckford's death, but its policy did not change. The *Whisperer* began its career February 17, 1770, in opposition to North's ministry, and Walpole declared that "the *North Britons* were milk and honey in comparison. The paper had a large circulation and was soon copied by the *Parliamentary Spy*. The *London Museum,* published by John Miller of the *London Evening Post,* and backed by John Almon, added another violently partisan journal to the field.[76]

The Bingley case inspired Candor to write *Another Letter to Mr. Almon,* which quickly secured a *Postscript.* Bingley's imprisonment came to an end when Attorney-General De Grey moved the Court of King's Bench for his discharge on May 28, 1770; the court refused to comply until De Grey insisted that the two-year imprisonment was adequate penalty for any crime for which the printer might have been convicted.[77] Candor now delivered himself of the legal opinion that judges were not "above the inspection of their country." If a "publisher of all sorts of libellous trash" like Bingley needed correction, let it come in a constitutional manner, by jury trial. Criticism does not stop the courts from functioning, but sworn interrogatories, if enforced, establish an "English inquisition." Bingley's case, declared the author, had shown both the evils and insufficiencies of such a system. "The only gainer was a shabby pamphlet-seller . . . who fattened and throve upon the reputation of patriotism . . . and who . . . was pretty indifferent about his personal liberty, provided his press moved freely, and found a large vent for his productions."

The activities of the press received immediate attention when parliament convened, but the role of the "obscure and anonymous writer of paragraphs" defied definition. John Glynn might maintain that the voice of the people was expressed in the daily newspapers, but the ministerial bench scoffed at "a few despicable mechanics . . . booksellers . . . the scum of the earth, the refuse of the people." "The press has been loudly complained of," noted Edmund Burke, "as exciting the public to a breach of their duty . . .

> but let the men who abused the liberty of the press on both sides be produced . . . I will venture to aver, that those on the side of administration are the worst. The experiment is now trying,

whether the liberty of the press be a curse or a blessing: it is easy to see that it will be differently determined by different parties.

By the end of January emotions ran high. Colonel Luttrell openly charged that a recent libel had come from Grenville's "near relation," Lord Temple. Grenville denied the accusation, demanded an investigating committee, and Luttrell was forced to recant even as Temple (who may have been present in the House of Commons) submitted a formal refutation.[78]

The administration was not helpless. Early in January action was taken against the *Morning Chronicle* for "A Catechism to Be Learned by Every Person before He Is Brought to Be Confirmed a Placeman or Pensioner by the Minister." Complaint was made by the Archbishop of Canterbury and the Bishop of London; the law officers quickly declared it a scandalous libel, and the secretary of state ordered them to prosecute.[79]

The House of Lords took the lead against the Wilkite *Middlesex Journal* on February 7 when William G. Edmunds, the printer, was ordered to attend the bar for breach of privilege in printing a minority protest. Richmond objected to the government's obvious effort to silence opposition. Temple reminded Sandwich of his own propagandizing, past and present, and pardoned the writers by remarking, "If a ridicule on his figure could give a dinner to a miserable crew of hireling scribblers, he could not be displeased." The Doorkeeper served the order that night, but Edmunds failed to appear on February 9, as directed. The Gentleman Usher had no better success in locating the printer in March, and not until May 7, did Edmunds surrender himself. Even then he refused to divulge any information except that he had absconded and fled to France. On the ninth, the Lords voted him "guilty of a high Contempt of the Authority of this House," fined him £100, and sent him to Newgate for a month and further until the fine was paid. Edmunds remained in prison until July 28, when the crown paid his fine.[80]

Governmental action against the *Whisperer* began after three numbers had been published. Upon the failure of a ministerial backbencher to move the House of Commons to prosecute the paper, the secretary of state's office proceeded in the usual fashion on March 6, and prosecution was ordered ten days later. Before that date, however, Sir William Meredith had objected to the licentiousness of the *Whis-*

perer and broached the subject in Commons. Honest disapproval of the personal libels which filled the daily papers had no place in the House of Commons. Debate quickly turned upon party lines, and the dubious merits of Johnson and Shebbeare were acidulously paraded. North refused to oppose the motion, throwing the taint of persecution upon the minority, and it was withdrawn.[81]

Political maneuvering could not protect the *Whisperer,* however. His Majesty was petitioned to prosecute William Moore, the printer of Nos. 5–6, on March 26; the House of Lords concurred with the Commons, and their joint resolution was accepted with alacrity. This action had no effect upon the *Whisperer.* In mid-April it was noted that "the paper still goes on, & the former Numbers of it are boldly advertized." A bill of indictment was subsequently found against the author, and in February, 1771, publisher James Mariner was sentenced to twelve months imprisonment, but the *Whisperer* continued to appear until the end of that year.[82]

Although the session was nearing its end, the House of Lords commenced action on May 9 against two more printers. Upon complaints that proceedings of the House had appeared in the *London Evening Post* and the *London Packet,* John Miller and William Oxlade were ordered into custody. The minority lords—Richmond, Temple, Albemarle, and Shelburne—protested in vain before an adamant majority. The two newspapermen escaped punishment, however, by avoiding detection until May 19, when parliament was prorogued.[83]

The opposition had struggled manfully throughout the session to express the discontents which were all too evident out-of-doors. North's successful parliamentary tactics and the king's refusal to be swayed by petitions, remonstrances, or riots left but one alternative—an appeal to public opinion which should carry the weight of party approval and bind the cause of the parliamentary opposition to that of popular opposition. Such a statement could not come from Chatham; the best efforts of Temple and Grenville had already been expended, but from the followers of Rockingham might come a manifesto of constitutional principles unblemished by personal or political vices. Unfortunately, the faction's penman was Edmund Burke, who "could not write even an occasional pamphlet without lifting current controversy into the realm of philosophical speculation."[84]

The projected pamphlet was taking shape as early as July, 1769, although the author was making little progress. The reunion of the

Grenvilles in October further distracted Burke and made him wish that his "little Scheme was in a way of being speedily completed." Though a union of the opposition was greatly to be desired, Burke thought first of showing the differences in constitution and persons between his own faction and all others. About the first of November his efforts became more serious; by the sixth he was able to inform Rockingham that "a good deal of it will be soon ready. . . . It will, I am afraid, be long." Some time in the next week or so the major portion was completed and forwarded to the marquis.

Burke had written from "first principles," but political sense had not abandoned him. To Rockingham he left the decision "whether a thing of this Nature should appear at all."

> It is . . . a formal attack upon that Object which has been nearest and dearest to the Court since the beginning of the reign—and . . . must put you on Terms irreconcileably bad, with the Court and every one of its adherents. . . . the other-bodies who compose the opposition will desire 'not to be comprehended in those declarations.' . . . So that you irritate past forgiveness the Court party, and you do not conciliate all the opposition.

Anticipating recognition as the author, Burke demanded "some tolerable support in Parliament. . . . I shall have enough of Odium; I could wish it a little divided." He therefore asked that the manuscript be submitted to the party for general approval.[85]

During December the draft copy circulated among Rockingham, Dowdeswell, Portland, Savile, and others of the marquis' friends. Suggestions were made by Rockingham and Portland to strengthen here and soften there, usually for the benefit of minority factions. "If they will assist us in pulling down what we wish to see demolished, why throw any obstacles in their way?" asked Portland. The embryo pamphlet was enthusiastically accepted as a pledge of future conduct to the nation, a banner to which "the young men of property, and independent people in both Houses" might rally. Burke meanwhile chafed impatiently for the return of his manuscript. The conclusion was causing him some difficulty, and not until Christmas did Rockingham dispatch the rough draft and corrigenda. For four more months nothing was heard of Burke's work. The author seems never to have been fully satisfied with his writing, and heavy parliamentary duties must have delayed the final touches. At last, on April 23, the pamphlet was published—its title, *Thoughts on the Cause of the Present Discontents*.[86]

"When the affairs of the nation are distracted," wrote Burke, "private people are . . . justified in stepping a little out of their ordinary sphere. . . . They may look into [the calamities of their country] narrowly; they may reason upon them liberally," and if they can rectify them, "they are certainly of service to the cause of Government." "I have nothing to do here with the abstract voice of the people," he continued, nor "a few puny libellers, acting under a knot of factious politicians." The people may err, but "between them and their rulers, the presumption is . . . in favour of the people." Burke turned next to the sovereign, describing the "great object of policy" which motivated the court: *the unlimited and uncontrolled use of its own vast influence, under the sole direction of its own private favour.*" This had been accomplished by separating the ministry from the court, by forming a court party, and by securing the acquiescence of parliament. As his critics immediately marked out, Burke eschewed the customary attack upon Bute; "it is the system," he declared, "and not any individual person who acts in it, that is truly dangerous."

In his remarks upon faction and party Burke reached dangerous ground. Condemning the court doctrine that "all political connexions are . . . factious, and . . . ought to be dissipated, and destroyed," he pleaded for party strength and cohesion: "Party is a body of men united . . . upon some particular principle in which they are all agreed." With scorn Burke dismissed "the cant of *Not men, but measures*; a sort of charm, by which many people get loose from every honourable engagement." He should not have wondered at Chatham's coolness, even had he not attacked the favorite measures of the whole Grenvillian brotherhood. Finally, Burke offered salvation and his party —or "if other ideas should prevail . . . the rage of civil violence; or . . . the dead repose of despotism."

The pamphlet quickly ran through several editions and was reprinted in newspapers and magazines. Within the week Burke was named the author.[87] In May, the radical element in the City—"a rotten subdivision of a faction," Burke had called them—passed judgment in the form of *Observations* written by Catherine Macaulay. The "republican virago" deplored "the baneful tendency" of the *Present Discontents* to extol a "junto of courtiers" rather than to support an "effectual reformation in the vitiated parts of our constitution and government." The *Observations* was short, generally dull, but rightfully pointed out that the Whigs of the Revolution had only themselves to thank for their present difficulties, and the people ought not unite with their successors "without exacting a political creed from leaders, who . . . are to all appearances only planning schemes of private emolument and private virtue." Burke jokingly remarked of Mrs. Macaulay's "patriotic scolding": "I have been afraid to answer her." Walpole riposted neatly by declaring it strong proof of the demerits of the *Present Discontents* that "the Court did not answer it at all.[88]

Reaction to Burke's pamphlet varied greatly. Shelburne referred to it as "excellent." Chatham accepted the author's good intentions, but found that the pamphlet had "done much hurt to the cause" by tending to destroy "a true public-spirited union of *all* who will not be slaves." The same criticism occurred to Horace Walpole, who saw in it "no one end but to deify Lord Rockingham, and to insinuate that Mahomet was his prophet. . . . It was a composition of great merit for ingenuity, eloquence, and knowledge, though at once too diffuse and too refined: it tired the informed, and was unintelligible to the ignorant."

As spring passed into summer the parliamentary opposition had little basis for optimism. Wilkes, at liberty once more, was scarcely an ally, and "he alone had all the popularity they were struggling to obtain." "Lord Chatham has talked on the Middlesex election till nobody will answer him," remarked Walpole, and "in Parliament their numbers are shrunk to nothing, and the session is ending very triumphantly for the Court."[90] Rockingham and Burke had gone to press with negligible results. There remained the chance that the press itself could change the course of politics. It could, at any rate, marshal a pen more barbed than that of Wilkes, more bombastic than the tongue of Chatham, a style whose periods put Burke to shame, and a constitutional ardor that outshone Grenville's. Its champion was Junius.

CHAPTER X

Junius and His Printers

IN AN AGE when anonymous newspaper letters made up the bulk of daily political comment, the name of Junius stood forth in unchallenged mastery of the field. For sheer invective he was unrivaled, and in the style of the eighteenth century, his ephemeral essays formed a model which the Earl of Chatham could recommend to young William Pitt. No political writer more freely bestowed his epithets in high places or with more telling effect, for Junius was accountable to no man. As Johnson remarked, "To him that knows his company, it is not hard to be sarcastic in a mask." This was the secret of Junius' power—anonymity which protected the writer and shielded his publisher—a shield which has never been pierced.*

On January 21, 1769, Henry Sampson Woodfall's *Public Advertiser* carried the first letter signed "Junius." It was a vigorous attack upon the Grafton ministry in behalf of

> a nation overwhelmed with debt; her revenues wasted; her trade declining; the affections of her colonies alienated; the duty of the magistrate transferred to the soldiery; . . . the whole administration of justice become odious and suspected to the whole body of the people.

The attack was not exceptional in itself and might have passed without notice had not Sir William Draper chosen to chastise this latest of "felonious robbers of private character [who] stab in the dark, without having the courage to sign their real names to their malevolent and

---

*It is not necessary to undertake the identification of Junius, an achievement which, were it possible, would not change the story significantly, for his shadow-figure possesses greater reality than many of those, both outstanding and obscure, who have been nominated for his honors. In spite of C. W. Everett's scholarly argument for Shelburne, and F. Cordasco's presumptive evidence for Laughlin Macleane, I remain faithful to the cause of Philip Francis, a man whose real talent, like Junius' identity, rests under a shadow.

wicked productions." Draper's letter in the *Public Advertiser* demonstrated his courage; Junius replied February 7, praising the goodness of his heart but not the depth of his understanding. For a month Draper maintained an unequal contest as Junius' blows fell with the speed and brilliance of lightning. On March 3, Junius took his leave of Draper to range for bigger game.

Throughout the spring and early summer Junius addressed his barbed epistles to the Duke of Grafton. Corruption, contumacy, immorality in public and private life were laid at the minister's door, and his Grace was denied every shred of respectability. When parliament rose, Junius roamed afield, striking at random among pamphleteers and politicians. The eminent Dr. Blackstone was warned "to be quiet"; the Duke of Bedford was made to writhe for his misdeeds.

The combination of ruthless sarcasm, keen invective, and political daring with which Junius lashed his enemies assured him of a great popular following. The publisher who offered Junius for sale might expect a ready market. Although the first two dozen Junius letters seem to have had little effect upon the circulation of the *Public Advertiser*,[1] other printers were prepared to give Junius more permanent form. Early in July, Francis Newbery, whose *Public Ledger* was an important rival of Woodfall's paper, brought out an unauthorized edition of the current Junian letters.[2] The author, who "did not expect more than the life of a newspaper," was flattered, but critical of Newbery's format. "If this man will keep me alive," he wrote to Woodfall, "let me live without being offensive." Woodfall took up the hint and proposed reprinting Junius himself. His correspondent was pleased and offered to write a preface should it be desired.

Newbery's piratical edition quickly ran into a second printing, to which a supplement was soon added.[3] Magazines and newspapers avidly snatched up Junius' letters as they appeared, and John Almon soon realized the profit inherent in a larger bound edition. His project was completed in December and entitled *A Collection of the Letters of Atticus, Lucius, and Junius.*

By the end of the year Junius was a familiar figure in political literature, prominent enough to cause H. S. Woodfall some misgivings concerning the attitude of Junius' victims toward his publisher. Junius was well aware that he walked a fine line. During the summer of 1769 he advised Woodfall, "Avoid prosecutions, if you can, but above all things, avoid the Houses of Parliament—there is no contending with them." With an eye to ducal sensitivity, Junius assured his publisher, "You have nothing to fear from the Duke of B[edford.] I reserve some things expressly to awe him, in case he should think of bringing you before the House of Lords." The personal nature of Junius' attacks and the threat of that vitriolic pen sufficed to ward off private actions against his publisher, but on December 19, 1769, Junius launched a letter to the king which was destined to make publishing history.

"When the complaints of a brave and powerful people . . . encrease in proportion to the wrongs they have suffered . . . every inferior consideration must yield to the security of the Sovereign, and to the general safety of the state." Junius then approached the throne as an honest man "unacquainted with the vain impertinence of forms . . . but not without respect." "Sir,—" he began, "It is the misfortune of your life . . . that you should never have been acquainted with the language of truth, until you heard it in the complaints of your people. It is not, however, too late to correct the error." Two courses Junius set before the king: "support the very ministry who have reduced your affairs to this deplorable situation . . . shelter yourself under the forms of a parliament, and set your people at defiance." Such a policy, "if it did not immediately shake your establishment . . . would rob you of your peace of mind forever." Or, act an honourable part. "Discard those little, personal resentments which have too long directed your public conduct." Silence Wilkes with a pardon—"it is only the tempest that lifts him from his place. . . . Come forward to your people . . . speak to your subjects with the spirit of a man, and in the language of a gentleman. . . . Tell them you are determined to remove every cause of complaint against your government; that you will give your confidence to no man who does not possess the confidence of your subjects." Adopt not Stuart principles: "The Prince who imitates their conduct, should be warned by their example; and while he plumes himself upon the security of his title to the crown, should remember that as it was acquired by one revolution, it may be lost by another."

The letter to the king was an immediate success. Woodfall's circulation had risen from an average of 2,800 to 3,400 as a result of Junius' early letters; it now jumped to 4,800, as 1,750 extra copies of the *Public Advertiser* were printed and sold within minutes of their appearance. Every paper not dedicated to the ministry reprinted it—Charles Say ran about 1,400 extra copies of the *Gazetteer* on this occasion—and the radical magazines snatched it up at the end of the month.[4] The letter seems to have been so widely known that it escaped detailed comment. Rockingham probably represented accurately the reaction of his class when he complained that it was "too much of a flagellation," too directly confronting his Majesty, cutting across the niceties of constitutional complaint. More common men saw in it a deeper meaning. Though "dictated by the spirit of party more than by real patriotism," wrote a minor government clerk, "yet in sober sadness there is but too much of truth in it."[5]

One measure of the effect of Junius' letter to the king was the alacrity with which action was taken against it. The paper was published December 19; the next day Weymouth asked for the attorney-general's opinion. On the twenty-first, De Grey reported that the letter was libelous and actionable, and "the most proper method of proceeding would be by information." He was ordered to begin his prosecution four days after the letter was printed.[6] Within the week Woodfall began to grow alarmed, aware, no doubt, of the action preparing against him. Junius sought to reassure him on the twenty-sixth, and advised the printer to "stand firm (I mean with all the humble appearances of contrition). If you trim or falter, you will lose friends without gaining others." When informations were filed against the publishers of the letter to the king, Woodfall's perturbation increased, and Junius repeatedly asserted his belief that no jury would find against the printer, "especially in these times." As added encouragement he held out a promise of reimbursement should Woodfall be found guilty—"but seriously . . . I think it is impossible."

The prosecutions commenced against Woodfall and the *Public Advertiser,* John Almon and the *London Museum,* John Miller of the *London Evening Post,* George Robinson's *Independent Chronicle,* the *Gazetteer's* publisher Charles Say, and Henry Baldwin and the *St. James's Chronicle* attracted widespread attention. Never before had such a general net of legal action been cast over the press. In the House of Commons, North defended the proceedings of the law officers on the grounds that "Junius is not a writer against administration; he flies at higher game." It was an appealing argument to which even Sir George Savile could give approval.[7]

In June the first printer came up for trial—surprisingly, not Woodfall, the original publisher, but John Almon. Although Attorney-General De Grey denied it, there may have been some truth in Almon's claim that his political activity in the press and in Westminster explained his precedence over Woodfall.*[8] More determinant perhaps was the hope that a clear-cut verdict against one who had only sold the letter (and who would be tried in Westminster) would ease the task of the crown lawyers against the original publisher in the City.[9] When the attorney-general might secure a special select jury—"six . . . incapable of understanding the question, three afraid of giving offence, and two more who will not take the trouble of thinking. Remains one who has sense, courage and application"—such considerations weighed heavily.[10]

Almon's case came on before Mansfield, June 2, 1770, in the Court of King's Bench. Like the other publishers, Almon was accused of having "by such wicked, artful, scandalous, and malicious allusions, suppositions, and insinuations . . . most unlawfully, wickedly and maliciously aspersed, scandalized and vilified our said present sovereign Lord the King." The evidence against him of having sold the *London Museum* containing Junius' letter had been secured by two unsavory characters whose trade it was "to supply the gentlemen of the Treasury with all political daily publications." The paper had been sent to Almon's shop January 1, and the proprietor being out of town, an unsuspecting clerk had placed it on sale. Almon returned that day, and learning of the ministerial intention to prosecute, ordered sales stopped and the remaining copies returned to John Miller, the printer. The delay had been sufficient, however, for evidence to be secured against him.

De Grey rested his case on two points: "that the publication concerns the king . . . [and] *that the defendant published this writing.*" It was not difficult to show that Junius' letter touched the king, and although Almon's counsel, Serjeant John Glynn, discredited the two messengers of the press, their testimony was irrefutable. "What signifies all the writers in the world," asked De Grey, "if they are confined to their garrets, and can't find publishers? . . . the man who introduces to the public the paper first written, is full as criminal as the writer."

Glynn made no attempt to defend the personal imputations against the king, but he insisted, "The freedom of political discussion is of the utmost consequence to all our liberty, and . . . the actions of this government may be canvassed, freely and consistently with the duty of a good subject." Turning to the crucial point of publication he noted

*The attorney-general's brother, Thomas De Grey, had spoken insultingly in the House of Commons of "base-born booksellers" and had been sharply rebuked by John Glynn, M.P. for Westminster, whose constituents voted him their thanks—at Almon's instigation.

that "Mr. Almon is singled out for a prosecution, as the *publisher* of a paper . . . that hath singly appeared in *all* newspapers that have been published." But "Mr. Almon . . . is not the publisher. Mr. Almon is a bookseller," and Glynn advised the jury that, according to custom, Almon's name had been inserted in the *London Museum* without his authorization, that it had been sold without his knowledge, and that he had voluntarily stopped the sale. "If these circumstances appear . . . how can you say that Mr. Almon is guilty of publishing this paper? If publication is an offence, Mr. Almon cannot be said to have committed it."

Any hopes of the defense were dashed when Mansfield instructed the jury—whose foreman was a clerk in the war office—that "a sale at a man's shop . . . by his servant, is evidence . . . to convict the master of publication. . . . If you believe these two witnesses, you will be satisfied by the sense put on the words by the information, you will find the defendant *guilty*."

The jury retired just before noon and returned in about two hours, one member desiring the chief justice to restate his dictum on the criminal responsibility of a master. Mansfield did so, but vouchsafed to the defendant's counsel, "If I am wrong, they may move the Court, and the trial will be set aside." All doubts erased by this instruction, the jury returned a verdict of guilty.[11]

Undaunted by one defeat, Glynn and Almon prepared to refute Mansfield's charge. A motion for a new trial was made June 19 and heard on the twenty-seventh when Glynn argued that "INTENTION is necessary for the CONSTITUTION OF GUILT. . . . I do conceive it, the undoubted maxim of the laws of this kingdom, that *no* man should be criminally answerable for the acts of his servant." Mansfield refused his attempt to question the first verdict on grounds of misconstruction and stubbornly upheld the dictum that "in order to convict a man of publishing a libel, the proof of its being bought in his shop is sufficient." The motion was set aside. On the thirtieth Almon and his counsel appeared to receive sentence. Affidavits were offered by Glynn extenuating Almon's conduct as a bookseller. Mansfield advised that certain corrections should be made and Almon should be brought up at a later date for sentencing. The delay, beneficial to the defendant, would also allow time to observe the punishment meted out to other printers whose guilt was more immediate. Both parties hoping to profit by this action, Almon's case was held over until the next term.[12]

The case of the crown against Henry S. Woodfall was heard on June 13 at the Guildhall. With the precedent of the Almon verdict, the attorney-general's task appeared easy; he based his case on the fact of publication and the meaning of Junius' letter. The spirit of the City was already manifest, and De Grey advisedly sought to ameliorate popular antagonism by pointing out that though six prosecutions were in hand, he had endeavored to pass over those publishers, equally guilty, who were poor and had large families. Three witnesses swore that Woodfall published the *Public Advertiser,* and the crown's case was complete.

As in Almon's case, Glynn was Woodfall's leading counsel. The serjeant had hewn close to legal argument eleven days before; he now began to play upon the jury. He flattered them on "the excellence of a London jury, and doubted not the liberties of the people were sufficiently safe, while there were trials by jury." He insisted that the phrases "false, scandalous, malicious" in the information were necessary of proof, likewise the criminal intent of the publisher—and he admitted Woodfall was the publisher. "But—if . . . the temper of the times was such, that the people needed that kind of information . . . if the acts of government . . . highly demanded public reprehension," then author and publisher had acted a most laudable part. If Woodfall were found guilty, Glynn told the jury, "the hands of every publisher would be tied" and "ministerial scribblers" would go unanswered.

Glynn's appeal might move a London jury, but it had no effect upon Lord Mansfield. The jury, said the chief justice, would not concern themselves with the terminology of the charges laid in the information—"they were mere formal words"—and as for the criminality of Junius' letter, "the Court were the only judges of that." "As for the liberty of the press," he concluded, "I will tell you what that is; the liberty of the press is, that a man may print what he pleases without a license: as long as it remains so, the liberty of the press is not restrained."

The jury withdrew at noon. By 3:30 they had not returned, and Mansfield, impatient at the delay, refused to sit longer than four o'clock. The jury were instructed to report their verdict to his house, and the court adjourned. By five o'clock, it was rumored, ten jurymen had agreed "to bring Woodfall in not guilty, but there were two who stood out, . . . the King's plasterer and a baker." Between 9:30 and 10:00, the jury rose and made its way to Bloomsbury Square, where standing in the hall with Mansfield's footmen, these twelve honest citizens returned their verdict: "Guilty of printing and publishing only."[13]

A question immediately arose as to the meaning of this ambiguous verdict. While lawyers on both sides prepared themselves for further action, Woodfall plaintively wrote, "I fear I must spend my Friday in Westminster Hall, and probably my Friday Night in the King's Bench, as my unfortunate Law Suit continues not only to be troublesome, Expensive, and vexatious, but draws to a very critical Period."[14]

On June 22 counsel for the defendant moved the court to stay judgment on the verdict, and the crown officers entered a cross-motion. The arguments were heard on July 3. Glynn maintained that the verdict acquitted his client. "Juries are judges of both law and fact," he declared.

> The jury therefore had a right to consider the paper charged as a libel. . . . They might take it upon them . . . or they might resort to the judges for advice. Here they have, by their word of exclusion, gone as far as to determine, that there is no guilt in the paper.

Crown counsel, led by Solicitor-General Edward Thurlow, adopted Mansfield's dictum. "When the jury have found sufficient matter of fact, your lordships will supply the matter of law," said Thurlow. "The jury have found the fact of printing . . . and that was the only thing they had to find. For what is the crime charged? It is the printing and publishing." Still Glynn insisted that the verdict was either an acquittal or no verdict at all and a new trial therefore necessary. The chief justice did not waver. "If the jury find, that the defendant published at all, they find the paper, as charged in the information, for that is their only enquiry. . . . I did not leave it to the jury whether the paper was innocent or not. I never do." Whatever his inclination, Mansfield declared the term too near its end for further action and, like Almon's, held Woodfall's case over to the next term.[15]

By mid-July popular sentiment in favor of Junius' publishers ran high. The *London Museum* had portrayed Mansfield and the king in "The Royal Chace" as hunting three fleeing printers, one of whom was Almon, while Junius hid in a tree. A doggerel verse celebrated the occasion:

> To Drive the Printers with hound and horn,
> 　George and Mansfield took their Way:
> The Child may rue that was unborn,
> 　The Hunting of that Day.

De Grey was satirized as performing a witch's dance before the king while tossing the names of Woodfall, Junius, Almon, and Say into a steaming caldron. The *Political Register* openly accused Mansfield of plotting to overthrow the liberty of the press: "Your present attempt will, perhaps, consign your name to [an] immortality in history, which you would not wish any friend to share."[16]

To the accompaniment of such raucous commentary the trials of John Miller and Henry Baldwin came on, July 18, at the Guildhall. Miller's case was heard at nine o'clock. Thurlow directed the prosecution and belabored the jury with all the brutal power at his command. He would not attack the liberty of the press, he said, but that liberty had been so abused by the author, printer, and publisher of Junius' letter that it effectively annihilated the liberty of all men. Carried away by the violence of the paper he described, Thurlow swore, "For God's sake, is that no libel?" If not, imagination cannot comprehend what a libel is. "If you . . . return a verdict of acquittal," he warned, "then you find a false verdict."

Thurlow sought to overwhelm the jury; Glynn sweetened their ears with the language of the City. He detested "those men who . . . prostitute their pen" to calumny, slander, and deprecation, but he bestowed "the higher measure of indignation and condemnation on that fountain from whence flows the encouragement to such pernicious prostitution. None of that sort has, however, been thought proper to be brought before you." In Junius he saw "a writer called forth by ardent zeal" for the safety of his nation.

> So far from thinking that paper obnoxious . . . I think the author
> . . . acted a justifiable part, to have obeyed the call on a good
> citizen, in conveying the alarm, and giving notice where he thought
> it necessary. . . . Is it criminal in a man to say, if he thinks so, that
> discontents prevail in this kingdom? is it criminal to state the
> grounds of it? . . . Gentlemen . . . you are the constitutional judges
> of the question. . . . It is left to you, whether . . . a citizen of London
> shall [suffer] for any paper published in such a way.

Glynn's second, Mr. Davenport, continued in the same vein, attacking the minister who, "with all his tribe of writers," was unable to defend himself without recourse to "the only instrument which is left in the hands of the Attorney General, the power of preferring an information."

Thurlow righteously protested the attempt to shift the argument from its true grounds. He viewed the jury as the last refuge of those who seek redress. "I protest to God, it appears to me . . . too strange a proposition to say liberty is concerned in protecting a man in writing injuriously and opprobriously" against another. If you deny those who apply for justice "there consequently is neither liberty, nor property, nor reputation, nor anything which this country has hitherto thought worth protection."

At the conclusion of the argument Mansfield summed up in most certain terms. The question for the jury was whether the defendant had published a paper of the tenor set forth in the information. There had been no objection to the meaning put to the paper, and the evidence of publication stood uncontradicted. "If you by your verdict find the defendant not guilty . . . there is an end of the prosecution. If you find that, . . . it is between God and your consciences." The verdict does not determine the character of the paper; that is a point of law to be considered by the court—and another jury, Mansfield reminded his auditors, had convicted Almon on the same charges. They were not bound by that, he said, but if juries act on passing impressions "there might be no law at all upon the subject."

As in Woodfall's case, the court adjourned before the jury returned its verdict. About 7:30 that evening they carried their verdict to Mansfield's house. "A vast concourse of people" soon filled Bloomsbury Square, and when word came that Miller had been found "not guilty," they "testified their joy, by the loudest huzzas." The conscience of the City of London was clear.[17]

The same day Henry Baldwin won obscure fame as the first of the printers to be acquitted. His trial began as soon as the Miller jury was locked up, and in four hours he was a free man. Twenty years later John Walter, publisher of *The Times,* explained the attitude of those London juries which took the law unto themselves and upheld the right of political criticism in a free society:

I was one of the jury who tried Junius's letters to the king . . . the printer of the *St. James's Evening* was acquitted as the jury did not choose to vest a power in the Court to give a sentence . . . of having wilfully, maliciously and seditiously published the papers when only the mere sale in the common course of his business was proved.

This was the simple reasoning of one ordinary businessman, but magnified ten-thousand-fold it was a certain portent of change.[18]

The obvious force of a popular opinion which could carry a jury against the violence of Thurlow and the commanding austerity of Mansfield was not to be denied. With but one clear-cut victory in four cases, the crown law officers could not be expected to pursue the remaining printers with great enthusiasm. George Robinson, whose *Independent Chronicle* had carried the letter to the king, was not tried until December 19, 1770. While the judge was delivering his charge to the jury, one of the members shouted, "You need not say any more, for I am determined to acquit him." The attorney-general promptly demanded his removal—for obvious reasons. Robinson's counsel, the indefatigable Glynn, objected, and the trial was put off until next term. Apparently no further action was taken against the printer, and as the *Independent Chronicle* was already defunct, the case seems to have been dropped.[19]

Charles Green Say of the *Gazetteer* presented different problems. When Junius' letter was inserted in his paper, Say was totally incapacitated as the result of an "apoplectic or paralytic fit." His servants had reprinted the letter as it appeared in other papers, and Say pleaded absolute ignorance of the entire transaction. Nonetheless, an information was filed against him. On May 18 the printer submitted a petition praying a stay of the proceedings in view of extenuating circumstances. Further, Say declared, he disapproved of Junius and "he had actually engaged, at a considerable expense, in defense of Government, a writer of well known abilities to supply the Gazetteer with proper answers to the letters signed 'Junius' . . . under the signature of 'Modestus.' "[20] The printer's petition was referred to the attorney-general but according to De Grey, a noli prosequi was not granted because Say's attorney could not provide substantiating affidavits. Trial was delayed for some time, however, and when it came on John Dunning, as solicitor-general, represented the crown. "It was stated, on the part of Mr. Say, that such and such [i.e., his debility] would be his defence." Dunning replied, "If that was the case the record should be withdrawn," and Say was never actually tried. As Dunning found nothing to comment upon in the former attorney-general's account of the case, it may be considered correct. Edmund Burke inserted a confusing partisan note by claiming that "when Woodfall was acquitted they did not then prosecute" Charles Say.[21]

The attempt to silence Junius by striking at his publishers had failed—and the humiliation of the crown lawyers and Mansfield was the glory of the City of London. There remained only Woodfall and Almon to deal with and there was little to be gained by a vengeful attitude which would only add fuel to the fires of discontent. The Court of King's Bench took up Woodfall's case again on November 20. Mansfield reviewed the arguments, the evidence, and concluded, "Guilty of printing and publishing, where there is no other charge is guilty: for nothing more is to be found by the jury. . . . Clearly there can be no judgment of acquittal. . . . The only question is, Whether . . . the word 'only' can have a meaning which would affect or contradict the verdict." Mansfield was clearly of the opinion that Woodfall ought to have been found guilty and that the jury did not intend to acquit the defendant; however, he declared, "Though the verdict be full, the Court may grant a new trial. And we are all of opinion . . . that there should be a Venire de Novo."

Woodfall's retrial was anticlimactic. The attorney-general informed the chief justice that he had lost the original newspaper by which publication could be proved. Mansfield "laconically replied, 'That's not my fault, Mr. Attorney;' and in this manner terminated the second trial." Woodfall escaped punishment, but his legal fees totaled about £120, and his ardor for radical publishing ventures was markedly cool thereafter.[22] For Glynn, whose conduct of the case had been flawless, Woodfall subsequently purchased a freehold at Brentford "in order to convince him . . . that I hold his Services in grateful Remembrance."[23]

John Almon appeared before the King's Bench, November 28, the lone publisher of Junius to be sentenced. Glynn had presented a formidable collection of affidavits in extenuation of Almon's guilt, and these were now read: that of John Miller showed that the defendant had objected to the use of his name in the *London Museum*; Almon's own statement of his innocent absence from Piccadilly and subsequent withdrawal of the paper after sixty-seven or sixty-eight of three hundred copies had been sold was supported by Robert Morris; Dilly vouched for the customary nature of this procedure in the trade; Adams (Almon's shopman) corroborated his master's evidence. The attorney-general was extremely harsh in denouncing Almon and his affidavits—both Mansfield and Aston rebuked him for his asperity—while Glynn quietly bespoke the court's leniency. When there was nothing further to be heard, Mansfield excused himself, in order to preside at the House of Lords, and Justice Aston delivered sentence.

John Almon had been found "guilty of publishing a most wicked, seditious, and malignant libel." However his own affidavit and that of Miller lessened the guilt. The others were not regarded—except that of Robert Morris. Politically obnoxious as a confirmed Wilkite, Morris had maintained in his affidavit that Junius' letter was not libelous. Aston digressed unnecessarily to declare that such an opinion was little short of treason. Returning to Almon, he said, "That the booksellers, in future times, might not screen themselves, by pleading ignorance of what they sold, it was necessary to repeat, that the bare fact of publication was sufficient conviction." Almon was fined ten marks and ordered to give security for two years in £400 himself, with two additional sureties of £200 each. The fees of Almon's legal counsel amounted to £139 0s. 11d., but the singularity of his conviction came to his aid. John Aubrey collected a purse of £100 for the publisher, and though Almon's sentence seemed harsh in view of the deliverance of Woodfall and Miller, it was difficult to discover a martyr in a man who was "reckoned to have made a fortune of £10,000 by publishing and selling libels."[24]

Popular interest in these cases encouraged a number of authors to publish the argument for the press. Early in August, Candor addressed *Another Letter to Mr. Almon, in Matter of Libel*. The pamphlet contained little new material, reviewed the cases of Almon and Woodfall, and while regretting the abuse of the press by "the present system of party-writing," opposed anything which might "give footing to a code of libel-polity, which may hereafter be turned to the destruction of all liberty of the press." Mansfield received his share of attention and was warned that "a man may happen to dislike the trial by jury, and an unlicensed press . . . but if the course of his profession and extraordinary talents were to bring such a man to be Chief Justice of England . . . he must . . . take the law of England as he finds it." In November, the author added a postscript animadverting on the judgments in both Almon's and Woodfall's cases. "The aim is so evident, that it is high time to ring out the alarum bell in the ears of all mankind, to hunt down such insidious enemies [i.e., Mansfield] to everything that is most dear and valuable to Englishmen, and to root out the grand canker-worm of the state."

More acrimonious was Robert Morris' *Letter to Sir Richard Aston.* The young lawyer felt the justice's remarks concerning his affidavit in Almon's case were a direct personal insult. He now appealed to the public, a court in which Aston could not impose silence. Morris' pamphlet expressed the opinion of the radicals in the City. The vendors of Junius' letter "would never have suffered a prosecution, if the public demand . . . had not shown, that mankind were pleased, not shocked," wrote Morris, "except in the court of King's Bench, or the supreme court at St. James's." How can that be a libel which the nation praises? And how is it that "printing . . . and publishing, which used to be lawful trades in this country, are become of a sudden criminal." Mansfield, the "arbitrary judge" who was "desirous to drive the printers into a petition for a licenser," was warned lest the cry arise among the people to abolish his court and punish its judges.[25]

Seldom did the chief justice escape condemnation. The anonymous author of *A Letter to the Jurors of Great Britain* might grudgingly admit his great talents and contributions to commercial law, but Phileleutherus Anglicanus compared Mansfield unfavorably with Jeffreys and Scroggs. "It is impossible," said the latter author, speaking of Almon's case, "to vindicate this sentence in any light; and it ought to produce a parliamentary inquiry."[26]

A spirit of criticism, investigation, and change was in the air. The vindication of Junius' commentaries and their free publication by the acquittal of Miller and Baldwin prepared the way for a broader, a higher, consideration of press law and the press in politics.

CHAPTER XI

Press and Parliament: The Opposition, 1770–1771

THE DEPENDENCE of law upon public opinion in a free society makes a capacity for change imperative in the statutory body if it is to retain a substantive character. In 1770 there were many who felt that the critical point had been reached by the law of libel as propounded by Mansfield and the Court of King's Bench. "The late doctrines . . . concerning the rights of juries to judge of *Law* and *Fact*, have spread universal alarm, and raised the justest indignation," said Chatham. "This is laying the axe to the root with a vengeance! Jurors who may not judge, electors who may not elect . . . compose a pretty system of English Government."[1]

Here was an issue, and Mansfield a target, upon which Chatham's guns might freely play. The old fire of opposition blazed in his heart as it had not for ten years past. The faction that had vainly tried to bring him into open opposition he now scorned: "the Marquis [of Rockingham] is an honest and honourable man," he wrote to his agent John Calcraft, "but . . . 'moderation, moderation!' is the burden of the song. . . . For myself, I am resolved to be in earnest for the public; and shall be a *scarecrow of violence* to the gentle warblers of the grove, the moderate Whigs and temperate statesmen."[2] Chatham's opinions soon came to the attention of Burke and Rockingham. It was reported that "verdicts and juries" were Chatham's "most favorite point . . . partly from political Views, and partly from his personal animosity to Lord Mansfield." Burke looked coolly upon the earl's projects. To Rockingham he described it as neither dignified nor respectful to engage themselves in Chatham's cause without due consideration and firm determination to persevere in the reform of abuses. "Malevolence and personal enmity" he could only regret as unnecessarily poor taste. The head of his faction could not afford to indulge Burke's personal inclinations; effective opposition depended upon union. The winter session of parliament was scheduled to begin November 13; on the preceding

188

Saturday, Rockingham visited Chatham and favorably impressed the earl with his "upright intentions."[3]

Chatham's own intentions toward the press at this point are not clear. On September 1, Calcraft had visited Lord Temple and they had discussed Almon's case at length. Apparently it was proposed to raise an issue upon the ruling that the jury could consider only the fact of selling. Sunday, November 11, Chatham entertained Serjeant Glynn— "the spirit of the constitution itself"—and parliamentary action upon press cases must have formed an important topic of conversation.[4]

The approaching session also brought Junius into the field. On Monday he sent to Woodfall the manuscript of a violent letter to Lord Mansfield which had just been completed. He implored the printer to let it appear on Wednesday, or, if he had any fears, to send it in sufficient time to John Miller that it might run in the *London Evening Post*, for "Miller, I am sure, will have no scruples." "We have got the rascal down," Junius gloated, "let us strangle him if it be possible."[5]

Parliament met November 13, and the opposition had seldom been more sympathetically united both indoors and out. But Chatham and his friends were absent from the first session as they paid silent tribute to the memory of George Grenville, who died that day. His loss was a cruel blow. Not only would his incisive grasp of constitutional principles be sadly missed, his death removed the only effective counterpoise between Chatham and Rockingham. Without their leader Grenville's followers gravitated away from opposition into the administration. "If poor Mr. Grenville dies," Lord George Sackville (now Germaine) had written, "what is to be the object of opposition? I hope not to make Lord Chatham minister."[6] And among the Grenvillians was Lord Temple, whose interest and knowledge of the political press were second to none. The earl's political career came to an abrupt termination with his brother's death, and one more voice was lost to the opposition. This may explain the failure of the opposition lords to raise Almon's case in the upper chamber. Chatham had no love for publishers and quickly devoted his efforts to another line of attack; only Temple might have bearded the House for a "base-born bookseller."

The spirit of the times was evident in the debate on the address of thanks. In the Commons, Sir William Meredith, referring to the current Anglo-Spanish crisis over the Falkland Islands, declared that Britain would never face a foreign enemy until justice had been done at home: "Britons . . . will never fight to arm despotism with new power, nor strike a blow which can only rivet their own chains."[7] On Wednesday, Junius' epistle to Mansfield appeared in the *Public Advertiser.* "Our language has no term of reproach, the mind has no idea of detestation, which has not already been happily applied to you, and exhausted," wrote Junius. He likened Mansfield to a woman—"timid, vindictive, and irresolute." He accused him of having "a settled plan to contract the legal power of juries. . . . Your charge to the jury, in the prosecution against Almon and Woodfall, contradicts the highest legal authorities, as well as the plainest dictates of reason. . . . When you invade the province of the jury in matter of libel, you . . . attack the liberty of the press, and, with a single stroke, wound two of your enemies." Junius concluded with a warning to "beware how you indulge the first emotions of your resentment. . . . The persecution of an innocent printer cannot alter facts, nor refute arguments.—Do not furnish me with farther materials against yourself."*

The crescendo of criticism rose another step when the City of London, in a "humble address, remonstrance, and petition" to the throne, noted the threat to "that sacred Bulwark of *English* Liberty, the Trial by Jury [from] the dangerous Designs of those, who have dared openly to attempt to mutilate its Power and destroy its Efficacy." The Address specifically complained of "juries forbid to judge of the whole Matter in Issue before them."[8]

In the face of this expression of public opinion Mansfield upheld his views in Woodfall's case on November 20—"quite incurable of his political leprosy," Chatham observed.[9] Two days later Sir Joseph Mawbey bluntly told ministers who called for unanimity, "There are those who believe there is a rooted intention to introduce arbitrary power. . . . Sir, there is a general feeling of dissatisfaction against the courts of justice, and against administration." So frequently was the treatment of the press brought up that North was forced to speak upon it and recognize the demand for action even though he might oppose it.[10] Chatham's virulent attack in the House of Lords upon ministerial foreign policy was heard by Philip Francis and printed by the *Middlesex Journal, London Evening Post, London Museum,* and *London Maga-*

---

*Attorney-General De Grey is said to have proposed further prosecution of Junius' publishers for this letter, but Mansfield wisely refused to allow a personal insult to become the basis of legal action from which neither advantage nor honor could be gained. Lord Campbell, *The Lives of the Chief Justices* (New York, 1873), III, 386.

zine as soon as copy could be prepared.[11] The public should know that its leaders were not silent.

The first parliamentary offensive was launched from Chatham's side. In conjunction with Shelburne it was tentatively arranged that Charles W. Cornwall should move the House of Commons for an inquiry into the proceedings of the Court of King's Bench in cases of libel. Cornwall, however, developed scruples against taking the leading part without giving prior notice to the Rockingham faction, although he realized that "any previous communication . . . might lead to insuperable difficulties." Satisfied by Cornwall's motives, Chatham was still in need of a spokesman. The names of Sir William Meredith and Richard Oliver were mentioned, but another solution appeared over the weekend. On November 24, Cornwall met with Constantine Phipps and William Dowdeswell, and learned that Phipps intended to move the House on November 27 for leave to bring in a bill concerning the attorney-general's power to file informations. Cornwall sought to expand the motion into a general inquiry, and Dowdeswell gave assurances of his assistance, although Shelburne feared he might "change his own notions . . . for the political notions of his party." With the smoke of battle in his nostrils, Chatham discounted the possibility of a divided opposition: "the wavering and the treacherous should be brought to the test. . . . My opinion still is, that all *will* follow, because they *must*."[12]

Phipps duly rose on November 27 to protest the political ramifications of the attorney-general's power to file informations. He avoided any personal attack upon ministers and based his request for leave to introduce "a bill to explain, amend, and render more effectual, the act . . . to prevent malicious Informations in the Court of King's Bench" upon constitutional grounds. Sir William Meredith seconded the motion, and Welbore Ellis opened the administration's defense. "A time of public disorder and confusion," he urged, when envenomed scurrility rages with lawless fury, is not the proper moment to tamper with the constitution.

Cornwall spoke next, according to the plan, pointing out the recent abuse of the press by the Court of King's Bench, but he described the motion as "too precipitate"; before a remedy might be suggested, inquiry was necessary. "From the facts that will then be elicited, we shall be able to arrive at the truth." Phipps defended his policy against this unexpected attempt at emendation, and De Grey rushed to widen the breach in the opposition ranks. How could his power be dangerous, he asked, when he had "hardly been able to bring a single offender to justice?" Glynn followed, heartily concurring in the motion, and delivering himself of a sound condemnation of Mansfield's legal doctrines. He was opposed by Solicitor-General Thurlow, who baited the opposition to further discord by declaring that "rumour is not a sufficient ground for proceeding." Alexander Wedderburn, a recent convert to the opposition camp and shortly destined to fill Thurlow's office, defended the conduct of the judges and opposed any rash step even as he supported the motion.

The palm of debate was carried off by Burke. Brilliantly he characterized the popular discontents, the abuse of power in Almon's case, the popular reaction which freed every other printer of Junius' letter. "How comes this Junius to have broke through the cobwebs of the law, and to range uncontroulled, unpunished, through the land?" This "great boar of the forest" has made "King, Lords, and Commons . . . the sport of his fury."

> But why . . . dwell upon Junius alone? . . . numberless other libellers . . . secure in the protection of the people . . . laugh . . . the terrors of information to scorn. All your messengers of the press, all your tribes of informers, are as much despised as they are detested. What is the cause of this general aversion to law, this universal conspiracy against government?

"The ministers are the grand criminals [who have] roused up in the nation this spirit of opposition, which tramples underfoot all law, order, and decorum." Only an inquiry, Burke insisted, could restore credit to the government.

Burke castigated De Grey for the prosecution of Almon, but the attorney-general was able to defend himself against Burke's charges. He could not, however, deny the great orator's rebuttal: "Libels have conquered the law. The liberty of the press has run into licentiousness . . . too strong for the government. The law is beaten down, and trampled upon." By this time the motion and the proposed inquiry were totally confused. In vain Meredith pointed out the dangerous divergence of the opposition effort, and Cornwall sought to heal the schism he had created. North hardly needed to speak well or do more than refer to a daily press teeming with slander and defamation, "the food and raiment of printers and booksellers."

The debate lasted six hours, and tempers became fiery. Phipps nearly crossed swords with a lord of the Admiralty; Glynn ill-liked the appellation "this liberty boy, this Bill of Rights man." The question was called for with "clamour and vociferation," and at 9:50 the House divided. The motion was lost 164 to 72, as many nominal opposition members felt that it was unsatisfactory even though it might tend in a desirable direction.[13]

The debate of November 27 had drawn the initial line of demarcation. Phipps's obstinacy and Dowdeswell's silence were ominous. Shelburne begged Chatham for instructions, while Chatham wrote to Calcraft, "I think all is ruined. . . . The times are pollution, in every quintessence; and the little manoeuvers in Opposition behind the scenes are deplorable." He would bring matters "to an explanation"; he would "separate from so unorthodox a congregation" before he would accept their views. This on the twenty-eighth; the next day he expressed himself as "much satisfied" with the same faction.[14]

Chatham's reconciliation with Rockingham was not very deep. Shelburne once again acted as as agent in securing the services of John Glynn to move for the inquiry into judicial proceedings which had been demanded in the recent debate. Almon's sentence was now known, and Glynn, feeling that the printer had little to hope for from an appeal to the House of Lords, seems to have considered the inquiry in the light of an appeal to the House of Commons.[15] On Monday, December 3, Glynn gave notice of his intention to offer a motion on Thursday. When a question was raised concerning the purport of the motion, Glynn's silence was defended by none other than Richard Rigby on the basis that "he did not imagine there would be any surprise upon the House; for, let the motion be what it would, he would be disappointed if he expected to carry it." To such a happy tune the Chathamites prepared to wage war upon Mansfield in spite of a ministerial majority and a dissentient opposition.[16]

The political error in Chatham's policy was all too obvious. "I take it for granted," wrote Calcraft's friend Philip Francis, "You are not sanguine enough to expect that, with the present Parliament, you will be able to punish Lord Mansfield, or even to reform the most trifling Abuse." If an attack on Mansfield is followed by a vote, defeat is certain. "You encourage a timid Man . . . to be active in doing Mischief. . . . You bring a disputed Point to a Decision, which you know will be against You; and You confirm his Doctrines." And to what end?

every attempt hitherto made to infringe the Liberty of the Press
has ended in Disgrace and Ridicule both to Government and to
the Court of King's Bench, The press, in spite of all their prosecutions, is actually as free as it need be for any good Purpose. Take
care how you raise a dangerous Question about it, when perhaps it
is the very best, if not the only Weapon, You have left to defend
the Constitution.[17]

The advice of a minor officeholder to a political agent of the great
Chatham carried no weight, but if Francis' words were those of Junius,
his comments are the more interesting for it; they could be no more
forceful.

While Glynn's motion was in preparation, Chatham himself took
up the cudgels in the House of Lords. After a two-hour speech, Wednesday, December 5, on the power of the Commons to exclude a chosen
representative, he digressed "upon the modern manner of directing a
jury from the bench, and giving judgment upon prosecutions for
libels." Such cases, said Chatham, were usually political and the question of libel determined on political rather than legal grounds. The
recent directions given by judges he described as "dangerous and unconstitutional . . . cruel and vindictive." This brought Mansfield to
his feet with the remark that such charges were "merely a fresh tub to
amuse the wretched whale of popularity."

> Before the noble lord . . . arraigns my judicial character, he should
> make himself acquainted with the facts; the scurrility of a news-
> paper may be good information for a coffee-house politician, but a
> peer of parliament should always speak from higher authority.

Unable to challenge Mansfield on the law, forced to confess that his
information came from the public prints, Chatham lamely expressed
an earnest desire that "a day may be appointed for examining into the
conduct of such judges as dare to establish this anti-constitutional
practice."

Camden came to the rescue with an offer to give an opinion upon
the direction to the jury in Woodfall's case, but debate was cut short.
Grafton declared that "the great crime of the sages in Westminster-
hall . . . is their not having prostituted the public ordinances . . . to
the purposes of sedition," and moved for adjournment. Only twenty
peers opposed the motion.[18]

If the silence of Rockingham's friends in the House of Lords seemed ominous on the fifth, their spokesmen in the lower chamber clarified their position the next day during the debate on Glynn's motion for a committee "to enquire into the administration of criminal justice . . . in cases relating to the liberty of the press, and the constitutional power and duty of juries." The motion was seconded by Richard Oliver, who declared the support of the "free and independent" citizens of London. Sir Joseph Mawbey represented the interest of the liberal element of Surrey, and John Sawbridge added to "the sentiments of the great city."

Charles Jenkinson and Grey Cooper began the administration's defense against the Chathamites. They pointed out that this was no more than a personal attack upon Chief Justice Mansfield, and George Onslow added, "It will prove as fatal to their cause as a court of justice to a libeller." In vain might Savile picture a deluge of "newspapers, pamphlets, puns, and pasquinades," if no action were taken. In vain might Glynn point out the weakness of precedent to support Mansfield's position. "Why . . . should we hesitate to put a negative upon a question which sprang from such a low source?" asked young Charles James Fox. "From dirt it came, and to dirt let it return."

Thus far only Chatham's friends and the radical city and county members had been heard. Burke now rose, and the effect of Chatham's politics became at once apparent, for Burke defended Mansfield. He abhorred the personal implications of the motion. He called the Chathamites "a parcel of factious people." Yet "no man laments more sincerely . . . the extreme disorder of the people. That monstrous, shameful, ruinous, and base crime of libelling." When Junius' letter to Mansfield is posted on both sides of Westminster hall, it behooves us to "look into it: examine it: scrutinize it to the bottom. . . . I was not in the confidence of the motion. I might have some little points, some little feelings, that might make me not so anxious to support it. But I do support it upon this one ground."

De Grey quickly took up the handle offered by Burke's speech. With obvious satisfaction he demonstrated that Mansfield rather than "a right judgment of the question" was the target of Glynn's motion. John Dunning replied with a lengthy legal argument, and a dangerous sort of support came from Lord George Germaine, who favored the motion as a means of clearing his friend the chief justice from the charges raised against him. Wedderburn gave feeble support, Thurlow "a direct negative." Calcraft and Barré used Almon's case to beat up the ministerial bench, but toward midnight Glynn and Onslow descended to personalities, and the question was demanded. The motion was cast out, 76 members voting with Glynn, 184 against.[19]

Despite the solid government majority, Chatham felt pleased with the debate and the division on Glynn's motion. Almon had been vindicated and "upon the whole, the day was a good and great one for the public."[20] A protest against Mansfield's law had been registered, but with no doubt remaining as to the position of the Rockingham Whigs, Chatham's next step can hardly be considered that of a statesman intent upon a successful reform. Camden had questioned Mansfield's actions in the Woodfall case, and on December 10, the chief justice, in accordance with notice given three days earlier, informed the House of Lords that he had left a copy of his judgment in Woodfall's case with the clerk that they might form their own opinions. As no motion was made encouraging debate, Chatham and Camden attempted to force the issue. Prompted by an anonymous communication which Calcraft had placed in his hands, an argument which had been drawn up by Philip Francis,[21] Chatham "threw out many oblique censures" and declared that Mansfield's conduct was "irregular." Mansfield was not so easily trapped. He refused even to have the paper entered in the *Journal,* thereby earning no small amount of criticism for timidity but retaining his judicial dignity and austerity.[22]

As Mansfield had avoided a political discussion of his judicial opinions, Camden took the lead in a legal inquisition. He drew up a set of six questions which he would lay before the chief justice and circulated them among the opposition lords. This latter conciliatory step was taken at a very late date, however, and was unsuccessful in warming the Rockinghams to the cause.[23] Tuesday, December 11, Camden informed the House that he considered Mansfield's opinion "a challenge directed personally to me," and asked that a day be set aside for debating the legality of the chief justice's opinion. For the present he submitted six questions for consideration: is the innocence or criminality of a paper of no significance? does the jury find the fact only, and not the law? what if a jury found the fact of publication but exonerated the charge of libel? would it be illegal for a judge to leave the entire question to the jury? what precedents could Mansfield cite in support of his position, and from what period of history were they taken?

This shotgun blast took Mansfield by surprise, but he had a ready answer—extracted from a recent press case—"He would not answer interrogatories." Camden pressed for a more satisfactory reply and received some assistance from Richmond, but Mansfield could not be moved. He pledged that the matter might be discussed, but refused to set a date. The Lords had already refused one motion for an inquiry; Mansfield's reticence put an effective end to all action in that House.[24]

Chatham might offer his congratulations to Camden for a "transcendent" effort, but it was clear that the campaign against Mansfield had failed. Reviewing these parliamentary skirmishes, Burke expressed surprise that Mansfield's defense had been so passive, and that Camden, "who had promised much to the public . . . seemed equally disposed to bury the matter in eternal silence." Obviously Mansfield had had no need to bestir himself from behind the sacred ramparts of the bench and the solid outworks of a ministerial majority. As for Camden, his health was not good at the moment, and Walpole's informant was probably correct when he said that Chatham "had driven him into the attack . . . which he did not like, and in which . . . he would meddle no further: he did not care to have all the twelve judges against him."[25]

Chatham's failure cleared the way for Rockingham's cohorts whose displeasure with the initial attack had already been expressed. They would not indulge in personal animosity against Mansfield, nor would they condemn the manner in which the law was propounded in the Court of King's Bench, yet they recognized the need for bringing law and public opinion into closer harmony by establishing once and for all the scope of the powers of a jury in cases of libel. The complexities of law and precedent might be avoided by legislative action, and to this end a bill was prepared.

By the first week in January, 1771, Rockingham was seeking converts. Chatham was given a copy of the bill drafted by William Dowdeswell, and his reactions, Rockingham noticed, "were just what we expected." They were probably similar to those of Constantine Phipps, who "seemed not to like it [because] it might furnish a loophole . . . for Lord Mansfield." Or, the marquis continued, rather "from his being desirous . . . for a declaratory bill, than a bill so far conceding . . . the matter to be subject at present to doubt and controversy."[26]

No surprise attack was attempted. Nor was it possible when the *London Chronicle* of January 17 printed the bill with "a caution to the public, lest they should approve it." Rockingham at once blamed the Chathamites and suggested that Dowdeswell and Burke write a reply pointing out that "personal contentions in the House of Lords will not finally produce any decision which may secure the public."

The marquis still hoped for a union of forces, however, and toward the end of the month the Duke of Richmond called upon Chatham in search of a common mode of action. The interview was a dismal failure. Chatham expressed dissatisfaction with Dowdeswell's bill, but indicated that his support might be won if the bill were altered and placed in Camden's hands. In addition he requested a general consultation of the opposition upon the legal aspects of the bill.[27]

The reaction of the Rockinghams was uniform. Burke advised that "not an Iota should be yielded. . . . If you yield now, the horseman will stick to you, whileever you live." He opposed any meeting with Chatham's legal friends but was willing to be reasonable concerning the phrasing of the bill. "If they Choose to break with you upon this point," Burke warned, "they mean to break if they cannot Tyrannize." Rockingham disapproved bringing Camden into the picture because his views were already sufficiently well known, as was the fact that in them he was unique among the judges. Camden's participation would also raise the point of personalities again. "I do not expect any great good being carried into effect in either House of Parliament in these times," said Rockingham, "but . . . our friends should show that . . . the *public advantage* is their object." The marquis felt that "Lord Camden has hard luck in all this matter," but he placed the blame squarely upon Chatham's "jealousy that our friends might get credit." Richmond also saw little to be hoped for from Chatham's side. The faction determined to pursue its own course, spurred on by a rumor that Chatham himself might "try to get the start and move a declaratory bill." "The possibility or probability of Lord's Chatham's lying quiet any time," the marquis warned Dowdeswell, "is not great."[28]

One more effort was made to link the two opposition factions. Richmond approached Camden and Chatham but found the former "determined not to agitate any question upon this subject," and the latter insistent upon a declaratory bill. Chatham was thereupon informed, February 20, that Dowdeswell would move his bill the next week. "I trust that the friends of the constitution, though temperate, will be found zealous and firm in asserting the essential rights of jurors, and in settling those doubts . . . in the minds of many well-meaning people," said Richmond. "We wish to leave the past just where it is, and shall be well satisfied if this bill can be carried through, and thereby security obtained on this great point for the future." That same day Dowdeswell gave Barré a copy of the bill and proposed a meeting of friends on Saturday the twenty-third. Chatham's militant spokesman snorted that it was impossible for him "to make a part of a company which was to discuss a measure which [he] not only disliked, but thought [him]self bound to oppose." Dowdeswell nonetheless expressed the hope that "after some conversation upon the subject, we should be all of the same opinion."[29]

Chatham's reply took the form of instructions to Colonel Barré: "friends of the constitution will, it is hoped, strenuously resist this compound of connection, tyranny, and absurdity—not to say collusion." He wrote in the same vein to Calcraft, and informed Richmond of his "determination to resist this dangerous bill, and promote a declaratory one." The effect of Chatham's attitude was evident by the twenty-first, when Dowdeswell gave notice of his bill, as Lord George Germaine advised dropping the project in view of the opposition schism. The caucus proposed for the twenty-third was held at Sir George Savile's house; Barré, despite his prior refusal, attended and reported happily to Chatham that no understanding was reached. The Rockinghams refused any measure to censure, and Chatham refused to think that Mansfield's law might be defensible and at the same time out of harmony with public opinion. He continued to plot with Shelburne a method whereby "the *wrong* bill [i.e., Dowdeswell's] . . . should be admitted to be brought in, in order to make it *right*; that is, *declaratory*, in the committee."[30] A last-minute conference between Chatham and Rockingham had no effect, and under such conditions Dowdeswell asked leave to introduce his bill on March 7.

Dowdeswell opened coldly to a thin house. He carefully described the position adopted by his party, accepting what was past, provided that the future directions of judges in libel cases should be different, and that "the jury should be held and reputed competent . . . in law and right . . . to decide upon the whole matter." He was seconded by Sir George Savile. The dissolution of the opposition was demonstrated by the next speaker, James Grenville, who voiced a warm antagonism to the measure as "unnecessary to protect juries in the possession of a right which has ever belonged to them." Calcraft declared he would vote against the bill in its final stages even though he might support it now. Constantine Phipps was "decidedly against any bill" and implored the ministry to back him as he moved for adjournment. Sir William Meredith seconded this surprise motion, but debate was allowed to continue.

Dunning, the leading lawyer on the floor while Glynn was on circuit, was explicit in condemning the proposed bill, as was Barré, who hoarsely declaimed, "I never will accept by statute, that which is my birthright." Burke spoke late in the debate. He maintained that "juries ought to take their law from the bench only; but . . . they should hear nothing from the bench but what was agreeable to the principles of the constitution." To the Chathamites he pointed out the hopelessness of any declaratory bill should it ever come before the law barons in the House of Lords, and he defended Dowdeswell's enacting measure as the only possible solution to the present controversy. At ten minutes past ten o'clock, the question for adjournment was put to a vote and carried, 218 to 72, against the opposition.[31]

The discomfiture of the minority was complete. The Treasury bench had maintained "a dead silence," and George III congratulated Lord North upon his tactics of leaving "the whole altercation" to the opposition: "if gentlemen can let their reason guide them to differ with their friends on what they might deem a popular question, it is to be hoped they will by this be encouraged to hold on future occasions the same propriety of conduct."[32]

"You see, my Lord," wrote Barré to Chatham, "what a glorious day yesterday was for the Opposition . . . ! Nothing under the humour of a Swift or a Rabelais can describe it." This "wise measure," he added, "has . . . put an end to parliamentary attendance."[33] Barré's prophecy was not quite accurate, for as he noted, "our city friends," who were absent on March 7, were busy preparing a new bomb which was destined to secure far more significant results than the puny efforts of the great Whig factions. The dependence of the liberty of the press upon a jury whose powers were complete in every sense, however, was delayed for twenty eventful years.

CHAPTER XII

Press and Parliament: The City, 1771

A CHRONICLER of the reign of George III, writing in 1770, remarked upon the eagerness with which parliament struck at any printer who dared unveil the actions of individual members to the public. "Under pretence of privilege they overturn liberty," he declared, "for the sake of which privilege was granted."[1] The session of 1770–1771 provided sufficient commentary upon his statement. The rights of electors, the rights of juries, the liberty of the press, all seemed destined to stumble upon the block of privilege upheld by a corrupt legislature supinely voting at the behest of its political managers and seeking to shield its actions from the public. A decade of parliamentary press relations had set the pattern, and on December 10, 1770, the House of Lords took the final step toward emancipation from the public by asserting its right to secrecy by closing the House to all strangers. Both Richmond and Chatham vehemently protested against this ministerial subterfuge but were overwhelmed by cries of "Clear the House." Unable to secure a hearing, some sixteen opposition lords signed a formal protest

> against the whole of this irregular conduct, as tending to suppress the sober and dispassionate deliberation which ought to guide the proceedings of this House, and to substitute clamour and violence in the place of reason and argument.[2]

The exclusion of reporters from the House of Lords, and the passive surrender of the liberty of the press to the judges by the House of Commons did little to win the sympathy of the trade for either chamber. Reports continued to appear whether speeches were heard or not. John Almon's political connections enabled him to secure accounts of debates for the *London Evening Post*; the *St. James's Chronicle* hired an obscure reporter, Wall, to write its account of parliamentary proceedings, and these were copied by the *Gazetteer*.[3] William Woodfall, brother of the *Public Advertiser*'s printer, began to exercise his prodigious memory to bring accuracy to parliamentary reporting.

Inevitably the press ran foul of the shoal of privilege. The first warning came on February 5, when Colonel George Onslow remarked upon the general misrepresentation of speeches by the newspapers and moved the reading of the resolutions concerning the printing of debates. Two days later, an objection to the exclusion of strangers demanded by a ministerial speaker brought Onslow to his feet again with a promise to clear the gallery as long as debates were reported. Burke admonished him that "misrepresentation . . . is more likely to take place from strangers being kept out. If they are not permitted freely to report the speeches . . . they will set about inventing them."[4] The press, led by the *Middlesex Journal* and the *Gazetteer*, was quick to vent its spleen upon "little Cocking George."

On the eighth, Onslow formally complained of that day's *Gazetteer* and the *Middlesex Journal* of the seventh, "as misrepresenting the Speeches and reflecting on several of the Members of this House . . . in breach of the privilege, of this House. . . . Sometimes I am held up as a villain; sometimes . . . as an idiot; and sometimes as both. To-day they call me 'little Cocking George.' They will find, Sir, I am a cock they will not easily beat. I never will give up this point." Upon such principles Onslow moved that the printers be ordered to attend on Monday, February 11, and the critical struggle over parliamentary reporting began. Opposition to Onslow's motion found Constantine Phipps and William Dowdeswell in agreement. Burke maintained that "a full and dispassionate inquiry into the conduct of a member . . . is not only right, but necessary. . . . As long as [the people] . . . feel an interest in examining into the proceedings of parliament, so long will you find a man that will print them." The majority, however, agreed to receive the offending papers in a division of 90 to 55, and John Wheble and R. Thompson* were ordered to attend for breach of privilege.[5]

The two printers did not come before the House on the eleventh, nor on the fourteenth as ordered, nor yet on the nineteenth, and Onslow's perseverance took a more serious turn. He moved that Thompson was guilty of contempt, but the opposition pointed out that the order for attendance that day had not been served. Onslow offered to withdraw his motion, but Dowdeswell, spearheading the printers' defense,

---

*The Commons' designation of "R. Thompson" caused (and still causes) great confusion; the *Gazetteer*'s publisher was Roger Thompson. See Haig, *Gazetteer*, pp. 107, 295 n. 10.

refused consent in hope that a negative vote might be secured. In order that his troops might see their standard, Lord North rose to express his regret that such a situation had developed, but he supported Onslow and amended the motion to a new order for attendance. North's tactics won Dunning's support, and the motion passed, 115 to 31, despite a warning that the House acted on "a precedent of parliament, which ... is damned, by universal consent, to all eternity."[6]

The new order produced no better results. On February 21, the messenger informed the House that he had seen neither Wheble nor Thompson but had left orders for attendance at their houses. After some debate the House adopted the speaker's suggestion that leaving a copy of the order at the place of abode was equivalent to personal service, and a new date, February 26, was set. At this point the possibility of embarrassing ramifications began to manifest itself. The king recommended to North "in the strongest manner ... that every caution may be used to prevent its becoming a serious affair." George III had no sympathy for "this strange and lawless method of publishing debates," but he felt that "the Lords have broader shoulders to support any schism that this salutary measure may occasion in the minds of the vulgar." North was already anticipating that a struggle with the printers might bring into the field the corporate authority of the City of London, an antagonist not to be lightly discounted.[7]

Tuesday the twenty-sixth arrived without a sign of Wheble or Thompson. Their orders had been duly served, and only one course was open to the House. Onslow moved that Wheble be taken into custody for contempt. The opposition might declare that "the whole French court, with their gaudy coaches and jack-boots, going to hunt a little hare, is nothing in comparison" to the figure made by the House of Commons pursuing two poor printers; prestige as well as privilege was at stake. Onslow knew his rights and those of the House, and he swore, "If I bring all the morning printers one day, and all the evening printers another, I certainly will persevere." He was supported in the division by 160 members against 17 who opposed the motion. Both printers were consequently ordered into custody. It was "a great majority," wrote Lord North, but in the minority, Dowdeswell, Savile and Burke, Dunning and Barré sufficiently represented the factions, and the City connections of five others bespoke a real popular opposition.[8]

By the first of March, North's premonition that the City might take up the printers' cause was a reality. "The City patriots will not give up the printers, and threaten if the sergeant-at-arms should attempt to seize them he shall be sent to Newgate."[9] Thus sped London gossip, and it ran true. Both Wheble and Thompson were in contact with John Wilkes and the radicals in the City and acted in accordance with Wilkes's instructions.*[10] The deputy sergeant-at-arms reported to the House, March 4, that he was unable to find the recalcitrant printers. Upon Onslow's motion the House requested the king to issue a royal proclamation for the arrest of John Wheble and R. Thompson. His Majesty issued the proclamation, with a £50 reward attached, on the seventh, and on March 9, it was printed in the London Gazette. All that the House could do at that point was await some move on the part of the printers.[11]

George Onslow, however, was not inactive. On Tuesday, March 12, he began to carry out his threat of bringing all the newspaper printers before the House of Commons. Having issued a surreptitious warning to the trade through John Williams, with strikingly poor success, he demanded that action be taken against William Woodfall (Morning Chronicle), Henry Baldwin (St. James's Chronicle), Thomas Evans (London Packet), T. Wright (Whitehall Evening Post), Samuel Bladon (General Evening Post), and John Miller (London Evening Post). The opposition was not long in finding its voice. "Why hunt six when you've not got two?" Onslow was asked. "Your warrants will not and cannot be executed." The legality of the royal proclamation was questioned, and Speaker Fletcher Norton, despite Constantine Phipps' protest that he should not influence debate, assured the House that their proceedings were legal. Reminiscent of another heated debate, John Sawbridge flung back at Norton, "I look upon it as so much waste paper . . . if anybody apprehended those printers in consequence of it, he would do an illegal act." Nonetheless, Woodfall's Morning Chronicle was delivered in and read with the approval of 140 members as against 43, and Woodfall was ordered to attend the House on Thursday. Baldwin's St. James's Chronicle was next brought up and received in a like manner. "He is attacking a hydra that will shoot out a hundred heads for every one he cuts off," cried one member—and seeing

*The part played by John Horne in the affair of the printers is not clear. Horne claimed to have initiated the action and he sought to direct the conduct of John Wheble of the Middlesex Journal, but Wilkes's greater influence in City politics enabled him to seize the lead and dominate subsequent events. Horne's claims are stated by Stephens, John Horne Tooke, I, 314 ff.; see also Haig, Gazetteer, pp. 104–5, 108.

the evening's entertainment develop in such fashion, gentlemen began to depart for White's and Almack's, where the play was more to their taste.

Members who kept their seats—and a sense of humor—were treated to a show the like of which Westminster Hall never witnessed before or after. One by one the printers were ordered to attend, but only by the tortuous process of twenty-one more divisions. The opposition used every conceivable device to wear out the majority, and attendance rapidly sank from about 190 to 80 or less. Barré, who enjoyed a strong joke, offered the absurd motion "that Jeremiah Weymouth, esquire, the d——n of this country, is not a member of this House." He got thirty votes for his proposition. Sir William Meredith promised to "either put a negative or move an adjournment upon every question," and proceeded to do so. When, with but three printers out of the way, Speaker Norton complained, "I am heartily tired of this business, and should be glad to put an end to it," Barré promptly moved to adjourn, and when he returned in defeat from the lobby, he moved that the last printer considered, Thomas Evans, should be allowed a delay in attending. Norton moaned, "I lament with all my soul, that I am in this situation; for I do not know how I am to get out of it." Upon which Burke opined, "This standing order has put a stand to the business of the nation." When an objection was raised to a minority motion that Evans' "compositors, pressmen, correctors, blackers, and devils" should also attend, Burke gleefully swore that "the devil is the most material evidence for the discovery of these contemners of your power." At length—at five o'clock in the morning—the House adjourned. The king, when North informed him of the night's work, remarked, "I apprehend the majority must have been much fatigued . . . but the litigiousness of the minority cannot give them any weight, on the contrary must offend every moderate man."[12]

March was not a month for moderation.

Wednesday the House of Commons recuperated from its marathon session, but on the fourteenth, four of Onslow's half-dozen printers appeared. Baldwin and Wright were reprimanded by the speaker as they knelt before the bar and were discharged upon paying their fees. Bladon expressed "a fixed Resolution of acknowledging his Offence" and escaped scot free. Evans withdrew even before he was called up, giving the novel excuse that his wife had broken her leg. He was ordered to attend the following Tuesday, but on that day he wrote to

the speaker declaring that he would not appear until the legal authority of the House had been determined and until "it is universally
known whether a British subject has, or has not a right to be tried by
a jury." The Commons had far greater problems to deal with than a
recalcitrant printer, and Evans escaped their grasp.[13]

William Woodfall did not attend the House of Commons on March
14, because he was before the bar of the House of Lords. His report of
the Lords' proceedings in the *Morning Chronicle* of March 8, had
attracted the attention of the upper chamber, and Woodfall was haled
before them. He admitted his error, pleaded the rush of business, and
threw himself upon their Lordships' mercies. He was fined £100 and
committed to Newgate for a month. Less than a week later his petition
for release was under consideration. It seemed that no accommodations
were available except among debtors or criminals. "Petitioner has the
most fatal Consequences to dread from the noxious Effluvia occasioned
by a Number of Bodies (many of them very uncleanly)," he wrote. "A
few Days Imprisonment, in the present Situation of Newgate, is equal
or more in Punishment to an Imprisonment for the Time of their
Lordships Order." Woodfall's prayer for "an immediate Enlargement"
was humanely granted upon the payment of his fine and fees.[14]

Colonel Onslow's first taste of printers' blood was rather meager.
Out of six intended victims, two had knelt in penance (the last ever to
do so), one had been immediately released by the very House whose
privileges he had so damaged, another simply went home of his own
volition. And all—though Onslow could scarcely have been impressed—
had declared the popular concern in this question. Baldwin said that
if he ceased printing the debates, "it would be attended with the Ruin
of his Paper." Wright concurred, and explained that his reports were
printed "at the Instance of several Applications from his Customers in
the Country." Bladon, despite his subservience, insisted that without
the debates in the *General Evening Post,* "He should have lost the sale
thereof."[15] Miller, Wheble, and Thompson still remained at large.

After more than a month of open defiance the City and its fugitive
printers seized the offensive. The campaign was mapped out by John
Wilkes, with the assent of the printers, and initiated on March 14.[16]
When his fellows made their submission to the House of Commons,
John Wheble submitted a lengthy legal brief, drawn up by Robert
Morris, denying the legality of the steps taken against him. The next
day, Wheble allowed himself to be arrested, on the strength of the royal

proclamation, by his servant Edward Carpenter and was taken before the justices sitting at the Guildhall—Lord Mayor Brass Crosby, Aldermen Richard Oliver, and John Wilkes. No legal cause of complaint was evidenced. As Wheble "had been apprehended in the City illegally, in direct violation of the rights of an Englishman, and the chartered privileges of a citizen of [London]," he was discharged.[17]

Wheble immediately instituted a suit for assault against Carpenter in order to test the validity of the royal proclamation. Carpenter was indicted by the grand jury on April 8, and brought to trial on June 30. He was adjudged guilty, fined one shilling, and committed to the Wood Street compter for two months. When Carpenter apprehended Wheble he was provided with a certificate which should have entitled him to the £50 reward. This was refused him, however. On March 20, Wedderburn, now solicitor-general, defended the administration's treatment of Carpenter in a witty speech describing the compact entered into between Wheble and his devil. "Whether the devil beats the printer, or the printer beats the devil is no concern of this House," he said. "There may, possibly, be the devil to do, and certainly there will be the devil to pay; but . . . if the devil has been paid already"—and here he bowed to Lord North—"he has fairly outwitted the noble lord near me."[18]

The line of action adopted in Wheble's case was followed in that of Thompson. He was arrested at his own door and carried before Alderman Oliver at the Mansion House. Accused of no crime, Thompson was at once released, and his captor was provided with a certificate of arrest in order to claim the promised reward. These actions demonstrated the City opinion of a royal proclamation but did not strike directly at the House of Commons. The direct conflict between the City and the House resulted from the plan adopted by Wilkes, John Almon, and the last of Onslow's half-dozen printers, John Miller.[19]

When Miller failed to appear before the bar on March 14, William Witham, a messenger, was instructed to apprehend the printer on the strength of a warrant signed by the speaker of the House of Commons. Witham found Miller at his shop on the fifteenth, and as he was in the act of placing him under arrest, the messenger suddenly found himself confronted by a City constable and charged with assault. Witham was then taken to the Mansion House. Despite the protests of the Commons' deputy serjeant-at-arms who rushed to his subordinate's assistance, Miller was freed and Witham charged with "assaulting and unlawfully imprisoning" the City printer.*[20]

This sudden turn of events shattered the façade of parliamentary supremacy like a bolt of lightning. Barré sent word to Chatham at once, noting the irreconcilable claims on both sides and the effect Wilkes's thrust must have in the City. Chatham was at a loss what to make of the situation and feared it would "not end well for the cause of liberty." George III bemoaned the rising storm and chided North, "You know very well I was averse to meddling with the Printers, but now there is no retracting; the honour of the Commons must be supported."[21]

The outcome of its attempt to assert authority was laid before the House of Commons on March 18. The printers shrank into oblivion as the City of London assumed the role of their protector and the enemy of privilege and prerogative. Lord Mayor Brass Crosby was a member of the House, as was Richard Oliver; Welbore Ellis moved that Crosby should attend in his place to explain his actions, his health permitting, and the House so ordered. The affair of the City printers was in that instant transformed into a struggle between the Commons and the City. The effect was immediately visible in the accession of strength to an opposition which almost doubled its numbers.[22]

The minority rejoiced. Chatham, at Hayes, whipped his cohorts into line. "Nothing but first rate geniuses in incapacity," he declared, could have accomplished the ministerial feat of placing themselves and the king in "a situation, wherein there is nothing they can do, which is not a fault." Crosby and Oliver defended themselves before the House with justifiable pride in their assertion of a liberty beyond the corruption of crown or parliament, and it was quickly realized that Wilkes was too hot to handle. The wildfire of excitement reached even to Stowe. Calcraft reported that "Lord Temple . . . was the eagerest politician in London, and resolved to come out [of retirement] on this business."[23] If the cause of the City was righteous, that of the House of Commons was no less sacred. North marshaled his big batallions and the government's majority increased in proportion to the popular fer-

---

*Witham was indicted by a grand jury on April 8, but the attorney-general entered a writ of noli prosequi for him on the grounds that "it is indecent that the name of the crown should continue as the prosecutor of a messenger of the House of Commons." On May 13, 1771, Witham's case was closed. *Annual Reg.*, XIV (1771), 106; *London Mag.*, XL (1771), 281; *Town and Country Mag.*, III (1771), 278.

ment in the City. Richard Oliver was committed to the Tower on March 25; the gout-ridden Lord Mayor followed two days later. "The Mansion House was sent in flannels to the Tower," wrote David Hartley. "They talk of violent measures."[24]

Well might the government of England—King, Lords, and Commons—bethink themselves of "violent measures." On the twenty-seventh the London mob passed members into the House through a veritable gantlet. Lord North barely escaped with his life, and Charles James Fox was rolled in the gutter. The cries of the mob penetrated into the chamber, where the minority vainly attempted to bring moderation to the counsels of the nation and challenged the king's minister to defend a policy which led to open conflict between the people and the parliament. North spoke quietly, simply, and to the point:

> At such a moment, when there is a disposition abroad to take occasion from every circumstance to shake the government of the country, because it is a government of law, and for no other reason, it is the bounden duty of every man to stand forward in his station. Unhappy I am, that it finds me in this situation; but being there, it is the more incumbent upon me to continue to perform my duty, until the Sovereign who placed me in it, shall think proper to dismiss me. There are but two ways in which I can go out now—by the will of my Sovereign, which I shall be ready to obey, or the pleasure of the gentlemen now at our doors, when they shall be able to do a little more than they have done this day.

He held the majority in absolute control and upheld the privilege of the House of Commons.[25]

The next day, March 28, a committee of twenty-one was chosen "to examine into the several Facts and Circumstances relative to the late Obstructions to the Execution of the Orders of this House." While the committee collected its evidence, the popular and parliamentary tumults continued, but the crisis had passed. Early in April, Chatham's hopes failed. He could not rouse Temple from his lethargy, he could not stomach Camden's disinterest, nor could he influence the Rockinghams in the slightest. He might move an address to the king to dissolve a parliament which sought to place "privilege above the laws of the land"; he could carry but a handful with him. The House of Commons, having vindicated itself as far as possible against the printers, showed rare discretion in dealing with Alderman John Wilkes. Thrice ordered before the House, Wilkes refused to appear in any character other than that of a duly elected member. The House finally ordered him to attend on April 8, and adjourned itself (and the problem of John Wilkes) until April 9. Like George III, members had no desire to meddle further with "that devil Wilkes."[26]

The secret committee of twenty-one reported on April 30, and the great results of its deliberations were soon displayed. Having sat daily from March 28 to April 30, Sundays excepted, the committee declared that "it highly concerns the Dignity and Power of the House, to maintain its Authority in this Instance, by re-taking the said J. Miller." Nothing more—and no intimation how its recommendation might be carried into effect. The opposition greeted the report with ridicule and moved a vote of thanks to the committee in such a manner that North, to save face, moved for adjournment.[27] A week later the session ended. The Lord Mayor and Alderman Oliver were at once enlarged; the printers, Miller, Wheble, Thompson, Evans, and Woodfall, were at liberty in defiance of the powers of the House of Commons, and their fellow printers were no less active than before. Indeed, the Bill of Rights Society had taken care to bolster publishing courage by voting the sum of £100 to Wheble, Thompson, and Miller for having "appealed to the laws of their country, and not having betrayed, by their submission, the rights of Englishmen."[28]

On All-Fool's Day an observant Irishman wrote:

> The indefatigable liberty of the press . . . industriously revealed the foul mystery of Parliament; it became necessary to confine the liberty of the press, or the exclusion of the people from their trustees was of no service. Privilege of parliament (a monster whose nature is unknown, whose power is undefined, who alarms, overbears, and perplexes mankind) was let out therefore, and resisted by the City. The motive of the City was constitutional, for it opposed corruption in the person of privilege.[29]

It derogates little from the fame of those who fought this sport of privilege that their motives were less exalted than their accomplishments. After 1771, no consistent effort was made to limit the political press by appealing to parliamentary privilege. If enforced at all, the complaint was misrepresentation rather than reporting. From time to time the galleries of the houses might be closed to strangers, but that poor weapon was easily turned by industrious publishers. Tacit acceptance of the publication of debates was a revolutionary step, implying, as it did, a certain parliamentary responsibility to the people. It was extorted at the last moment before the controlling influence of the king and his minister settled like a shroud over the political life of England.

CHAPTER XIII

Calm after Storm, 1771-1774

THE END of the parliamentary session in 1771 marked a distinct epoch in the history of the press in politics. The administration of Lord North stood as firm as the throne of George III; the implied relationship was not far removed from reality. During the next three years politics seemed to pass through an artificial channel which allowed little deviation. The press continued to describe the ebb and flow of events in no less violent terms than it had utilized in the preceding decade. But the spirit was changed. Increasing interest in American affairs may be partially accountable, so also the understandable hesitancy of government to aggravate when there was no need, and only in the City of London, where John Wilkes, John Horne, and Junius led the pack, did these years seem related to the conflict-ridden opening of the reign.

Even as the City of London defied the power of the House of Commons, division of interest was apparent among its leaders. Wilkes's rise to political prominence in the City won him enemies as well as friends, and his insistent care for the personal interests of John Wilkes—particularly where money was concerned—alienated many of the latter. The first serious breach occurred when John Horne proposed that the Bill of Rights Society should subsidize the martyred printer William Bingley. Wilkes, already personally at odds with the parson of Brentford, insisted that his own needs should be met by the society before it enlarged its activities, and he won the majority of the members to his cause. Horne therefore attempted to dissolve the Bill of Rights, and failing this, withdrew to establish the Society for Constitutional Information, whose membership included Aldermen James Townsend, John Sawbridge, and Richard Oliver.[1]

The champions had been corresponding through the columns of the *Public Advertiser* and the *Gazetteer* since October 31, 1770; by the spring of 1771, their letters had become highly acrimonious. The situation was complicated by an open breach between Wilkes and Oliver at the official level of City politics,[2] and by May, the political letters in the London newspapers fairly smoked as Wilkes, Horne, and their friends exchanged shots. The printers of the leading papers were forced to walk a narrow line between the antagonists in order to avoid disastrous effects upon their circulation.[3]

John Horne was a vigorous combatant, but he fell far short of Wilkes's polished, practiced finesse, and his opposition to Wilkes made him vulnerable to the charge of defection from the public cause. This shaft was hurled at Horne on July 24, by no less a hero than Junius: "to gratify your personal hatred of Mr. Wilkes, you sacrificed . . . the cause of the country." Junius held no brief for Wilkes as an individual, but he realized that the radical schism would enable the court party in the City to secure political control.

> You will not suspect me of setting up Wilkes for a perfect character. The question to the public, is, where shall we find a man, who, with purer principles, will go the lengths, and run the hazards that he has done? The season calls for such a man, and he ought to be supported.[4]

In August, Junius supplemented his public letters on City politics by opening a private correspondence with John Wilkes. He urged moderation upon the patriot but failed to influence his policy. Friendly relations were maintained between the two great propagandists, however, and Wilkes was shown the Dedication and Preface prepared by Junius for Woodfall's edition of his letters. This "official" collection was designed to compensate the printer, "a man who has deserved well of me, and of the public," wrote the author, "and who, on my account has been exposed to an expensive, tyrannical prosecution."[5]

The great unknown was approaching the end of his career. His publisher became reticent in the spring of 1771, and Junius found it necessary to assure him that "the Ministry are sick of prosecutions. Those against Junius cost the Treasury above six thousand pounds, and after all they got nothing but Disgrace."[6]

Before he became embroiled with Wilkes and Horne, Junius had received the blunt attentions of Dr. Samuel Johnson. At the end of January, 1771, Junius wrote upon the controversy with Spain concerning the Falkland Islands. Johnson, defending the ministry, described his rival in worthy terms as

> a meteor formed by the vapours of putrefying democracy, and kindled into flame by the effervescence of interest struggling with con-

viction; which after having plunged its followers in a bog, will leave us inquiring why we regard it.

Johnson supplies his own answer to the riddle of Junian power:

> It is not by his liveliness of imagery, his pungency of periods, or his fertility of allusion, that he detains the cits of London and the boors of Middlesex. Of stile and sentiment they take no cognizance. They admire him for virtues like their own, for contempt of order, and violence of outrage, for rage of defamation and audacity of falsehood.[7]

Harsh words, perhaps, but what finer tribute could be offered a propagandist?

The last days of Junius were accompanied by widespread conjecture as to his identity. The comparative merits of the pseudonymous penman and the greatest orator in the House of Commons, Edmund Burke, led many eyes astray and caused Burke no little embarrassment.[8] Junius had other worries, real fears of actual discovery. One of the proprietors of the *Public Advertiser* was the actor-dramatist David Garrick. Like most men dependent upon the public, Garrick retained close contacts with the press and its directors. About the first of November, 1771, Henry Sampson Woodfall advised Garrick "in a letter nowise relative to the subject, *without any previous impertinent inquiries on* [*Garrick's*] *part*, or the least desire of secrecy on [Woodfall's], that *Junius would write no more.*" Two or three days later Garrick sent a message concerning the theater to a correspondent at court and mentioned this interesting rumor. Further, Garrick admitted, "I wrote no letter to any of my friends without the mention of so remarkable an event." On November 8, Junius suddenly warned Woodfall, "Beware of David Garrick. He was *sent* to pump you, and *went* directly . . . to tell the King I should write no more." Two days later he sent Woodfall a private letter for the actor in which he advised, "Meddle no more, thou busy informer!—It is in *my* power to make you curse the hour in which you dare to interfere with JUNIUS." To Woodfall Junius admitted, "I must be more cautious than ever. I am sure I should not survive a Discovery three days; or, if I did, they would attaint me by bill."

Henry Sampson Woodfall at once began to anticipate unfortunate repercussions. He informed Garrick of Junius' violent warning but apparently did not send him the letter. At the same time, he reassured Junius of Garrick's honor and sought to shift the discussion to his own dangers. Junius was at first pacified by Woodfall's explanation. He was unimpressed by the publisher's fears, for, he wrote, "Punishing *you* (unless it answered the purpose of stopping the press) would be no gratification to the King. . . . They talk of farther informations, but they will always hold that language *in terrorem*." Garrick made his amends to Junius on November 20, denying the act or intent of betrayal and putting up a bold front of injured honor. Junius was not convinced, but he allowed the supposed traitor to escape as he turned his attention for the last time to Lord Mansfield.[9]

The campaign against the chief justice which closed Junius' career was designed to bring into line the most vigorous forces of the opposition. John Wilkes was privy to the plans as early as November 6 and favored Junius with materials and advice. Mansfield was belabored twice in November by letters in the *Public Advertiser,* and in December, Junius prepared a long paper which was intended to appear on January 21, 1772, when parliament met, and to form a public impeachment of Mansfield. At the same time Junius hoped to strike a blow in the House of Lords. To this end he wrote to Chatham on the fourteenth, submitting his whole scheme and asking the earl to attend the opening session "prepared to take down [Mansfield's] words, and thereupon to move for committing him to the Tower." When the twenty-first arrived, Junius and Woodfall did their part; Mansfield was indicted in a tiresome, lengthy article full of legal arguments. Their efforts were wasted, however, for neither Chatham nor Camden attended the opening of parliament. With one final appeal to Camden, Junius retired from a field upon which no further honor was to be gained.[10]

William Strahan, the King's Printer, told a friend in February, 1772:

> Even *Junius* has now fairly written himself down. . . . his last Letter . . . is universally decried as frivolous and groundless in the highest Degree. —We are, at length, I hope, after a violent and tedious Hurricane, on the eve of as long a Calm in Politicks. Indeed I can see nothing to prevent it. Lord North goes on calmly, steadily, and firmly.[11]

It was a fair description of the times. Junius himself, when Woodfall sought to recall him to life, declared,

> In the present state of things, if I were to write again, I must be as

silly as any of the horned Cattle that run mad through the city. . . .
I meant the cause and the public. Both are given up. I feel for the
honour of this Country, when I see that there are not ten men in it
who will unite and stand together upon any one question. But it is
all alike, vile and contemptible.[12]

So passed into history and literary legend the greatest of the anonymous
writers of the late eighteenth century. His contribution to the development of the English newspaper cannot be measured but was unques-
tionably great. However, the press might well have declared with
Henry Sampson Woodfall, "Though I derived much honour from his
preference, I suffered much by the freedom of his pen."[13]

The durability of John Wilkes surpassed that of Junius. Wilkes was
his own "cause"; his goal, political control of the City; his weapon, the
press. None surpassed Wilkes in dexterity. His pen was both feared
and hated by rivals who constantly complained of an influence they
could not counteract. At the Common Hall for electing a Lord Mayor,
September 28, 1771, Sawbridge declared that anonymous hostile paragraphs in the newspapers had had such an effect that he must call "this
inventor of intelligence . . . who is not less known for not having signed
his name, and who is now present . . . to stand forth and become my
accuser." Wilkes was no unfledged parvenu; he kept his place and was
not stirred up by the succeeding taunts of Alderman Townsend, who
had suffered similarly.

When the voting ended, October 5, William Nash and John Sawbridge led the poll. That evening Wilkes replied—in the newspapers—
to the charges laid against him at the Common Hall. "You well know
it is not usual to authenticate *paragraphs* with the name of the author,"
he told Sawbridge and Townsend, and he upbraided them for having
dared to accuse him only behind his back. Why, asked Wilkes, should
those who have encouraged "*anonymous paragraphs*" for over three
years suddenly undergo a total change of sentiment? "For my own part
. . . I have truly and faithfully informed the public of every affair
interesting to them [and] . . . I will steadily persevere in the same line
of conduct to the last moment of my political career."

The Court of Aldermen chose Nash on the eighth, and Wilkes took
advantage of the assembly to demand proof of the charges brought
against him in September. Townsend at once named Wilkes as the
accused and defied him to clear himself. The Livery, Wilkites to a
man, greeted Townsend with hisses. Their hero blandly admitted, "He

had wrote many paragraphs in news-papers . . . but these paragraphs were for the public good." He charged Townsend with "deserting the cause of the printers," and only the intervention of the Lord Mayor enabled Townsend to be heard above the groans and hisses that accompanied his weak refutation of Wilkes's thrust. Sawbridge fared slightly better when he, and then Wilkes, politely denied that he had meant to reflect upon the other.[14]

The Livery demonstrated their opinion of comparative political merits on January 24, 1772, when a £200 cup and two £100 cups were awarded to Crosby, Wilkes, and Oliver "for the noble stand they made in the business of the Printers, against an arbitrary vote of the H[ouse] of C[ommo]ns." Wilkes replied in the same vein. On April 6, the Sheriffs' address to the Livery (obviously drawn by Wilkes) noted that the House of Commons had apparently surrendered "their late usurpation of the personal rights and privileges of the people" and that "the Lords have not dared . . . to impose any fines at their arbitrary will, for offences cognizable by Juries. No man has been committed at their bar for what their votes, not the laws, declare seditious, nor for what they so readily find a libel on a brother Peer."[15]

Wilkes's utilization of the press created dangers for his printers. James Townsend was elected Lord Mayor in 1772, and Wilkes, the defeated candidate, proceeded to make his mayoralty miserable by lambasting him in the newspapers. Townsend reciprocated as best he could. By extorting an admission of the source of the attack from Henry S. Woodfall, the Lord Mayor sought to embarrass Wilkes. His only achievement, however, was to force the moderate printer of the *Public Advertiser* into wholehearted cooperation with his author. When Townsend demanded the source of certain articles in the *Public Advertiser* for December, 1772, Woodfall wrote Wilkes, "I have no Idea of giving answers to any impertinent Questions of this Kind," and to Townsend's emissary he said that he "had not time to dance to the Mansion house every time his Lordship should please to send for me."[16]

By 1773, Wilkes's power in the City had become so great that only the avowedly partisan vote of the Lord Mayor defeated his election for the highest municipal office. As in preceding years, Wilkes filled the papers with propaganda. He accused Townsend's administration of "violence, tyranny, neglect of public business, a contempt of all order and decorum . . . [and] the most sordid parsimony." When publicly criticized for such libelous abuse, Wilkes added to his list, "partiality and cruelty." The Court of Aldermen attempted to bring him to account for his audacity, but Wilkes retired from the November 17 meeting "in doleful dumps, chusing rather to leave his character to the mercy of his opponents, than to support the combat on such unequal ground." The court was then moved that as there existed "the clearest evidence that Mr. Wilkes had infamously abused the liberty of the press, by many false and defamatory paragraphs . . . tending to inflame the minds of the people, and to degrade the dignity of the magistrates of this city," his conduct deserved the severest censure. The motion was withdrawn at Townsend's behest, however, possibly for fear it would not pass, possibly out of consideration for Wilkes's certain reprisal.[17]

While Junius was passing into oblivion, and Wilkes was carving a niche for himself in the City of London, the government quietly went about refuting those charges it could meet and developing some sort of order out of the chaos of 1770. At the height of Junius' attack upon Mansfield, old pensions were honored, and Philip Francis became the recipient of his late father's gratuity. William Strahan, King's Printer and middle-man between Samuel Johnson and the Treasury secretaries, wrote occasionally under the pseudonym *Britannicus,* but he thought little of such efforts as "the License of the Papers is now so great, that nobody minds what they contain."[18]

Lord North succeeded where other ministers had failed to bring the great Johnson into the open as a propagandist. In the spring of 1771, an anonymous pamphlet was published which supported the administration's foreign policy and was quickly recognized as the Doctor's offspring. "Mr. Johnson's Pamphlet," remarked David Hume, "is a good one, and very diverting from the Peculiarity and Enormity of the Style. One sees he speaks from the Heart." The lifeblood of Johnson's *Falkland's Islands* had been furnished by the ministry, and its flow was regulated by Lord North. When he discovered an unfortunate reflection upon the late George Grenville, the minister ordered the sale stopped and the offending passage removed. Johnsonian wit was scarcely worth the risk of antagonizing recently won allies.[19]

Lesser writers carried the burden of North's defense. ZENO and A BARRISTER-AT-LAW undertook to refute Junius in the *Public Advertiser.* Caleb Whitefoord contributed anonymous paragraphs for which Woodfall found ample space and type of the same size used for Junius' letters. Under-secretaries continued their watchful vigil over the London papers but asserted more of a corrective than a punitive influence.

Parson James Scott, once a leading propagandist, wrote from his rectory at Simonburn, "We constantly after Dinner drink the King and his Friends, and despise John Wilkes and his whole Gang. . . . I long to be at them again, but . . . I cannot think of launching my little Bark into the troublesome Ocean without being asked."[20] Apparently he received no invitation. The key to a favorable press which North utilized may have been shaped to fit the purses of London publishers—the subsidy policy which was a major influence in the next decade.

No attempt was made to turn the failure of the attack upon Mansfield's interpretation of the law in libel cases or the confirmation of the attorney-general's power to file informations ex officio to ministerial advantage. Credit for North's policy of toleration cannot be accurately assigned, but the minister himself was probably responsible. The impression is borne out by the results of a royal suggestion in July, 1774, that the printer of the *Whitehall Evening Post* ought to be prosecuted for a libel against a young relative of Lords North and Dartmouth. The king believed that "the prosecution of a Printer by so worthy a Man as Lord Dartmouth must be attended with success, and would greatly tend to check that licentiousness which disgraces the freedom of the Press." Lord North replied that as there was no truth to the story related in the paper, Dartmouth had no intention of prosecuting, and the affair was dropped.[21]

Such an attitude was far more politic than that of the Earl of Sandwich, who, in 1773, instituted an action of *scandalum magnatum* against John Miller of the *London Evening Post* for publishing a letter accusing Sandwich with having attempted the sale of an Admiralty commissioner's post for £200. The earl asked £10,000 damages. Miller retained John Glynn as counsel and was brought up for trial before Mansfield and a special jury on July 8. The defense attempted to vindicate the printer by proving his charges. This, declared Attorney-General Thurlow, only aggravated the offense. Glynn thereupon maintained that Sandwich was conducting "a direct attack upon the liberty of the press . . . if the freedom of political discussion was denied to a free people, men in office might . . . trample upon the rights of humanity, yet go unpunished." Thurlow replied that "he hoped no man would pretend to call a base attack upon public characters, political discussion." Inasmuch as the author had not been named (nor any attempt been made to discover him), "the printer . . . is the responsible party." Mansfield advised the jury that since the truth of the charges was not proven, and publication was proven, they should "find for the plaintiff; but I shall not say one word about the damages." After an hour and three-quarters, the jury returned a verdict and £2,000 damages for Sandwich.[22]

Juries continued to show a liberal spirit toward injured private honor. In 1774, Henry Baldwin, printer of the *St. James's Chronicle*, was fined £500 for a libel upon a naval officer, and John Williams of the *Morning Post* was sentenced to one month's imprisonment and fined £100 and costs for a paragraph reflecting upon Charles James Fox.[23] Such actions were a necessary check upon the licentiousness of the press, and except for the case of Fox, whose fame gave a political tinge to Williams' case, they were in no way an infringement upon the liberty of the press.

The sole affair during these years which smacked of the violence of the preceding decade was that of the "South Briton." In February, 1774, Charles James Fox called the attention of the House of Commons to a letter in the *Public Advertiser* and the *Morning Chronicle*, signed "A South Briton," which he described as a libel upon the Glorious Revolution and the constitution. Fox, "an enemy to all libels—to all licentiousness of the press—though a friend to the legal liberty of it," was deliberately seeking to commit the ministry to a policy of repression in order to embarrass Lord North. Though still an officeholder, he would join the opposition in a matter of days, and it is of considerable interest that this was the only article during fifteen years of the most partisan writing to be officially noticed from what might be termed a "Whiggish" point of view. As North took the position, "I am not answerable for measures in which I had no concern," the majority in the Commons supported Fox, and the attorney-general was ordered to prosecute the authors, printers, and publishers.[24]

Both William and Henry Sampson Woodfall, publishers of the *Morning Chronicle* and the *Public Advertiser*, were brought to trial before Lord Mansfield on July 11. William Woodfall was tried first. His counsel sought to excuse the "South Briton's" article as "a stupid performance," but Mansfield declared, "It does not follow that the libel must be so cleverly written as to have its effect. . . . the author is not the less criminal for doing all the mischief he could, and intending more." After five hours the jury found the defendant guilty. Henry S. Woodfall was convicted an hour later, despite a shrewd plea by his counsel that the publisher, not the paper, was being considered, and as Woodfall was in confinement at the time of publication, no intention to publish could be shown. Mansfield disallowed the argument on technical and general grounds: "Whenever a man publishes he publishes at his peril." The jury found the printer guilty of publishing the paper, but did not find the article a libel—a verdict which had no significance to Mansfield who took it to mean simply "guilty." Sentence was delivered by Justice Aston on November 26, and the brothers suffered both fine and imprisonment.[25]

The only other case of parliamentary action between 1771 and 1774 was almost a reversal of precedent and a startling example of the debility of the House of Commons. Early in February, 1774, William Tooke, a prominent member of the Constitutional Society, became involved in a dispute concerning an enclosure bill presented to the House of Commons in behalf of a ministerial supporter. As political affiliation seemed likely to determine the question, Tooke's friend John Horne suggested a change of tactics. "To accomplish this end," said he, "I intend to begin by writing a libel on the speaker." Horne's facile pen produced a letter in the *Public Advertiser*, February 11, entitled "Strike, but Hear," which accused Speaker Fletcher Norton of abetting Tooke's rival.

The ruse succeeded admirably. Norton complained of the insult that same afternoon. Although all parties in the House expressed satisfaction with his conduct and the speaker declared himself "perfectly easy as to . . . this scandalous libel," a motion was offered to call the printer of the *Public Advertiser* to the bar. A division of opinion at once appeared. Some were for avoiding any contact with printers whatsoever; others, including Dowdeswell and Meredith, declared that such obvious license demanded punishment. Lord North, hopeful that action by the Commons would not lead to conflict with the City, found himself held to the motion by Charles Fox's vigorous assertion that the House must enforce its rights or surrender to printers the privilege of libeling whomsoever they pleased. Without a division the letter was found to be a libel, and Henry S. Woodfall was ordered to attend the House.[26]

George III, when he learned of the letter and the Commons' action, expressed hearty concurrence in the proceedings. On Monday, February 14, Woodfall attended and named Horne as his author. The House agreed he was guilty of breach of privilege but was divided in opinion as to suitable punishment. Charles Fox moved for commitment to

Newgate. North favored a moderate policy that would secure general approval, for "he meant no harm to the liberty of the press [which was] . . . on a very good footing, as it was at the printer's peril what he published." Thinking it "highly imprudent to force themselves into a contest with the city," North moved for commitment to the Gatehouse in order to pacify Fox, but he instructed his followers to support commitment to the serjeant-at-arms. Schism on the Treasury bench forced North to vote with Fox, while the majority divided with the opposition to allow Woodfall the greatest possible lenience.[27]

The king, pleased by North's success, urged an end to the "half measures" which had been formerly pursued. Horne, however, was no ordinary libeler. He declined the summons to attend on Wednesday the sixteenth, claiming in a letter to the speaker, that he was not the *Reverend* John Horne, but simply *Mr.* John Horne. Such a *jeu d'esprit* had no effect upon the House; John Horne, being guilty of contempt, was ordered into custody. The next day Horne was brought in and pleaded "not guilty" of the charge against him. For two days debate raged, and Horne professed a happy technical innocence which could not be disproved. On Friday he was discharged, protesting even the payment of the usual doorkeepers' fees.[28]

The ease with which Horne defied the House of Commons had numerous repercussions. By the seventeenth, George III was trusting that "the House will make the Printer feel its resentment; for if he escapes easily, the Press will grow more insolent." Not only the press and "the evil every thinking Man now complains of" were to be considered, but also Charles Fox, who had demonstrated his powers as an *agent provocateur* in ministerial garb. The king was "greatly incensed" at his presumption. He wrote to North, "That Young Man has so thoroughly cast off every principle of common honour and honesty that he must become as contemptible as he is odious."[29] Fox sought something more tangible than honor among the Dysons, Jenkinsons, and Robinsons on the Treasury bench, however, and failing to find it, he welcomed North's laconic notice that "His Majesty has thought proper to order a new Commission of Treasury to be made out, in which I do not see your name."[30] While Fox secured his release from the Treasury, Woodfall was unable to escape the custody of the serjeant-at-arms. His petition for discharge was refused on February 24, and not until March 2 did the House listen favorably to his request. Two weeks' imprisonment and the consequent gratuities cost the poor printer £72, not counting business losses but including eighty-eight bottles of port, sherry, and daily beer.[31]

The Horne affair, to quote Walpole, left "the majesty of the senate . . . a little singed,"[32] and the same phrase might be applied to the entire three-year period following the 1771 struggle with the City. Wilkes plotted a second campaign with Junius and that "fine Oliverian soldier" John Miller, but neither House would rise to the bait.[33] Emboldened, the printer of the *London Evening Post* began to publish the "Votes and Proceedings" as well as a "Faithful Narrative of the Proceedings of Parliament." The *Morning Chronicle* followed suit under William Woodfall's guidance. No effort was made to suppress his reports, so Woodfall announced, June 13, 1772: "This important matter may therefore be looked upon as settled, and the electors of Great Britain will hereafter be allowed the wonderful privilege of knowing how faithfully their representatives discharge their duty."[34] Veteran reporters like Almon and Woodfall were soon joined by others. In 1773, the *Morning Post* hired Arthur Young as a regular parliamentary reporter at the reputed (but unlikely) salary of five guineas a week.[35] The next year John Almon resolved to compile periodical reports of the debates in both houses, and these were published as *The Parliamentary Register,* a journal patronized and supported by numerous members of parliament.[36]

The years just prior to the American Revolution were fruitful in journalistic enterprise. New men and new papers appeared and thrived upon the broadening political interests of Englishmen and the commercial possibilities of advertising. The *Morning Post,* founded in 1772, enjoyed instant success. The *London Evening Post* and the *Morning Chronicle,* owing their importance to the parliamentary reports of John Almon and William Woodfall, were soon rivaled by the *London Packet* when the two reporters combined to support it as well as their own publishing interests. In this period of vigorous expansion, the newspaper came of age.[37]

CONCLUSION

JOHN WILKES epitomized the accomplishment of the years 1760–1774 when he wrote:

> The people are now made the Judges of the conduct of their representatives, and the full exertion of the liberty of the press, the great bulwark of all our liberties, in support of the constitution, with the other acquisitions for the public, will render this aera ever memorable in our annals.[1]

The statement has a genuine Wilkite tone, but it rings true.

A young Frenchman setting out to describe the English constitution at the close of the period found in the new exercise of the liberty of the press a thrilling supplement to the much admired constitutional checks and balances. Turning not to the tomes of Blackstone or the pontifications of Mansfield, but to the vital arguments of Serjeant John Glynn, he observed that the right of every Englishman "to lay his complaints and observations before the Public, by means of an open press," and the wonderful multiplication of all kinds of public papers, "this public notoriety of all things," was the real force keeping "within their respective bounds, all those persons who enjoy any share of public power." The representative nature of parliament might be sharply restricted and its vaunted omnipotence recognized only by itself, but through the medium of a free press "a whole Nation holds a Council, and deliberates."[2]

"What is England now?" asked Horace Walpole. "A sink of Indian wealth, filled by nabobs and emptied by Maccaronies! A senate sold and despised! . . . A gaming, robbing, wrangling, railing nation, without principles, genius, character, or allies; the overgrown shadow of what it was!"[3] True enough, but these things pass, and the people learn —though Burke might feel they had "fallen into a total indifference to any matters of publick concern."[4] Their emergence was slow; it was labored, but it was legal and peaceful. With it came a new concept of the liberty of the press—a liberty which included responsibility to society and was based upon economic maturity—a process which began in the early years of the reign of George the Third.

224

APPENDIX A

Chronology

1760

October 25   Seven Years War with France; PITT-NEWCASTLE ministry
    Accession of George III
    Press attack against Pitt's war policy

1761
March 25   Bute enters the ministry as secretary of state
October 2–5   Pitt's proposal of war with Spain rejected,
       Pitt and Temple resign

1762
January 2   War with Spain begins
May 26   Newcastle resigns, BUTE ministry
June 5   Wilke's *North Briton* No. 1
    The War of the Weeklies
December 9   Preliminaries of peace debated and approved

1763
February 10   Treaty of Paris signed
April 8   Bute resigns, GRENVILLE ministry
April 23   *North Briton* No. 45
April 26   General warrant issued
April 30   Wilkes arrested and sent to the Tower
May 3–6   Pratt frees Wilkes on plea of parliamentary privilege
July   Cases of the journeyman-printers *vs.* the messengers
       arising from *North Briton* No. 45
    Wilkes reprints the *North Briton* and the *Essay on Woman*

August   Unsuccessful efforts to unite Pitt and Newcastle
November   Parliamentary attack on Wilkes begins
December 3   *North Briton* burned
December 6–10   Cases of Wilkes *vs.* Wood and Leach *vs.* Money effectively end
       the use of general warrants
    Wilkes, wounded in a duel, retires to France

1764
January 19–20   Wilkes is expelled from the House of Commons
February 13–18   Opposition attack on general warrants fails
February 21   Wilkes convicted *in absentia* in Court of King's Bench
February 25   *Droit le Roi* burned
April   The Conway affair. Hartley's *The Budget*
May   *Monitor* cases against Halifax begin

July	Trials of John Williams and George Kearsley
August	Almon's *Defence of the Minority*
November	Candor's *Letter concerning Libels*

1765

January 29	Meredith's motion to condemn general warrants fails
February 17	John Williams pilloried
March 4	Calvert's motion against informations fails
May 1	Almon's trial for the *Letter concerning Libels*
June	Negotiations with Pitt fail
July 16	ROCKINGHAM ministry formed
November 27	Camden's decision in Entick *vs.* Carrington

1766

April–May	House of Commons resolutions against general warrants and the seizure of papers
July 30	CHATHAM ministry formed, press attack upon his peerage

1767

February	Chatham incapacitated; GRAFTON leads the ministry
May	Almon's *Political Register*
July	Negotiations among the factions collapse disastrously
December	Bedford's faction supports the ministry

1768

February	Wilkes returns to England
March–April	General elections; Wilkes chosen for Middlesex
April 27	Wilkes imprisoned
May 10	Riots in St. George's Fields
	The "Unreported Parliament" opens
June 18	Wilkes sentenced to twenty-two months imprisonment
	John Bingley's case begins

1769

January 21	Junius begins to write for the *Public Advertiser*
January 23	Wilkes is refused privilege of parliament
February 3–4	Wilkes is expelled from the House of Commons
April	Colonel Luttrell is finally seated for Middlesex
	Popular opposition and petitions favoring Wilkes
October	Recovery of Chatham and reunion of the Grenvilles
December 19	Junius' "Letter to the King"

1770

January 23	Grafton resigns; NORTH ministry formed
April 23	Burke's *Cause of the Present Discontents*
June 2	Trial of John Almon for Junius' "Letter to the King"
June 13	Woodfall's trial
July 18	Trial and acquittal of Miller and Baldwin
November 13	Death of Grenville weakens the opposition
November–	Parliamentary attack upon Mansfield and upon the use of

December	informations divides Chatham and Rockingham; efforts of Glynn and Camden defeated

1771

February 5	Colonel Onslow begins his attack upon parliamentary reporting
March 8	Dowdeswell's bill defeated
	The City, led by Wilkes, takes up the printers' cause
March 12	Onslow's attack reaches its peak
March 15	Messenger of the House of Commons arrested in the City
March 18–	Parliamentary struggle between the House of Commons
April 30	and the City of London
	Rivalry between Wilkes and Horne

1772

January	Junius' final attack upon Mansfield
	Wilkes embroiled in City politics

1773

July	Sandwich *vs.* Miller

1774

February	Fox attacks the Woodfalls for the "South Briton" letter
	John Horne's "Strike, but Hear"

APPENDIX B

Biographical Sketches

ALBEMARLE. George Keppel, 3rd Earl (1724–1772). Head of one of the great old Whig families, Albemarle enjoyed a notable military career which culminated in the taking of Havana in 1762; politically attached to the Newcastle-Rockingham faction.

ALMON, John (1737–1805). Author, bookseller, and publisher, Almon was Lord Temple's propagandist, suffered for it in the courts of law, but enjoyed considerable financial success. Almon's memoirs and other writings shed much light upon the political press, to which he made a number of significant contributions.

ASTON, Sir Richard (d. 1778). Barrister, lord chief justice of Common Pleas, Ireland, 1761; knighted and transferred to the King's Bench, England, 1765; an otherwise undistinguished judge.

BAKER, Sir William (d. 1770). A leading City financier, alderman of London, one of Newcastle's advisers on financial matters.

BARRÉ. Isaac (1726–1802). Colonel in the army, served under Wolfe; losing the sight of one eye, he turned to politics and made a name for himself as a very rough and ready debater.

BATH. William Pulteney, Earl of Bath (1684–1764). One of the brilliant young Whig politicians of the early eighteenth century, Pulteney broke with Sir Robert Walpole in 1725, wrote for Bolingbroke's *Craftsman,* and by 1742 had gained such pre-eminence that he was asked to form a ministry; he refused and settled for a peerage and relative political obscurity.

BECKFORD, William (1709–1770). West Indian planter of great wealth and political influence, active supporter of Pitt and the French war, Lord Mayor of London 1762, 1769.

BEDFORD. John Russell, 4th Duke of Bedford (1710–1771). Head of one of the greatest and wealthiest of the old Whig families, Bedford was lord lieutenant of Ireland 1756–1761, ambassador to France in 1762, lord president of the privy council 1763–1767; his faction was known as the Bloomsbury Gang and gained something of a reputation for venal office-seeking.

BURKE, Edmund (1729–1797). Irish man of letters, politician, and pamphleteer; wrote the political sections of the *Annual Register* in the 1760's, became Rockingham's private secretary and M.P., 1765. Although he was the brain of Rockingham's faction, Burke's origins limited his hope of political advancement; his speeches, though brilliant, were often so tediously long that he became known as "the dinner bell of the House of Commons." Burke's greatest period was that of the American Revolution, at the conclusion of which he was able to take the lead in achieving numerous reforms. His later years were filled with the drawn-out proceedings against

Warren Hastings (a cause shared with Philip Francis) and his great literary assault upon the principles of the French Revolution.

BUTE. John Stuart, 3rd Earl of Bute (1713–1792). Scottish peer whose influence with the Princess of Wales and ascendancy over the young George III won him highest office in 1761. Having achieved an end to the war, and recognizing that his unpopularity as a royal favorite and a Scot reflected upon the king, Bute resigned office, but continued to enjoy an influence with the king which was neither as great nor lasting as his enemies claimed.

CALCRAFT, John (1726-1772). An army contractor attached to Henry Fox until 1763, Calcraft made a fortune after the manner of his patron, then turned his support to Pitt. He had the best head for intrigue in the Chathamite faction and helped to reunite Chatham and Temple in 1768.

CHESTERFIELD. Philip Dormer Stanhope, 4th Earl of Chesterfield (1694–1773). Wit and letter-writer, Chesterfield's independence frustrated his political career, but he was at times closely associated with Newcastle. By the reign of George III, he was content to view politics from the outside and write most devastatingly accurate descriptions of his contemporaries.

CHURCHILL, Charles (1731–1764). Sometime curate and outstanding satirical poet, Churchill became a man of fashion and Wilkes's close friend and collaborator.

CONWAY, Henry Seymour (1721–1795). A respectable military career and good connections brought Conway high command during the Seven Years War, but he was dismissed for political reasons in 1764. He was secretary of state 1765–1768, and commander-in-chief 1782–1783. A close friend and correspondent of Horace Walpole, who busied himself with Conway's political career, the general was too well equipped with connections to ignore and too poorly supplied with ability to be of much use to anyone.

COOPER, Grey (d. 1801). Secretary of the treasury 1765–1782; lord of the treasury 1783–1784; noted for his financial acumen and dependable service on the treasury bench.

CORNWALL, Charles Wolfran (1735–1789). Charles Jenkinson's brother-in-law, a Treasury lord 1774–1780, speaker of the House of Commons 1780–1789.

DARTMOUTH. William Legge, 2nd Earl of Dartmouth (1731–1802). Noted for his piety and support of Methodism, Dartmouth was president of the Board of Trade 1765–1766, and colonial secretary 1772–1775.

DASHWOOD, Francis, Baron Le De Spencer (1708–1781). A notorious rake and founder of the Medmenham Abbey brotherhood or Hellfire Club, Dashwood was chancellor of the exchequer 1762–1763, and postmaster-general 1770–1781.

DE GREY, William (1719–1781). Barrister, attorney-general 1766–1770, chief justice of Common Pleas 1771–1780.

DODINGTON, George Bubb, Lord Melcombe (1691–1762). Dodington long placed his hopes on the reversionary interest of Frederick, Prince of Wales, and then his son George. An inveterate intriguer, Dodington offered Bute much sound advice, and in 1761, he received his baronage as a reward.

DOWDESWELL, William (1721–1775). A competent and politically minded country gentleman whose opposition to the cider bill won Rockingham's favor; chancellor of the exchequer 1765–1766, he led the opposition to Townshend's economic policies in 1767, and was one of the chief spokesmen for the Rockingham faction; his moderation and lack of confidence probably explain his failure to play a more prominent role in political affairs.

DRAPER, Sir William (1721–1787). Commander of the British forces that captured Manila in 1762, Draper became a lieutenant-general and was lieutenant-governor of Minorca 1779–1782.

DUNNING, John, Lord Ashburton (1731–1783). Barrister, solicitor-general 1768–1770, created baron 1782; although most often remembered for his motion in 1780 condemning the power of the crown, Dunning was, next to Glynn, the outstanding press lawyer of his time.

EGREMONT. Charles Wyndham, 2nd Earl of Egremont (1710–1763). George Grenville's brother-in-law, Egremont possessed no outstanding capacities, but he was well thought of among the back-benchers; secretary of state 1761–1763.

ELLIS, Welbore, Baron Mendip (1713–1802). A successful placeman and supporter of royal policy, secretary at war 1762–1765.

FITZHERBERT, William (d. 1772). Member of the Board of Trade 1763, 1765–1772; affiliated with Rockingham, to whom he recommended Burke as a secretary, and for whom he negotiated with Wilkes.

Fox, Charles James (1749–1806). A younger son of Henry Fox, Charles enjoyed a life of dissipation combined with a brilliant parliamentary career. The most gifted orator in the House of Commons after Pitt, young Fox began his career in 1768, and until 1774, he supported the ministry, winning an unpopularity that was as great as his subsequent popularity, foreign secretary 1782, secretary of state 1783, foreign secretary 1806.

Fox, Henry, Lord Holland (1705–1774). Secretary at war 1746–1754, secretary of state 1755–1756, paymaster-general 1757–1765, created a peer in 1763. The elder Fox was the most unpopular of contemporary statesmen; as paymaster-general he secured a fortune manipulating public funds, but his real ability as an administrator and debater made him Pitt's greatest rival and a useful man in office.

FRANCIS, Rev. Philip (1708?–1773). Private chaplain in the Fox household, the elder Francis also wrote propaganda for Henry Fox and those ministers Fox supported; father of the younger Philip Francis.

FRANCIS, Philip (1740–1818). Clerk at the war office 1762–1772, councilor to the governor-general of India 1774–1780, and one of Warren Hastings' most bitter enemies. Francis has been the most popular nominee for Junius' honors.

GARRICK, David (1717–1779). Actor, producer, manager of the Drury Lane theater, like most of his profession, Garrick maintained close contacts with the press.

GLYNN, John (1722–1779). Outstanding lawyer and spokesman of Wilkite radicalism as M.P. for Middlesex 1768–1779. As Wilkes's counsel in 1763, Glynn assumed the leading role among those of his profession who supported the popular cause, and he was the most prominent press lawyer of his day.

GRAFTON. Augustus Henry Fitzroy, 3rd Duke of Grafton (1735–1811). Young Grafton was a well-meaning nonentity who was constantly torn by his admiration for Pitt and his natural connection with the Rockingham faction. Secretary of state 1765–

1766, effective head of the Chatham administration 1767–1770, he held office under North 1771–1775, and rejoined Rockingham in 1782.

GRENVILLE, George (1712–1770). Temple's brother and Pitt's brother-in-law, Grenville remained with the ministry after their retirement in 1761; selected by Bute to succeed as first lord of the treasury 1763–1765, Grenville's ministry was plagued by inherited problems ranging from Wilkes to American colonial administration. Grenville was a competent administrator and a good House of Commons man.

HALIFAX. George Montagu Dunk, 2nd Earl of Halifax (1716–1771). Lord lieutenant of Ireland 1761–1763, president of the Board of Trade 1748–1761, Halifax became secretary of state in 1762; he was one of the triumvirs who succeeded to Bute's power in 1763.

HARDWICK. Philip Yorke, 1st Earl of Hardwicke (1690–1764). Solicitor-general 1720, attorney-general 1724, chief justice 1733, lord chancellor 1737–1756. Hardwicke was Newcastle's adviser in legal and most other matters; in his later years he worked behind the political scene but sought to advance his family interest and particularly the career of Charles Yorke.

HARTLEY, David (1732–1813). Statesman, scientist, and political writer, Hartley was a friend of Benjamin Franklin and helped negotiate the treaty ending the American Revolutionary War in 1783.

HOGARTH, William (1697–1764). Painter and engraver best known for his portrayal of eighteenth-century society in "The Rake's Progress," "The Harlot's Progress," etc. He excelled in caricature and satire.

HORNE, John (1736–1812). Philologist and politician, Horne was first a Wilkite, then a far more significant Radical in his own right. His vigorous speech and writing got him into difficulties during both the American and French Revolutions. In 1782, he added the name Tooke to his own.

JENKINSON, Charles, 1st Earl of Liverpool (1727–1808). Most successful of those public servants whose loyalty to the crown won them the appellation "King's Friends." Jenkinson's talents as a "man of business" secured him a treasury secretaryship 1763–1765, posts as secretary at war 1778 and president of the Board of Trade 1786, and his peerage. His son was the well-known nineteenth-century prime minister.

JOHNSON, Samuel (1709–1784). Lexicographer, essayist, occasionally a political writer, Johnson, was the leading literary figure of his time and, thanks to Boswell, far and away the best known.

KNOX, William (1732–1810). A competent colonial agent and authority on American affairs, Knox was under-secretary of state for America 1770–1782.

LLOYD, Charles (1735-1773). George Grenville's secretary after 1763, a competent pamphleteer and man of business for the faction.

LUTTRELL, Henry Lawes, 2nd Earl of Carhampton (1743–1821). Wilkes's replacement for Middlesex, 1769, was a soldier and politician with a reputation for bravado.

MACAULAY, Mrs. Catherine (1731–1791). An eccentric historian, controversialist, and ardent Radical; Mrs. Macaulay was one of the most notorious feminists of her day.

MACPHERSON, James (1736–1796). Scottish author and purported translator of the

Gaelic poet Ossian, Macpherson enjoyed Bute's support and was employed by Lord North.

MANSFIELD. William Murray, 1st Earl of Mansfield (1705–1793). Solicitor-general 1742, attorney-general 1754, lord chief justice 1756. Mansfield's house was burned during the Gordon riots of 1780, as a result of his unpopularity. Mansfield was an extremely able jurist and debater, and his views on libel stood until Fox's Libel Act of 1792.

MAUDUIT, Israel (1708–1787). Businessman, colonial agent for Massachusetts, pamphleteer.

MEREDITH, Sir William (d. 1790). M.P. for Liverpool 1761–1780, veered toward the Rockingham faction and secured minor office in 1765, but was generally independent and a supporter of various reform movements.

MORRIS, Robert (d. 1794). Lawyer, secretary of the Bill of Rights Society.

MURPHY, Arthur (1727–1805). Author and actor, occasional political writer, biographer of Johnson and Garrick.

NEWCASTLE. Thomas Pelham-Holles, Duke of Newcastle (1693–1768). Greatest of the Whig borough-mongers, Newcastle was a staunch Hanoverian and an indefatigable electioneer. With his brother Henry, Newcastle dominated the political scene 1746–1756, but the dismal beginning of the Seven Years War forced him to share power with Pitt. Newcastle devoted his life to politics and never rose to the level of statesmanship.

NORTH. Frederick, 2nd Earl of Guilford (1732–1792). Usually known by his courtesy title, Lord North, he was an undistinguished junior lord of the treasury prior to the accession of George III. North became a stalwart supporter of the king's policy, chancellor of the exchequer 1767, first lord of the treasury 1770–1782. In 1783 he joined forces with Charles Fox in a notorious and short-lived coalition.

NORTON, Fletcher, 1st Baron Grantley (1716–1789). Solicitor-general 1762, attorney-general 1763–1765, speaker of the House of Commons 1770–1780; nicknamed Sir Bull-face Double-fee because of his extortionate violence.

ONSLOW, George (1731–1792). Politician, soldier, and supporter of the ministry in office, his place in history depends upon the results of his reaction to the epithet, Little Cocking George.

PHIPPS, Constantine, 2nd Baron Mulgrave (1744–1792). A naval officer and explorer of some distinction, Phipps could usually be counted among the king's friends.

PITT, William, 1st Earl of Chatham (1708–1778). The foremost orator of the House of Commons in the eighteenth century, Pitt's haughty independence excluded him from office until the crisis of the Seven Years War when his coalition with Newcastle (1757) was formed. Physical infirmity limited his activity in his last years, but in 1775 and 1777 he attempted to influence policy toward America.

PRATT, Charles, Earl Camden (1714–1794). Attorney-general 1757, chief justice of Common Pleas 1761, elevated to the peerage 1765, lord chancellor in Chatham's administration 1766–1770, lord president of the privy council 1782–1783, 1784–1794.

ROCKINGHAM. Charles Watson-Wentworth, 2nd Marquis of Rockingham (1730–1782). Politically insignificant prior to 1762, Rockingham was stirred to action by Newcastle's fall, and he inherited the mantle of leadership of the duke's faction. He was neither a statesman nor an ardent politician, and he depended greatly upon Burke and others. He returned to office in 1782, and lived just long enough to initiate peace negotiations.

SACKVILLE, George (1716–1785). Sackville enjoyed a distinguished military career until 1759, when his inaction at Minden led to a court-martial, dismissal from the service, and a declaration that he was unfit to serve in any military capacity. He assumed the name of Germain in 1770, and was colonial secretary 1775–1782.

SANDWICH. John Montagu, 4th Earl of Sandwich (1718–1792). Diplomat, naval administrator, secretary of state 1763, first lord of the admiralty 1771–1782. For turning against his fellow libertine Wilkes, he was popularly hailed as "Jemmy Twitcher."

SAVILE, Sir George (1726–1784). One of the most highly respected and active members of the House of Commons, Savile sat for Yorkshire throughout his career and was active in every reform movement.

SCOTT, James (1733–1814). Political writer and popular divine who wrote for Sandwich under various pseudonyms 1765–1771.

SHEBBEARE, John (1709–1788). Surgeon and political writer who was pilloried for libel in 1758, but continued to write as a government hack. His fame greatly exceeded his influence or merit.

SHELBURNE. William Petty, 2nd Earl of Shelburne (1737–1805). After disdaining Bute and deserting Grenville, Shelburne became a loyal supporter of Pitt. A man of great intellect and a notable patron of the arts and sciences, he failed to inspire faith among politicians, who labeled him the Jesuit of Berkeley Square. Home secretary under Rockingham, 1782, then first lord of the treasury, he was overthrown by the Fox-North coalition. Thought by some to have had a major part in the preparation of Junius' letters.

SHERIDAN, Thomas (1719–1788). Actor, elocutionist, and father of the famous Richard Brinsley Sheridan; apparently dabbled in politics just sufficiently to secure himself a pension.

SMOLLETT, Tobias George (1721–1771). Outstanding novelist and journalist—until he turned to politics; author of *Roderick Random* (1748) and *Humphrey Clinker* (1771).

TEMPLE. Richard Grenville, Earl Temple (1711–1779). George Grenville's brother, Pitt's brother-in-law, Temple supported Pitt as first lord of the admiralty, 1756, and lord privy seal 1757–1761. Squire Gawky to his contemporaries.

THURLOW, Edward (1731–1806). A brilliant lawyer who became solicitor-general in 1770, attorney-general 1771, lord chancellor 1778–1783, 1784–1792; his great abilities were marred by political inconstancy and coarse manners and speech.

WALES, Augusta, Princess of (d. 1772). Augusta of Saxe-Gotha married Frederick, Prince of Wales and son of George II in 1736. After the death of her husband in 1751, the princess favored the Earl of Bute and placed her hopes upon her son, the future George III. George was fiercely loyal to his mother and bitterly resented the common slander that Bute was her lover.

WALPOLE, Horace, 4th Earl of Orford (1717–1797). A younger son of Sir Robert Walpole, Horace enjoyed the fruits of his father's labors and only dabbled in politics. A significant author and scholar, his fame rests upon his memoirs and correspondence; both are major historical sources, but the memoirs were compiled to direct the course of future scholarship and may be intentionally misleading.

WARBURTON, William (1698–1779). Religious controversialist, chaplain to Frederick, Prince of Wales, bishop of Gloucester 1759.

WEBB, Philip Carteret (1700–1770). Antiquary and politician, treasury solicitor 1756–1765.

WEDDERBURN, Alexander, 1st Baron Loughborough (1733–1805). Scots lawyer who came to London in 1757 and became a close friend of Bute; solicitor-general 1771, attorney-general 1778, chief justice of Common Pleas 1780–1793, lord chancellor 1793–1801.

WHATELY, Thomas (d. 1772). Politician and pamphleteer, secretary to the treasury 1764–1765, under-secretary of state 1771–1772.

WHITEFOORD, Caleb (1734–1810). Political writer, secretary of the peace commission 1782; his interest in politics and propaganda, as reflected in his correspondence, was considerably greater than his actual contributions.

WILKES, John (1727–1797). Son of a London brewer, member of the Hellfire Club, M.P. for Aylesbury at the time of the *North Briton* affair. In 1774, Wilkes took his seat in the House of Commons for Middlesex and held it until 1790; he was Lord Mayor of London, 1774, and city chamberlain 1779–1797. Wilkes was, in spite of appearances, a sincere and moderate Radical, but, as he observed, never a Wilkite and never a crusader.

WILMOT, Sir John Eardley (1709–1792). Barrister, judge in King's Bench 1755, commissioner of the great seal 1756–1757, chief justice of Common Pleas 1766–1771.

YATES, Sir Joseph (1722–1770). Barrister, judge in King's Bench 1764, transferred to Common Pleas 1770.

YORKE, Charles (1722–1770). Younger son of the Earl of Hardwicke, solicitor-general 1756–1761, attorney-general 1762–1763, 1765–1767. In 1770, Yorke was finally named lord chancellor, but his death (rumored to be suicide) brought his career to an end just short of his father's hopes.

NOTES

INTRODUCTION

1. William Cobbett (ed.), *The Parliamentary History of England* (London, 1813), XVI, 892. Cited hereafter as *PH*.

2. Sir Lewis Namier, *England in the Age of the American Revolution* (2nd ed.; London, 1961), p. 51.

3. *The Letters of Horace Walpole*, ed. Mrs. Paget Toynbee (Oxford, 1903–18), VII, 335. Cited hereafter as *Letters* (Toynbee).

4. J. E. Pomfret, "Some Further Letters of William Strahan, Printer," *Pennsylvania Magazine of History and Biography*, LX (1936), 471.

5. Albert von Ruville, *William Pitt, Earl of Chatham* (London, 1907), III, 260.

6. E. Fitzmaurice (ed.), *Life of William, Earl of Shelburne* (London, 1876), III, 356–57, 363–64.

7. Tobias Smollett in *Briton*, No. 15, September, 1762.

8. Romney Sedgwick (ed.), *Letters from George III to Lord Bute 1756–1766* (London, 1939), p. 208.

9. Mrs. Elizabeth Montagu in W. J. Smith (ed.), *The Grenville Papers* (London, 1852), IV, 452. Cited hereafter as *Grenville Papers*.

10. Horace Walpole, *Memoirs of the Reign of King George the Second*, ed. Lord Holland (London, 1846), II, 331.

11. Horace Walpole, *Memoirs of the Reign of King George the Third*, ed. G. F. Russell Barker (London, 1894), II, 75. Cited hereafter as *Memoirs*.

12. Alexander Stephens, *Memoirs of John Horne Tooke* (London, 1813), I, 369–70.

13. Tobias Smollett, May 18, 1770: W. A. S. Hewins (ed.), *The Whitefoord Papers: being the Correspondence and other Manuscripts of . . . Caleb Whitefoord from 1739–1810* (Oxford, 1898), p. 149.

14. Walpole, *Letters* (Toynbee), IV, 447.

15. C. W. Everett (ed.), *The Letters of Junius* (London, 1927), p. 9. Hereafter cited as *Junius*.

16. Edmund Burke, *Thoughts on the Causes of the Present Discontents* (London, 1770), p. 2.

17. Thomas B. Macaulay, *Works* (London, 1873), V, 229. On the effect of this change see Laurence Hanson, *Government and the Press 1695–1763* (London, 1936), and Fredrick S. Siebert, *Freedom of the Press in England 1476–1776* (Urbana, 1952).

18. William Blackstone, *Commentaries on the Laws of England* (Chicago, 1873), Book IV, Ch. xi, pp. 150–59.

19. Rex *v.* Tutchin, 1704, in T. B. Howell (ed.), *A Complete Collection of State Trials* (London, 1816), XIV, 1128. Hereafter cited as *ST*.

20. *PH*, X, 1331–32. My italics.

21. *Works* (New York, 1902), XI, 156.

22. *PH*, XVI, 1166.

23. *Works* (Troy, 1903), X, 43, and VIII, 34–35. See also Edward A. Bloom, *Samuel Johnson in Grub Street* (Providence, 1957), Ch. vii.

24. *Present Discontents*, p. 3.

25. Commission on Freedom of the Press, *A Free and Responsible Press* (Chicago, 1947), p. 113.

26. Camden's concluding remarks in Entick *v.* Carrington in *ST*, XIX, 1024. For Mansfield see Rex *v.* the Dean of St. Asaph, *ibid.*, XXI, 1040.

27. *North Briton*, No. 1, June 5, 1762.

28. James Boswell, *Life of Johnson*, ed. G. B. Hill, rev. L. F. Powell (Oxford, 1934), II, 60. Cited hereafter as Boswell (Hill-Powell).

29. *Idler*, No. 30.

30. On the reading public see A. S. Collins, *Authorship in the Days of Johnson* (London, 1927), pp. 232–59, and James Lackington, *Memoirs* (London, 1794), p. 250. On the number and financial status of newspapers see A. Aspinall, "Statistical Accounts of the London Newspapers in the Eighteenth Century," *English Historical Review*, LXIII (1948), 208–28. The significance of the vested interest of the press was suggested by W. T. Laprade, "The Power of the English Press in the Eighteenth Century," *South Atlantic Quarterly*, XXVII (1928), 431.

31. Siebert, *Freedom of the Press*, Ch. xv. See also Edward Hughes, "English Stamp Duties, 1664–1764," *Eng. Hist. Rev.* Vol. LVI (1941).

32. Siebert, *Freedom of the Press*, p. 357.

33. Boswell (Hill-Powell), III, 19; Walpole, *Letters* (Toynbee), V, 154.

34. For example, Henry Sampson Woodfall's petition, *Journals of the House of Commons*, XXXIV, 492.

35. Public Records Office, H. O. 42/32.

36. Charles Welsh, *A Bookseller of the Last Century* (London, 1885), pp. 19, 41–44, 336.

37. R. A. Austen-Leigh, "William Strahan and His Ledgers," *Transactions of the Bibliographical Society*, 2nd ser., III (1922–23), 268–76.

38. Arthur Aspinall, *Politics and the Press* (London, 1949), pp. v, 66.

39. See the testimony in Rex *v.* Almon in *ST*, XX, 829–31.

40. See P. C. Webb, *Copies . . . of Warrants Issued by Secretaries of State, for Seizing Persons Suspected . . . . of being the Authors, Printers and Publishers of Libels* (London, 1763), p. 75, and the "First Report of the Commissioners Appointed . . . to Enquire into the Fees, Gratuities, Perquisites, and Emoluments . . . received in the Several Public Offices therein mentioned. Secretaries of State," *Parliamentary Papers. Reports*, X, No. 103 (London, 1793), 3.

41. *Parliamentary Papers. Reports*, X, No. 103, 5–7.

42. F. G. Stephens (ed.), *Catalogue of Prints and Drawings in the British Museum. Division I: Political and Personal Satires* (London, 1870——), Vol. IV; and M. Dorothy George, *English Political Caricature to 1792* (Oxford, 1959).

43. *Auditor*, No. 12, September, 1762.

44. *Critical Review*, XIX (March, 1765), 231.

45. *Ibid.*, XVI (July, 1763), 70–71.

CHAPTER I

1. Namier, *England*, p. 84. See also Romney Sedgwick (ed.), *Letters from George III to Lord Bute, 1756–1766* (London, 1939).

2. The most complete account of these negotiations is provided by Namier, *England*, pp. 120 ff.

3. H. P. Wyndham (ed.), *The Diary of the Late George Bubb Dodington* (Salisbury, 1784), p. 434.

4. See Namier, *England*, pp. 171 ff., and *The Structure of Politics at the Accession of George III* (2nd ed.; London, 1957), pp. 196 ff.

5. Namier, *Structure of Politics*, p. 229. For records of payment, see the "Secret Service Accounts of the Duke of Newcastle," pp. 427 ff.

6. Edward Porritt, "The Government and the Newspaper Press in England," *Political Science Quarterly*, XII (1897), 668–69.

7. Walpole, *Memoirs*, I, 75.

8. John Almon, *A Letter to the Right Honourable Charles Jenkinson* (London, 1781), p. 6.

9. H. R. Fox Bourne, *English Newspapers* (London, 1887), I, 196–97; Stanley Morison, *The English Newspaper* (Cambridge, 1932), p. 151.

10. Israel Mauduit, *Considerations on the German War* (London, 1760), p. 90.

11. Dodington, *Diary*, pp. 419, 427.

12. J. A. Lovat-Fraser, *John Stuart, Earl of Bute* (Cambridge, 1912), p. 30.

13. Von Ruville, *Pitt*, III, 15, denies Bute's responsibility and blames Fox for the attack upon Pitt; he overstates the case, to say the least.

14. Albert Hartshorne (ed.), *Memoirs of a Royal Chaplain, 1729–1763* (London, 1915), p. 334.

15. W. S. Lewis (ed.), *The Yale Edition of Horace Walpole's Correspondence* (New Haven, 1937——), IX, 330. Cited hereafter as *Corr*. (Yale).

16. *Critical Rev.*, XVI (1763), 280.

17. Walpole, *Memoirs*, I, 25; IV, 93. Walpole, *Letters* (Toynbee), V, 7. D. C. Tovey (ed.), *The Letters of Thomas Gray* (London, 1904), II, 204. For variant views on Hardwicke's inspiration see Basil Williams, *The Life of William Pitt, Earl of Chatham* (London, 1913), II, 66–67, and Brian Tunstall, *William Pitt, Earl of Chatham* (London, 1938), pp. 282, 516.

18. J. Wright (ed.), *Sir Henry Cavendish's Debates* (London, 1841–43), I, 574 n.

19. *Ibid*.

20. J. Russell (ed.), *Correspondence of John, Fourth Duke of Bedford* (London, 1843), II, 426. Cited hereafter as *Bedford Corr*.

21. John Almon, *The History of the Late Minority* (London, 1765), p. 13; Walpole, *Memoirs*, I, 25.

22. Edmund Burke, *Present Discontents*, p. 12.

23. Williams, *Pitt*, II, 82–83, which see also for a summary of pamphlet material on this subject.

24. *Grenville Papers*, I, 363.

25. Lloyd Sanders, *Patron and Place-hunter* (London, 1919), pp. 261–62; W. S. Taylor and J. H. Pringle (eds.), *Correspondence of William Pitt, Earl of Chatham* (London, 1840), II, 148 n. 1. Cited hereafter as *Chatham Corr*.

26. On the summer's politics see Namier, *England*, pp. 283 ff., and D. A. Winstanley, *Personal and Party Government* (Cambridge, 1910), pp. 43 ff.

27. Tunstall, *Pitt*, p. 308; P. C. Yorke (ed.), *The Life and Correspondence of Philip Yorke, Earl of Hardwicke* (Cambridge, 1913), III, 330; G. F. S. Elliot, *The Border Elliots* (Edinburgh, 1897), p. 370.

28. Almon, *Late Minority*, pp. 35–36.

29. *Notes and Queries*, 1st ser., I (1850), 66.

30. Walpole, *Letters* (Toynbee), V, 132.

31. *Bedford Corr.*, III, 51.

32. John Almon, *Anecdotes of the Life of the Right Honourable William Pitt* (London, 1796), I, 371–72.

33. *Letters* (Toynbee), V, 132.

34. From *Owen's Weekly Chronicle*: *Grenville Papers*, I, 418.

35. *Bedford Corr.*, III, 52–53.

36. *Chatham Corr.*, II, 158–59.

37. George Harris, *The Life of Lord Chancellor Hardwicke* (London, 1847), III, 260; the Earl of Albemarle (ed.), *Memoirs of the Marquis of Rockingham* (London, 1852), I, 49–51. Cited hereafter as *Rockingham Memoirs*.

38. *Letters* (Toynbee), V, 132. See also Henry Fox's "Memoir on the events

attending ... the accession of George III," in Ilchester and Stavordale (eds.), *The Life and Letters of Lady Sarah Lennox* (London, 1901), I, 53–54.

39. *Rockingham Memoirs*, I, 49–51; Harris, *Hardwicke*, III, 266.

40. Yorke, *Hardwicke*, III, 334; *Rockingham Memoirs*, I, 49, 53; *Bedford Corr.*, III, 63.

41. *Addresses Presented from the Court of Common Council to the King* (London, 1778), pp. 23–24.

42. Bonamy Dobrée (ed.), *The Letters of Philip Dormer Stanhope, 4th Earl of Chesterfield* (London, 1932), VI, 2385.

43. Harris, *Hardwicke*, III, 266.

44. John Adolphus, *The History of England from the Accession to the Decease of King George the Third* (London, 1840), I, 121, 573.

45. *Letters* (Toynbee), V, 147.

46. Walpole, *Memoirs*, I, 96–97. For a general survey of the pamphlet literature see *Gentleman's Magazine*, XXXI (1761), 460–69, 513–21, 579–83; *Annual Register*, IV (1761), 42–48; *Critical Review*, XII (1761), 304 ff., 394 ff., 476 ff.

47. Almon, *Letter to Charles Jenkinson*, pp. 5–6; N. S. Jucker (ed.), *The Jenkinson Papers* (London, 1949), pp. xii, 14–16.

48. *B. M. Cat. of Prints*, III, 2; Walpole, *Memoirs*, I, 13–14; Walpole, *Corr.* (Yale), IX, 320.

49. John Almon, *The Correspondence of the Late John Wilkes* (London, 1805), I, xi; *Memoirs of John Almon* (London, 1790), pp. 14–15; Robert L. Haig, *The Gazetteer 1735–1797* (Carbondale, 1960), pp. 50–51.

50. *Annual Reg.* IV (1761), 45.

51. Namier, *England*, pp. 302 ff.; Winstanley, *Personal and Party Government*, pp. 94 ff.

52. Collins, *Authorship*, p. 200.

53. Boswell (Hill-Powell), I, 372–75; G. B. Hill (ed.), *Letters of Samuel Johnson* (New York, 1892), I, 92–93. See also Joseph Wood Krutch, *Samuel Johnson* (New York, 1945), pp. 190–93; John Forster, *Oliver Goldsmith* (London, 1848), II, 387.

54. For a similar but clearer case see Robert R. Rea, "Some Notes on Edward Gibbon's *Memoire Justificatif*," *Studies in Bibliography*, Vol. V (1952).

55. British Museum Additional MSS 38305, fol. 19; *Jenkinson Papers*, pp. 203–4, 390–91; Boswell (Hill-Powell), I, 380, 520.

56. Almon, *Letter to Charles Jenkinson*, p. 8.

57. *Jenkinson Papers*, pp. xii–xiii, 69–70, 144, 246–47.

58. *Ibid.*, pp. 63, 67, 76.

59. *B. M. Cat. of Prints*, IV, 52–53.

60. Ilchester, *Henry Fox* (New York, 1920), II, 154.

61. *Critical Rev.*, XIV (1762), 316.

62. *Letters* (Toynbee), V, 213, 253.

63. *B. M. Cat. of Prints*, IV, xxxviii, lix, lxxiv.

64. *Letters* (Toynbee), V, 268.

65. John Nichols, *Illustrations of the Literary History of the Eighteenth Century* (London, 1817–18), VIII, 280.

66. *Whitefoord Papers*, 148–49.

67. Henry Fox's "Memoir," in Ilchester and Stavordale, *Lady Sarah Lennox*, I, 71, 76.

68. J. S. Corbett, *England in the Seven Years' War* (London, 1907), II, 353, 363; *Grenville Papers*, I, 468.

69. Boswell (Hill-Powell), I, 425.

70. *Whitefoard Papers,* p. 143; see also Fox's "Memoir," in Ilchester and Stavordale, *Lady Sarah Lennox,* I, 68; Walpole, *Letters* (Toynbee), V, 213.
71. Keith G. Feiling, *The Second Tory Party, 1714–1832* (London, 1938), p. 72.
72. B.M. Add. MSS 32939.
73. *Memoirs of John Almon,* p. 15.
74. Haig, *Gazetteer,* pp. 54–55.
75 Fox's "Memoir," Ilchester and Stavodale, *Lady Sarah Lennox* I, 77; *Bedford Corr.,* III, 154.
76. Walpole, *Memoirs,* I, 175; Almon, *Anecdotes of William Pitt,* I, 347.

CHAPTER II

1. *Grenville Papers,* III, xxxvii.
2. *ST,* XIX, 1033.
3. D. M. Low (ed.), *Gibbon's Journal* (London, 1929), pp. 145–46.
4. *Wilkes Corr.,* I, 59; *Political Register,* II (1768), 413.
5. *Wilkes Corr.,* I, xi; III, 168.
6. George Nobbe, *The North Briton* (New York, 1939), pp. 31, 44.
7. L. M. Knapp, "Smollett and the Elder Pitt," *Modern Language Notes,* LIX (1944), 250–57; Arnold Whitridge, *Tobias Smollett* (Brooklyn, 1925), p. 60.
8. E. S. Noyes, "Another Smollett Letter," *MLN,* XLII (1927), 232.
9. L. M. Knapp, *Tobias Smollet* (Princeton, 1949), p. 245; Whitridge, *Smollett,* p. 60.
10. According to William Knox, who may have heard something of it from Wedderburn himself. H.M.C. *Various,* VI, 267–68. E. S. Noyes suggests that John Home, Bute's secretary, "persuaded Smollett to conduct the *Briton,*" but has no proof to offer. *The Letters of Tobias Smollett, M. D.* (Cambridge, Mass., 1926), p. 204.
11. Whitridge, *Smollett,* p. 70. Wilkes noted it in *North Briton,* Nos. 1 and 3.
12. Whitridge, *Smollett,* p. 63.
13. John Almon, *A Review of Lord Bute's Administration* (London, 1763), p. 55.
14. See *North Briton,* No. 1.
15. John Almon, *Biographical, Literary, and Political Anecdotes* (London, 1797), II, 10.
16. Nobbe, *North Briton,* p. 102.
17. *Auditor,* No. 2.
18. See *Gentleman's Mag.,* Vol. XXXII (1762), *passim.*
19. Noyes (ed.), *Letters of Tobias Smollett,* p. 73; Whitridge, *Smollett,* Appendix. See also *Wilkes Corr.,* I, 46–50.
20. See Wallace Cable Brown, *Charles Churchill* (Lawrence, 1953), pp. 89 ff., and Edward H. Weatherly (ed.), *The Correspondence of John Wilkes and Charles Churchill* (New York, 1954).
21. Nobbe, *North Briton,* pp. 94–96; J. M. Beatty, "An Essay in Critical Biography—Charles Churchill," *PMLA,* XXXV (1920), 238 ff.
22. *Grenville Papers,* I, 546–58.
23. *Grenville Papers,* I, 459–60; Nobbe, *North Briton,* p. 44.
24. Weatherly, *Corr. of Wilkes and Churchill,* p. 3; *Grenville Papers,* I, 460–61.
25. *Auditor,* No. 10.
26. J. Redington and R. A. Roberts (eds.), *Calendar of Home Office Papers of the Reign of George III* (London, 1878–99), I, 195. Cited hereafter as *Cal. H. O. Papers.*
27. Walpole, *Memoirs,* I, 141.
28. *ST,* XIX, 1161–62; Nobbe, *North Briton,* pp. 66–67.

29. Nobbe, *North Briton*, pp. 76–83.

30. *North Briton*, No. 15, September 11, 1762.

31. *Works* (London, 1797), VIII, 1; Noyes, "Another Smollett Letter," *MLN*, XLII (1927), 232; Noyes, *Smollett Letters*, pp. 78–79.

32. H.M.C., *Various*, VI, 267–68; Nobbe, *North Briton*, pp. 160–68.

33. See *Monitor*, October 9, 16, 22 (Wilson & Fell), and October 23 (Scott).

34. H.M.C., *10th Report*, Part I, p. 346; *Late Minority*, pp. 59–60.

35. *Cal. H. O. Papers*, I, 201, 204, 248.

36. *Grenville Papers*, II, 3.

37. This was Wilkes's story in 1769: *A Letter to the Rt. Hon. George Grenville*.

38. *Cal. H. O. Papers*, I, 203, 205, 248.

39. Weatherly, *Corr. of Wilkes and Churchill*, pp. 34–35.

40. *North Briton*, No. 26.

41. Weatherly, *Corr. of Wilkes and Churchill*, p. 35.

42. Nobbe, *North Briton*, pp. 136–37.

43. *North Briton*, No. 27.

44. *Chatham Corr.*, II, 193.

45. MS note by Wilkes in his copy of the *Late Minority*, quoted by Nobbe, *North Briton*, p. 47. Horace Bleackley suggested that Wilkes's anti-Scottisms antagonized Pitt: *John Wilkes* (London, 1917), p. 76.

46. H.M.C., *13th Report*, Part VII, p. 131.

47. Rose Mary Davis, *The Good Lord Lyttelton* (Bethlehem, 1939), p. 277.

48. Yorke, *Hardwicke*, III, 400–401.

49. *Rockingham Memoirs*, I, 113–14.

50. Yorke, *Hardwicke*, III, 426.

51. Harris, *Hardwicke*, III, 312.

52. H.M.C. *12th Report*, Part V (Rutland MSS, II), p. 278.

53. Henry Ellis, *Original Letters* (London, 1827), 2nd ser., IV, 452–53.

54. *Bedford Corr.*, III, 168.

55. Yorke, *Hardwicke*, III, 379.

56. *North Briton*, No. 30.

57. Ellis, *Original Letters*, 2nd ser., IV, 454.

58. Smollett, *Works*, VIII, 1. According to Walpole, *Memoirs*, I, 197, the *Auditor* was stopped at Fox's command.

59. Sedgwick, *Letters*, p. 167.

60. On the political scene in January–March, 1763, see Winstanley, *Personal and Party Government*, pp. 144–53.

61. Walpole, *Corr.* (Yale), XXII, 116; *Memoirs*, I, 190.

62. Sedgwick, *Letters*, p. 190.

63. B.M. Add. MSS. 35353, fol. 312.

64. Yorke, *Hardwicke*, III, 367.

65. Namier, *England*, pp. 380–81.

66. Winstanley, *Personal and Party Government*, pp. 144–45.

67. Nobbe read the opposite meaning into Hardwicke's letter of April 18, 1763, but it is impossible to agree with him.

68. Yorke, *Hardwicke*, III, 445.

69. Walpole, *Corr.* (Yale), X, 52.

70. *Gentleman's Mag.*, XXXIII (1763), 200; *Annual Reg.*, VI (1763), 71.

71. MS note by Wilkes in his *Late Minority*, quoted by Nobbe, *North Briton*, pp. 191–92.

72. Walpole, *Corr.* (Yale), X, 58.

73. *North Briton*, No. 44.
74. Walpole, *Corr.* (Yale), X, 60.
75. Mure, *Caldwell Papers*, Part II, I, 176.
76. *Wilkes Corr.*, I, 94–95; but see also Nobbe, *North Briton*, p. 208.
77. *North Briton*, No. 45.
78. Walpole, *Memoirs*, I, 217.
79. Walpole, *Letters* (Toynbee), V, 315.

CHAPTER III

1. H.M.C., *13th Report*, Part III (Fortescue MSS I), p. 144; Nichols, *Literary History*, VII, 283.
2. *Jenkinson Papers*, pp. 146–47.
3. H.M.C., *10th Report*, Part I, p. 355.
4. For the warrant see Almon, *Late Minority*, p. 141; *An Authentick Account of the Proceedings Against John Wilkes, Esq.* (London, n.d.), pp. 6–7; *A Complete Collection of the Genuine Papers* (Berlin, 1769), pp. 18 ff.
5. See Fitzmaurice, *Shelburne*, I, 274.
6. B.M. Add. MSS 35353, fol. 316; Yorke, *Hardwicke*, III, 481, 489.
7. Nobbe, *North Briton*, p. 214, but see also R. W. Postgate, *That Devil Wilkes* (London, 1930), p. 53.
8. Yorke, *Hardwicke*, III, 481; Almon, *Late Minority*, pp. 140–46; Sedgwick, *Letters*, pp. 232–33; Nobbe, *North Briton*, pp. 214–17. See C. H. Timperley, *A Dictionary of Printers and Printing* (London, 1839), p. 710, for a partial list of those arrested on April 29.
9. Almon, *Memoirs*, pp. 15–16; *Wilkes Corr.*, I, 101–2; Almon, *Late Minority*, p. 150. Wilkes's account is to be found in his second "Letter to the Duke of Grafton," *Wilkes Corr.*, III, 197–200.
10. See *An Authentick Account*, pp. 8–10; Sedgwick, *Letters*, pp. 232–33; *Wilkes Corr.*, III, 201–9; Nobbe, *North Briton*, pp. 219–20.
11. Yorke, *Hardwicke*, III, 489, and Basil Williams, "The Eclipse of the Yorkes," *Transactions of the Royal Historical Society*, 3rd ser., II (1908), 135–36.
12. B.M. Add. MSS 35353, fol. 316.
13. Yorke, *Hardwicke*, III, 490.
14. *Ibid.*, pp. 487–91.
15. Sedgwick, *Letters*, pp. 232–34.
16. H.M.C., *10th Report*, Part I, pp. 355–56.
17. *Cal. H. O. Papers*, I, 277–79.
18. Winstanley, *Personal and Party Government*, p. 161; see also Harris, *Hardwicke*, III, 347.
19. Yorke, *Hardwicke*, III, 492–93.
20. *ST*, XIX, 985–87.
21. Yorke, *Hardwicke*, III, 493.
22. W. R. Anson, *Autobiography of the Duke of Grafton* (London, 1898), pp. 190–92; *Grenville Papers*, II, 54.
23. *ST*, XIX, 987–90.
24. Yorke, *Hardwicke*, III, 494; *Wilkes Corr.*, I, 116–24.
25. *Wilkes Corr.*, I, 124–29; *Cal. H. O. Papers*, I, 280–81.
26. R. R. Moore, *Hogarth's Literary Relationships* (Minneapolis, 1948), p. 11.
27. *Cal. H. O. Papers*, I, 282; Nobbe, *North Briton*, pp. 233–34.
28. Yorke, *Hardwicke*, III, 495–97.
29. Tunstall, *Pitt*, p. 335; Williams, *Pitt*, II, 158.
30. Fitzmaurice, *Shelburne*, I, 254–55.

31. Yorke, *Hardwicke,* III, 497–99.

32. *Ibid.,* p. 499.

33. *Ibid.,* pp. 506–8; Harris, *Hardwicke,* III, 362–63.

34. Yorke, *Hardwicke,* III, 500–503.

35. *Ibid.,* pp. 498, 502–4; Sedgwick, *Letters,* p. 235.

36. *Grenville Papers,* II, 83–84; Yorke, *Hardwicke,* III, 512–15.

37. Yorke, *Hardwicke,* III, 516–19.

38. *Ibid.,* pp. 519–21.

39. *Grenville Papers,* II, 193–202; Yorke, *Hardwicke,* III, 523–28.

40. Yorke, *Hardwicke,* III, 521–24.

41. *Ibid.,* p. 529; Winstanley, *Personal and Party Government,* pp. 184–86.

42. Yorke, *Hardwicke,* III, 530–33; Winstanley, *Personal and Party Government,* p. 186.

43. Yorke, *Hardwicke,* III, 533–35; *Chatham Corr.,* II, 260–62.

44. *Chatham Corr.,* II, 263–64; Yorke, *Hardwicke,* III, 535–36.

45. Yorke, *Hardwicke,* III, 536–37.

46. *Ibid.,* pp. 539–44; *Grenville Papers,* II, 149.

47. Yorke, *Hardwicke,* III, 545–48.

48. *Ibid.,* pp. 548–53; *Grenville Papers,* II, 218–19.

CHAPTER IV

1. Almon, *Late Minority,* pp. 184–88; *Biographical Anecdotes,* II, 27; *Wilkes Corr.,* I, 131–32; *Grenville Papers,* II, 57; *Annual Reg.,* VII (1764), 18–19.

2. *Grenville Papers,* II, 60–62.

3. On these cases see *Gentleman's Mag.,* XXXIII (1763), 359; *London Mag.* XXXII (1763), 390; *Annual Reg.,* VI (1763), 88. *Chatham Corr.,* II, 230–35; *Grenville Papers,* II, 70–73; Yorke, *Hardwicke,* III, 509–10; Harris, *Hardwicke,* III, 364–68.

4. Yorke, *Hardwicke,* III, 510–11; *Jenkinson Papers,* pp. 167–68. See also the trenchant remarks of the printer William Strahan, in J. E. Pomfret, "Some Further Letters of William Strahan," *Penn. Mag. of Hist. and Biog.,* LX (1936), 469.

5. *Grenville Papers,* II, 78–79; D. C. Tovey (ed.), *The Letters of Thomas Gray* (London, 1904), III, 18.

6. *Gentleman's Mag.,* XXXIII (1763), 564; *London Mag.,* XXXII (1763), 671, and XXXIII (1764), 377; *Royal Mag.,* X (1764), 332; *Annual Reg.* VI (1763), 88, and VII (1764), 81.

7. *Annual Reg.,* VI (1763), 115; *London Mag.,* XXXII (1763), 673; H.M.C. *10th Report,* Part I, p. 361.

8. *Rockingham Memoirs,* I, 246–48.

9. *ST,* XIX, 1003–28; W. S. Holdsworth, *A History of English Law* (Boston, 1938), X, 667–72; M. A. Thomson, *The Secretaries of State 1681–1782* (Oxford, 1932), pp. 123–24; *Grenville Papers,* III, 50.

10. *Annual Reg.,* VI (1763), 82, 98, and VII (1764), 73–74; *Gentleman's Mag.,* XXXIII (1763), 312, 462; *London Mag.,* XXXII (1763), 333, and XXXIII (1764), 158; *Royal Mag.,* X (1764), 162.

11. *Annual Reg.,* VII (1764), 73–74; *London Mag.,* XXXIII (1764), 266, 269; *Gentleman's Mag.,* XXXIV (1764), 246, 248. The final hearing in this case apparently occurred between May 23 and May 26.

12. *London Mag.,* XXXIII (1764), 277.

13. *Ibid.,* p. 326; *Gentleman's Mag.,* XXXIV (1764), 301; *Annual Reg.,* VII (1764), 81; *Royal Mag.,* X (1764), 331.

14. *London Mag.,* XXXIII (1764), 378; *Gentleman's Mag.,* XXXIV (1764), 347; *Royal Mag.,* XI (1764), 54; *Annual Reg.,* VII (1764), 87; *ST,* XIX, 1030–36.

15. *London Mag.*, XXXIII (1764), 654–55; *Gentleman's Mag.*, XXXIV (1764), 600–601; *Annual Reg.*, VII (1764), 112–13 and VIII (1765), 64; *Royal Mag.*, XI (1764), 329.

16. Holdsworth, *History of English Law*, X, 672.

17. *ST*, XIX, 1030–74; *Annual Reg.*, VIII (1765), 88, 101, 146.

18. *Annual Reg.*, XII (1769), 150–51.

19. Weatherly, *Wilkes-Churchill Corr.*, p. 63.

20. *Grenville Papers*, II, 137.

21. *ST*, XIX, 1153–68.

22. *Grenville Papers*, II, 239.

23. Holdsworth, *History of English Law*, X, 670. See also Siebert, *Freedom of the Press*, pp. 374–80.

CHAPTER V

1. Walpole, *Memoirs*, I, 272.

2. Almon, *Late Minority*, p. 204; *Biographical Anecdotes*, II, 30; *Wilkes Corr.*, I, 139.

3. *A Letter ... On the Seizure of Papers* (London, 1763), pp. 27–28. On the authorship see *Grenville Papers*, II, 53; Almon, *Biographical Anecdotes*, II, 37; III, i, 177 ff.

4. *Grenville Papers*, II, 57, 60, 74–75.

5. Charles W. Dilke, "Wilkes and the 'Essay on Woman,' " *Notes and Queries*, 2nd ser., IV (1857), 1–2, 41–43. The British Museum copy, P.C. 31, k7, gives evidence of being authentic except for the title page.

6. *Grenville Papers*, II, 190–91.

7. The story is best told by Postgate, *That Devil Wilkes*, pp. 71–84, and much admittedly remains unknown.

8. *Chatham Corr.*, II, 253; A. W. Evans, *Warburton and the Warburtonians* (London, 1932), p. 241; *Grenville Papers*, II, 154–55.

9. *Grenville Papers*, II, 135, 151–52; Lord North, "Lord North, the Prime Minister: A Personal Memoir," *North American Review*, CLXXVI (1903), 783; R. J. Lucas, *Lord North* (London, 1913), I, 32.

10. *Caldwell Papers*, Part II, I, 197, 199.

11. *Journals of the House of Commons*, XXIX, 668 (cited hereafter as *JHC*); *PH*, XV, 1356–61; Sir John Fortescue, *The Correspondence of King George the Third* (London, 1927), I, 53–57; Walpole, *Letters* (Toynbee), V, 385–86; *Caldwell Papers*, Part II, I, 200–203; Yorke, *Hardwicke*, III, 556.

12. *Journals of the House of Lords*, XXX, 415–16, 420–22, 458–59 (cited hereafter as *JHL*); *PH*, XV, 1347, 1349–52; Fortescue, *Correspondence*, I, 50–51; Walpole, *Letters* (Toynbee), V, 387–88; Turberville, *House of Lords*, p. 317; Evans, *Warburton*, pp. 242–43.

13. R. Blunt (ed.), *Mrs. Montagu "Queen of the Blues"* (London, n.d.), I, 74; Almon, *Late Minority*, p. 208.

14. *Critical Rev.*, XVI (1763), 479; *Gentleman's Mag.*, XXXIV (1764), 44; *Annual Reg.*, VII (1764), 46.

15. *JHC*, XXIX, 674–78, 685, 689; *JHL*, XXX, 425, 432; *PH*, XV, 1361–64; Yorke, *Hardwicke*, III, 556; *Grenville Papers*, II, 228–29.

16. *Grenville Papers*, II, 230; *JHL*, XXX, 426–29; *PH*, XV, 1371–78; Harris, *Hardwicke*, III, 384–85; Almon, *Anecdotes of the Life of Pitt*, I, 488–90.

17. Dobrée, *Chesterfield Letters*, VI, 2558, 2563; Yorke, *Hardwicke*, III, 557–58; Walpole, *Letters* (Toynbee), V, 420.

18. *Grenville Papers,* II, 232, 237; R. R. Sharpe, *London and the Kingdom* (London, 1894–95), III, 76; *PH,* XV, 1382–85; *JHL,* XXX, 437–38; *JHC,* XXIX, 696, 698–99.

19. *Grenville Papers,* II, 234–35; Walpole, *Memoirs,* I, 219, 263.

20. *JHC,* XXXIX, 721–23; *PH,* XV, 1393; *Chatham Corr.,* II, 273–77; Blunt, *Mrs. Montagu,* I, 87–88; *Grenville Papers,* II, 484, 255.

21. Yorke, *Hardwicke,* III, 562; Walpole, *Letters* (Toynbee), V, 450–51; VI, 1–2.

22. *PH, XV,* 1394–1400; *JHC,* XXIX, 838–43; Walpole, *Letters* (Toynbee), VI, 3–6; *Grenville Papers,* II, 261–64, 490–91.

23. *Grenville Papers,* II, 491; Walpole, *Letters* (Toynbee), VI, 11; Yorke, *Hardwicke,* III, 563.

24. *JHC,* XXIX, 846; *PH,* XV, 1400–13; Almon, *Anecdotes of the Life of Pitt,* II, 15; Walpole, *Letters,* VI, 9–11; Yorke, *Hardwicke,* III, 563–64; Almon, *Late Minority,* pp. 272–83; Namier, *Structure of Politics,* pp. 150 ff.

25. Namier, *Structure,* p. 153.

26. Almon, *Anecdotes of Pitt,* II, 16.

27. *Grenville Papers,* II, 493.

28. *ST,* XIX, 1075–77; *Annual Reg.,* VII (1764), 50; *London Mag.,* XXXIII (1764), 108.

29. *Jenkinson Papers,* p. 193; *Cal. H. O. Papers,* I, 495.

30. On Kearsley's case see *Gentleman's Mag.,* XXXIV (1764), 348, 354, 399; XXXV (1765), 45. *Annual Reg.,* VII (1764), 87, 108, 113–14; VIII (1765), 59. *Royal Mag.,* XI (1764), 55, 327. *London Mag.,* XXXIII (1764), 378, 487, 544, 654; XXXIV (1765), 54, 109. Almon, *Late Minority,* p. 296; Timperley, *Dictionary,* p. 713; Plomer, *Dictionary,* p. 143–44.

31. On the case of Rex *v.* Williams see *London Mag.,* XXXIII (1764), 595; XXXIV (1765), 54, 109–10, 376. *Annual Reg.,* VII (1764), 87, 108; VIII (1765), 59, 65. *Gentleman's Mag.,* XXXIV (1764), 348, 554; XXXV (1765), 45, 96. *Royal Mag.,* XI (1764), 55. Almon, *Late Minority,* 296; *Biographical Anecdotes,* I, 236–37, *B.M. Cat. of Prints,* IV, 346–51. Earl of Malmesbury, *Letters of the First Earl of Malmesbury* (London, 1870), I, 121–23; Walpole, *Memoirs,* II, 57; *Letters* (Toynbee), VI, 191; John Wilmot, *Memoirs of the Life of the Rt. Hon. John Eardley Wilmot* (London, 1811), pp. 228–35. Timperley, *Dictionary,* p. 713; Plomer, *Dictionary,* pp. 264–65. *Grenville Papers,* II, 429–30; Stephens, *John Horne Tooke,* I, 58–67; M. C. Yarborough, *John Horne Tooke* (New York, 1926), pp. 22–24; and Robert R. Rea, "The *North Briton* and the Courts of Law," *Alabama Lawyer,* Vol. XII (1951).

CHAPTER VI

1. *Chatham Corr.,* II, 289; Yorke, *Hardwicke,* III, 565; *Grenville Papers,* II, 267, 296, 493.

2. Walpole, *Memoirs,* I, 303.

3. *Annual Reg.,* VIII (1765), 17.

4. Walpole, *Memoirs,* I, 303.

5. *Grenville Papers,* II, 504; *Chatham Corr.,* II, 296–97.

6. Walpole, *Memoirs,* I, 303.

7. *Annual Reg.,* VIII (1765), 17.

8. H.M.C., *4th Report,* p. 400.

9. Walpole, *Memoirs,* I, 303.

10. *Annual Reg.,* VIII (1765), 17–18.

11. L. S. Sutherland, "Edmund Burke and the First Rockingham Ministry," *Eng. Hist. Rev.,* XLVII (1932), 54.

12. *Addresses Presented from the Court of Common Council to the King* (London, [1778]), pp. 55–56.

13. H.M.C., *Stopford-Sackville MSS.*, I, 60–61.

14. H.M.C., *11th Report*, Part IV, pp. 398–99; Porritt, "Government and the Newspaper Press," *Pol. Sci. Qtly.*, XII (1897), 669.

15. Walpole, *Memoirs*, II, 2–3.

16. *Wilkes Corr.*, II, 54.

17. Almon, *Memoirs*, pp. 16–17.

18. In *A Letter to the Right Honourable the E[arl] T[emple]* (London, 1766).

19. *Grenville Papers*, II, 430–31.

20. *Ibid.*

21. B.M. Add. MSS. 30868, fols. 136–37.

22. *Grenville Papers*, II, 457–58.

23. B.M. Add. MSS. 30868, fols. 136–37.

24. Walpole, *Memoirs*, II, 3–5; *Grenville Papers*, II, 428.

25. *Grenville Papers*, II, 403–5.

26. *Rockingham Memoirs*, I, 177–81.

27. *Grenville Papers*, II, 428.

28. Walpole, *Memoirs*, II, 5–6.

29. *Jenkinson Papers*, pp. 308–12.

30. *Ibid.*

31. *Critical Rev.*, XIX (1765), 231.

32. Almon, *Biographical Anecdotes*, II, 147–48; G. H. Guttridge, *David Hartley, M.P.* (Berkeley, 1926), p. 243.

33. H.M.C., *10th Report*, Part I, p. 358; Porritt, "Government and the Newspaper Press," *Pol. Sci. Qtly.*, XII (1897), 669; *Grenville Papers*, II, 137.

34. *Gentleman's Mag.*, XXXIII (1763), 475–76, 516; *Grenville Papers*, II, 137; *An Appeal to the Public in behalf of George Johnstone, Esq.; Governor of West-Florida. In Answer to the North-Briton Extraordinary* (London, 1763).

35. H.M.C., *10th Report*, Part I, pp. 366, 372–73; *Cal. H. O. Papers*, I, 420, 432.

36. H.M.C., *10th Report*, Part I, pp. 372, 375; *Cal. H. O. Papers*, I, 463.

37. Laprade, "Stamp Act in British Politics," *Amer. Hist. Rev.*, XXXV (1930), 744 n. 2.

38. B.M. Add. MSS. 30868, fols. 136–37; *Enquiry into the Doctrine Lately Propagated, Concerning Libels, Warrants, and the Seizure of Papers* (London, 1764), p. 94.

39. *Gentleman's Mag.*, XXXIII (1763), 325–29.

40. Tovey, *Gray's Letters*, III, 36–37.

41. Nichols, *Literary Anecdotes*, IX, 725–27; *London Mag.*, XXXIV (1765), 327–32; Almon, *Biographical Anecdotes*, II, 347.

42. *Jenkinson Papers* pp. 144–46, 199, 211–12, 242–43.

43. *Grenville Papers*, II, 270–71; J. Shebbeare, *An Answer to the Queries, Contained in a letter to Dr. Shebbeare* (London, [1775]), p. 29; J. R. Foster, "Smollett's Pamphleteering Foe Shebbeare," *PMLA*, LVII (1942), 1090–92.

44. Walpole, *Memoirs*, I, 262; Parkes and Merivale, *Francis*, I, 87; *Annual Reg.*, VI (1763), 111; VIII (1765), 179; *Gentleman's Mag.*, XXXIII (1763), 563–64.

45. Walpole, *Memoirs*, II, 5.

46. *Grenville Papers*, II, 250–51, 254–55; Parkes and Merivale, *Francis*, I, 360–61; Walpole, *Memoirs*, II, 26; *Jenkinson Papers*, pp. 342–44.

47. Walpole, *Memoirs*, I, 304.

48. *JHL*, XXX, 476–77, 480–83; *JHC*, XXIX, 874–75; *PH*, XV, 1418–20; Walpole,

Letters (Toynbee), VI, 21; Walpole, *Memoirs,* I, 304–6; *London Mag.,* XXXIII (1764), 157; *Gentleman's Mag.,* XXXIV 1764), 96.

49. Almon, *Biographical Anecdotes,* I, 45.

50. Pomfret, "Further Letters of William Strahan," *Penn. Mag. of Hist. and Biog.,* LX (1936), 469.

51. *Caldwell Papers,* Part II, I, 196–98.

52. H.M.C., *Lothian MSS,* p. 250.

53. *Critical Rev.,* XVII (1764), 391.

CHAPTER VII

1. P. C. Webb, *Copies Taken from the Records . . . of Warrants Issued by Secretaries of State, for Seizing Persons Suspected of Being . . . the Authors, Printers and Publishers of Libels* (London, 1763); Boswell (Hill-Powell), II, 73.

2. *Grenville Papers,* II, 426–28.

3. J. H. Jesse, *Memoirs of George Selwyn* (Boston, 1902), I, 293; Almon, *Biographical Anecdotes,* I, 78–80; Walpole, *Letters* (Toynbee), VI, 111; *Wilkes Corr.,* II, 88; Walpole, *Memoirs,* II, 6–7.

4. Jesse, *Selwyn,* I, 303.

5. Almon, *Biographical Anecdotes,* I, 78–80.

6. See *A Postscript to the Letter on Libels . . . in Answer to a Postscript in the Defence of the Majority* (2nd ed.; London, 1765), and the 2nd ed. of Lloyd's pamphlet, to which is added *A Postscript in Answer to . . . the Reply to the Defence of the Majority* (London, 1765).

7. D. E., "The Candor Pamphlets," *Notes and Queries,* 2nd ser., V (1858), 121; Parkes and Merivale, *Francis,* I, 74.

8. Parkes and Merivale, *Francis,* I, 81; William James Smith, "The Candor Pamphlets, and the Authorship of 'Junius,' " *Notes and Queries,* 2nd ser., V (1858), 240.

9. *Grenville Papers,* II, 459.

10. D. E., "The Candor Pamphlets," *Notes and Queries,* 2nd ser., V (1858), 122; Parkes and Merivale, *Francis,* I, 86.

11. Almon, *Memoirs,* p. 21; *Grenville Papers,* II, 65; III, 46 n. 1; *Wilkes Corr.,* II, 95 n.

12. Walpole, *Letters* (Toynbee), VI, 154–55 (see also Walpole, *Memoirs,* II, 26–27, wherein Walpole calls it "perhaps the ablest [pamphlet] ever written"); *Gray's Letters,* III, 56–57; *Wilkes Corr.,* II, 94–95.

13. Almon, *Biographical Anecdotes,* I, 79.

14. Lloyd, *Defence of the Majority* (2nd ed.), pp. 48, 52–53.

15. Walpole, *Letters* (Toynbee), VI, 154–55; *Memoirs,* II, 26–27; *Wilkes Corr.,* I, 245 n.; II, 95 n.; Almon, *Biographical Anecdotes,* I, 80; D. E. "Candor Pamphlets," *Notes and Queries,* 2nd ser. V (1858), 161.

16. *Gentleman's Mag.,* XXXV (1765), 45; Almon, *Memoirs,* p. 23.

17. Almon, *Memoirs,* p. 23; Walpole, *Memoirs,* II, 48; *Annual Reg.,* VIII (1765), 177–79.

18. *JHC,* XXX, 70; *PH,* XVI, 6–15; *Annual Reg.,* VIII (1765), 26–32; H.M.C. *10th Report,* Part I, pp. 381–82; Winstanley, *Personal and Party Government,* pp. 214–16.

19. *PH,* XVI, 40–45; Walpole, *Memoirs,* II, 60; *Grenville Corr.,* III, 8–11.

20. See Winstanley, *Personal and Party Government,* pp. 220–41; G. M. Imlach, "Earl Temple and the Ministry of 1765," *Eng. Hist. Rev.,* Vol. XXX (1915); and B.M. Add. MSS 30868.

21. Almon, *Memoirs,* p. 32; B.M. Add. MSS 30868; *Grenville Papers,* III, 49.

22. *Gentleman's Mag.*, XXXV (1765), 243, 282; *London Mag.*, XXXIV (1765), 261; Almon, *Memoirs*, pp. 24 ff.

23. Almon, *Memoirs*, pp. 26 ff.; *Grenville Papers*, III, 46–49, 51–52.

24. *Grenville Papers*, II, 65–68; Almon, *Memoirs*, p. 31.

25. Almon, *Biographical Anecdotes*, I, 79, 258; Almon, *Memoirs*, p. 31; Harris, *Hardwicke*, III, 456.

26. Wilmot, *Memoirs*, pp. 243–71; *English Reports*, XCVII, 94–106; J. C. Fox, "The King v. Almon," *Law Quarterly Review*, XXIV (1908), 185–89, 277–78; A. E. Hughes, "Contempt of Court and the Press," *ibid.*, XVI (1900), 296.

27. *JHC*, XXX, 753–54, 772; *PH*, XVI, 208–9; *Bedford Corr.*, III, 333–34; *Rockingham Memoirs*, I, 325–29; H.M.C., *Stopford Sackville MSS.*, I, 110.

28. *JHC*, XXX, 780; *JHL*, XXXI, 401, 405, 410; *PH*, XVI, 209–10.

29. Burke, *A Short Account of a Late Short Administration*.

30. *Wilkes Corr.*, II, 199 ff.; Almon, *Pitt Anecdotes*, II, 68–75; Treloar, *Wilkes*, pp. 43–46; Postgate, *Wilkes*, pp. 110–14.

CHAPTER VIII

1. Almon, *Biographical Anecdotes*, I, 92–94; *Rockingham Memoirs*, I, 309.

2. *Annual Reg.* VIII (1765), 45.

3. Dobrée, *Chesterfield Letters*, VI, 2662–63; *Bedford Corr.*, III, 317.

4. *Grenville Papers*, III, 110; Walpole, *Memoirs*, II, 191; Fortescue, *Correspondence*, I, 225, 228.

5. B.M. Add. MSS 30869; *Wilkes Corr.*, II, 229–31.

6. *Grenville Papers*, III, 244–52.

7. *Ibid.*, pp. 247, 251–52, 316.

8. *Chatham Corr.*, II, 345.

9. *Grenville Papers*, III, 267; B.M. Add. MSS 30869.

10. *Chatham Corr.*, III, 21.

11. *Rockingham Memoirs*, II, 3; Mary Bateson (ed.), *A Narrative of the Changes in the Ministry 1765–1767* (London, 1898), p. 86.

12. Walpole, *Memoirs*, II, 254; Sutherland, "Burke and the First Rockingham Ministry," *Eng. Hist. Rev.*, XLVII (1932), 59.

13. B.M. Add. MSS 30869, Dobrée, *Chesterfield Letters*, VI, 2740, E. F. D. Osborn (ed.), *Political and Social Letters of a Lady of the Eighteenth Century* (London [1890]), p. 248.

14. B.M. Add. MSS 30869.

15. Walpole, *Letters* (Toynbee), Supplement I, p. 136.

16. Bateson, *Narrative*, p. 98; *Grenville Papers*, III, 292–93, 306–7; Almon, *Pitt Anecdotes*, II, 84.

17. *Grenville Papers*, III, 307; Sedgwick, *Letters*, p. 256; Osborn, *Political and Social Letters*, pp. 146–48; Ellis, *Letters*, 3rd ser., IV, 387; Davis, *Good Lord Lyttelton*, pp. 356–57.

18. Dobrée, *Chesterfield Letters*, VI, 2755–56.

19. Almon, *Memoirs*, p. 34.

20. Walpole, *Letters* (Toynbee), Supplement I, p. 148.

21. *Jenkinson Papers*, p. 433.

22. *Chatham Corr.*, III, 218–19.

23. *Ibid.*, pp. 227, 248; B.M. Add. MSS 30869, fol. 106.

24. *Rockingham Memoirs*, II, 33–34.

25. Almon, *Biographical Anecdotes*, II, 108–11; *Grenville Papers*, IV, 70, 170; Walpole, *Memoirs*, III, 83.

26. Porritt, "Government and the Press," *Pol. Sci. Qtly.*, XII (1897), 667–68;

H.M.C. *Various,* VI (Knox MSS), 94; Forster, *Goldsmith,* p. 434; *Grenville Papers,* IV, 232–33.

27. Walpole, *Memoirs,* III, 83.

28. B.M. Add. MSS 30869, fols. 107, 110, 119.

29. *Ibid.,* fol. 157.

30. *Rockingham Memoirs,* II, 32; Cavendish, *Debates,* I, 581.

31. Anson, *Grafton,* p. 147.

32. See Winstanley, *Whig Opposition,* pp. 171–96; John Brooke, *The Chatham Administration 1766–1768* (London, 1956), pp. 162–217; B.M. Add. MSS 30869, fol. 151.

33. *Bedford Corr.,* III, 382–83.

34. B.M. Add. MSS 30869, fol. 151; Walpole, *Memoirs,* III, 83.

35. Earl Fitzwilliam and R. Bourke (eds.), *Correspondence of the Right Honourable Edmund Burke* (London, 1844), I, 147–48; *Rockingham Memoirs,* II, 54–56.

36. Fitzwilliam and Bourke (eds.), *Burke Corr.,* I, 147–48.

37. Cavendish, *Debates,* I, 584; *Rockingham Memoirs,* II, 57.

38. Winstanley, *Whig Opposition,* p. 192.

39. Almon, *Biographical Anecdotes,* II, 108–11; *Grenville Papers,* IV, 200–204, 240.

40. Almon, *Memoirs,* p. 47.

41. *Grenville Papers,* IV, 346–47. For a fuller discussion see Robert R. Rea, "The Impact of Party Journalism in the *Political Register,*" *Historian,* XVII (1954), 1–17.

42. *Grenville Papers,* IV, 312–13, 316–21, 344, 359, 363; H.M.C. *Various,* VI (Knox MSS), 95–101.

43. *Grenville Papers,* IV, 368–69.

44. S. Smiles, *Memoir and Correspondence of the Late John Murray* (London, 1891), I, 4–5.

45. *Grenville Papers,* IV, 390–91, 394–95.

46. *Ibid.,* pp. 390, 392.

47. Walpole, *Memoirs,* III, 222.

48. *Ibid.,* p. 182.

49. *Grenville Papers,* IV, 468–69.

50. *Ibid.,* p. 338.

CHAPTER IX

1. William Bollan, *The Freedom of Speech and Writing upon Public Affairs Considered* (London, 1766), p. 137.

2. *JHC,* XXIX, 109, 120, 123, 129.

3. *Ibid.,* pp. 206–7.

4. See Benjamin B. Hoover, *Samuel Johnson's Parliamentary Reporting* (Berkeley, 1953).

5. *JHL,* XXX, 508, 511; Walpole, *Letters* (Toynbee), VI, 33; Walpole, *Memoirs,* I, 311–12; Almon, *Biographical Anecdotes,* I, 403–4; *Wilkes Corr.,* V, 51–62.

6. Walpole, *Memoirs,* I, 311–12; *JHL,* XXX, 511; Almon, *Biographical Anecdotes,* I, 403–4.

7. Almon, *Biographical Anecdotes,* I, 405–6.

8. H.M.C., *Stopford-Sackville MSS.,* I, 61.

9. Almon, *Memoirs,* p. 118.

10. *JHL,* XXXI, 65.

11. *Ibid.,* pp. 212–15.

12. Walpole, *Memoirs,* I, 312.

13. *Bedford Corr.,* III, 319–20.

14. *JHL*, XXX, 839, 842–44.

15. *Ibid.*, XXXI, 463.

16. Francis Blackburne, *Memoirs of Thomas Hollis* (London, 1780), pp. 652–54.

17. B.M. Add. MSS 30869, fol. 106.

18. *JHC*, XXX, 427, 432; Charles Gray's Parliamentary Notebook, H.M.C. *14th Report*, Part IX, p. 316.

19. *JHC*, XXXI, 580, 584, 589, 596, 617; Haig, *Gazetteer*, pp. 76–77.

20. B. Dobrée, *The Letters of King George III* (London, 1935), pp. 53–54.

21. Cavendish, *Debates*, I, 4.

22. B.M. Add. MSS 30869.

23. *Chatham Corr.*, III, 242–43.

24. B.M. Add. MSS 30869, fol. 119.

25. *Ibid.*, fol. 123.

26. *Ibid.* On Wilkes's *History of England*, of which only an *Introduction* was published, see Robert R. Rea, "John Almon: Bookseller to John Wilkes," *Indiana Quarterly for Bookmen*, IV (1948), 20–28.

27. B.M. Add. MSS 30869, fol. 139. A different version of the story is given by Wilkes in the *Grenville Papers*, IV, 188–89; the original letter is published in *Wilkes Corr.*, III, 28 ff.

28. B.M. Add. MSS 30869, fol. 139.

29. B.M. Add. MSS 30869; *Grenville Papers*, IV, 188–89.

30. *ST*, XIX, 1077–1117.

31. Walpole, *Letters* (Toynbee), VII, 191–92.

32. *ST*, XIX, 1117–1124; Fortescue, *Correspondence*, II, 30.

33. J. Y. T. Greig (ed.), *The Letters of David Hume* (Oxford: The Clarendon Press, 1932), II, 182.

34. *Chatham Corr.*, III, 324 n.

35. *Genuine Papers*, pp. 228–32; *Political Reg.* III (1768), 36.

36. Anson, *Grafton*, pp. 210–11.

37. *Political Reg.* III (1768), 36–37; *Gentleman's Mag.*, XXXVIII (1768), 298 ff., 396, 539, 586; *London Mag.*, XXXVII (1768), 326, 441, 606–7, 700–701; *Annual Reg.*, XI (1768), 120–24, 156, 184, 188, 196; *The Extraordinary Case of William Bingley* (London, 1770).

38. Quoted in Winstanley, *Whig Opposition*, p. 225; Anson, *Grafton*, p. 199.

39. *Public Advertiser*, October 18, 1768; Fitzmaurice, *Shelburne*, II, 164–65; *Grenville Papers*, IV, 383; *Wilkes Corr.*, III, 293–95.

40. Cavendish, *Debates*, I, 617; Fortescue, *Correspondence*, II, 62; Harris, *Hardwicke*, III, 426; *JHL*, XXXII, 204–14.

41. *JHC*, XXXII, 108–9, 113, 117; Cavendish, *Debates*, I, 106–15; Harris, *Hardwicke*, III, 427–28.

42. Cavendish, *Debates*, I, 111.

43. *Ibid.*, pp. 68, 616; *JHL*, XXXII, 180–81, 186–87.

44. *JHC*, XXXII, 97, 99, 113, 116; Cavendish, *Debates*, I, 101–2.

45. *JHC*, XXXII, 129–30; *PH*, XVI, 533–38; Cavendish, *Debates*, I, 116–20; Fortescue, *Correspondence*, II, 61.

46. *PH*, XVI, 538–40; Cavendish, *Debates*, I, 127; *JHC*, XXXII, 157.

47. *JHC*, XXXII, 169–72; *PH*, XVI, 541–43.

48. Walpole, *Letters* (Toynbee), VIII, 251.

49. *JHC*, XXXII, 175–76; *PH*, XVI, 544; Cavendish, *Debates*, I, 140–47; Fortescue, *Correspondence*, II, 76–79.

50. Fortescue, *Correspondence*, II, 79.

51. *JHC*, XXXII, 178; *PH*, XVI, 545–74; Cavendish, *Debates*, I, 151–85; *Chatham Corr.*, III, 350; H.M.C. *2nd Report*, p. 29; H.M.C. *10th Report*, Part I, p. 412; Fortescue, *Correspondence*, II, 79.

52. *PH*, XVI, 575–88.

53. See for instance B.M. Add. MSS 30869, fol. 142.

54. *Wilkes Corr.*, IV, 6–7; *Grenville Papers*, IV, 450; Walpole, *Memoirs*, III, 220.

55. Cavendish, *Debates*, I, 372, 381–82; *JHC*, XXXII, 451.

56. Thomas W. Copeland (ed.), *The Correspondence of Edmund Burke* (Chicago, 1958——), II, 51–52, 78.

57. *Grenville Papers*, IV, 433; H.M.C. *Various*, VI, 103.

58. *Grenville Papers*, IV, 471–72; *The Speech of a Rt. Hon. Gentleman* (London, 1769), Advertisement.

59. *Grenville Papers*, IV, 475; H.M.C. *Various*, VI, 104–5.

60. *Grenville Papers*, IV, 479.

61. *Wilkes Corr.*, III, 300.

62. *London Mag.*, XXXVIII (1769), 51, 53, 95, 193; *Gentleman's Mag.*, XXXIX (1769), 51.

63. *A Petition of the Freeholders of the County of Middlesex* (May 24, 1769); *English Liberty* (London, 1769), II, 206–17.

64. *Extraordinary Case of William Bingley*, pp. 81–92; *Annual Reg.*, XII (1769), 69; *London Mag.*, XXXVIII (1769), 52; *Gentleman's Mag.*, XXXIX (1769), 53, 108, 161.

65. John Hope, *Letters* (London, 1772), pp. 42–43; *Extraordinary Case of William Bingley*, pp. 93–100.

66. *Annual Reg.*, XII (1769), 108, 153; *Gentleman's Mag.*, XXXIX (1769), 316; Timperley, *Dictionary*, pp. 723–24; *A Sketch of English Liberty!* (London, 1793?); *Extraordinary Case of William Bingley*, pp. 111–21.

67. B.M. Add. MSS 30870, fols. 186, 201, 215.

68. *Annual Reg.*, XII (1769), 105, 150; *Bedford Corr.*, III, 409–10; *Grenville Papers*, IV, 482.

69. Morison, *English Newspaper*, pp. 153–54; G. F. Barwick, "Some Magazines of the Eighteenth Century," *Transactions of the Bibliographical Society*, X (1908–9), 127.

70. H.M.C. *15th Report*, Part I (Dartmouth MSS, III), p. 191. For Wilkes's correspondence with the Boston patriots see B.M. Add. MSS 30870.

71. "Correspondence between William Strahan and David Hall, 1763–1777," *Penn. Mag. of Hist. and Biog.*, XI (1887), 233–34. See also Pomfret, "Further Letters of William Strahan," *ibid.*, LX (1936), 481–82.

72. Wilmot, *Memoirs*, p. 155; Greig, *Letters of David Hume*, II, 208–9.

73. Malmesbury, *Letters*, I, 202. See also H.M.C. *10th Report*, Part I, p. 418.

74. Collins, *Authorship*, pp. 201, 207; Nichols, *Literary Anecdotes*, IX, 725–27; *B.M. Cat. of Prints*, IV, 662–63; *Cal. H. O. Papers*, II, 483; *Grenville Papers*, IV, 521; *Annual Reg.*, XVII (1774), 198; D. M. Clark, "The Office of Secretary to the Treasury in the Eighteenth Century," *Am. Hist. Rev.*, XLII (1936), 22–45; *Whitefoord Papers*, pp. xxiv–xxv, 146, 148; Noyes, *Smollett Letters*, pp. 104–5.

75. Fortescue, *Correspondence*, II, 126.

76. Walpole, *Memoirs*, IV, 112; Morison, *English Newspaper*, p. 155; Walpole, *Letters* (Toynbee), VII, 369; Timperley, *Dictionary*, p. 721; Fred J. Hinkhouse, *The Preliminaries of the American Revolution as Seen in the English Press, 1763–1775* (New York, 1926), p. 27; Leslie Stephen, "Chatham, Francis, and Junius," *Eng. Hist. Rev.*, III (1888), 238.

77. *Annual Reg.*, XIII (1770), 110; *London Mag.*, XXXIX (1770), 322; *The Case of William Bingley ... Compiled by a Barrister of the Middle Temple* (London, 1773), pp. 123–26. Bingley continued his publishing career with *Bingley's Journal;* or, the *Universal Gazette* (1770–73), and in 1773 was publishing the *Independent Chronicle and Universal Evening Post.* He was no businessman, however, and was gazetted a bankrupt in August, 1771. *Case of William Bingley*, Adv., 5; *Gentleman's Mag.*, XLI (1771), 380; E. S., "A Forgotten Journalist," *Athenaeum* (May 20, 1899).

78. *PH*, XVI, 696–704, 762, 806–7.

79. *Cal. H. O. Papers*, III, 4.

80. *PH*, XVI, 829–30; *JHL*, XXXII, 425, 429, 488, 570–75; *Gentleman's Mag.*, XL (1770), 387; *Annual Reg.*, XIII (1770), 135–36; Timperley, *Dictionary*, p. 722.

81. H.M.C., *10th Report*, Part I, pp. 420-21; *Cal. H. O. Papers*, III, 17, 22–23; Cavendish, *Debates*, I, 514–16.

82. *JHC*, XXXII, 827–28, 832–33; *JHL*, XXXII, 506, 511; Cavendish, *Debates*, I, 514, 624; H.M.C., *10th Report*, Part I, p. 423; *Annual Reg.*, XIII (1770), 100; Timperley, *Dictionary*, p. 721; Plomer, *Dictionary*, pp. 162, 175; *Cal. H. O. Papers*, III, 403.

83. *JHL*, XXXII, 576; *PH*, XVI, 978.

84. G. D. H. Cole, *Politics and Literature* (London, 1929), p. 84.

85. *Burke Corr.* (Copeland), II, 49, 101, 107–9.

86. *Rockingham Memoirs*, II, 144–47; *Burke Corr.* (Copeland), II, 114; Walpole, *Memoirs*, IV, 86. For somewhat more extensive treatment see Donald C. Bryant, "Burke's *Present Discontents:* The Rhetorical Genesis of a Party Testament," *Quarterly Journal of Speech*, XLII (1956), 115–26; and Carl B. Cone, *Burke and the Nature of Politics* (Lexington, Ky., 1957), pp. 195–209.

87. *Political Reg.*, VI (1770), 345 ff.; P. B. Gove, "Early Numbers of *The Morning Chronicle* and *Owen's Weekly Chronicle*," *Trans. Bibliog. Soc.*, 2nd ser., XX (1940), 413.

88. *Burke Corr.* (Copeland), II, 150; Walpole, *Memoirs*, IV, 87.

89. Fitzmaurice, *Shelburne*, II, 204; Rockingham *Memoirs*, II, 194; Walpole, *Memoirs*, IV, 86.

90. *Bedford Corr.*, III, 413; Walpole, *Letters* (Toynbee), VII, 378.

CHAPTER X

1. *The Athenaeum* (July 29, 1848), p. 748.

2. L. J., "The Early Piratical Editions of Junius," *Notes and Queries*, 1st ser., VI (1852), 240.

3. *Ibid.*

4. Everett, *Junius*, p. 135 n.; *Athenaeum* (July 29, 1848), p. 748; Haig, *Gazetteer*, p. 70.

5. *Rockingham Memoirs*, II, 147–48; C. F. Hardy (ed.), *Benenden Letters* (London, 1901), p. 77.

6. *Cal. H. O. Papers*, II, 544.

7. Cavendish, *Debates*, I, 515–16.

8. *The Trial of John Almon* (London, 1770), pp. 35–36; *PH*, XVI, 669, 696; *Political Reg.*, VI (1770), 110–13.

9. Walpole, *Memoirs*, IV, 106.

10. Prothero, *Letters of Edward Gibbon*, I, 221.

11. Almon, *Trial*, pp. 5–65; *ST*, XX, 820–36; Almon, *Memoirs*, pp. 61 ff., 175–85; Walpole, *Memoirs*, IV, 105; *London Mag.*, XXXIX (1770), 323; *Annual Reg.*, XIII (1770), 115.

12. *ST*, XX, 842–50; Almon, *Memoirs*, pp. 193–99, 235; Walpole, *Memoirs*, IV,

106; *Annual Reg.*, XIII (1770), 121.

13. *ST*, XX, 895–903; *Grenville Papers*, IV, 519; *Annual Reg.*, XIII (1770), 117.

14. *Whitefoord Papers*, pp. 150–51.

15. *ST*, XX, 903–14.

16. *B.M. Cat. of Prints*, IV, 601–2, 624–26; *Political Reg.*, VI (1770), 102–7.

17. *ST*, XX, 869–96; *Annual Reg.*, XIII (1770), 129; *London Mag.*, XXXIX (1770), 383–84; *Gentleman's Mag.*, XL (1770), 342.

18. *The History of The Times* (New York, 1935), I, 56–57; Walpole, *Memoirs*, IV, 107; *London Mag.*, XXXIX (1770), 383–84.

19. *Annual Reg.*, XIII (1770), 172; Plomer, *Dictionary*, p. 215; Morison, *English Newspaper*, p. 154; Nichols, *Literary Anecdotes*, III, 445.

20. *Cal. H. O. Papers*, III, 39; Everett, *Junius*, p. 118.

21. Cavendish, *Debates*, II, 95–107; *PH*, XVI, 1130, 1139, 1149; Plomer, *Dictionary*, p. 222; Haig, *Gazetteer*, p. 82–85.

22. *ST*, XX, 896-97, 917–21; *Annual Reg.*, XIII (1770), 164.

23. Everett, *Junius*, p. 322.

24. *Gentleman's Mag.*, XL (1770), 541; Almon, *Memoirs*, pp. 76, 186; Almon, *Trial*, p. 65; *Annual Reg.*, XIII (1770), 165; *ST*, XX, 843–47; R. Morris, *A Letter to Sir Richard Aston, Knt.* (London, 1770), pp. 9–10; Walpole, *Memoirs*, IV, 106.

25. Morris, *Letter to Sir Richard Aston, passim;* Walpole, *Memoirs*, IV, 154–55.

26. Phileleutherus Anglicanus, *A Summary of the Law of Libel* (London, 1771), pp. 11–12, 32.

CHAPTER XI

1. Lord Mahon, *History of England* (London, 1858), V, App. xliii.

2. *Chatham Corr.*, III, 469.

3. *Burke Corr.* (Copeland), II, 160–61; *Chatham Corr.*, III, 481.

4. Almon, *Memoirs*, pp. 63, 76; *Chatham Corr.*, III, 483.

5. Everett, *Junius*, p. 306.

6. H.M.C., *Stopford-Sackville MSS.* I, 131–33.

7. *PH*, XVI, 1038.

8. *Addresses Presented from the Court of Common Council to the King* (London [1778]), p. 26.

9. *Chatham Corr.*, III, 495.

10. Cavendish, *Debates*, II, 68–69, 76.

11. Parkes and Merivale, *Francis*, I, 363; L. Stephen, "Chatham, Francis, and Junius," *Eng. Hist. Rev.*, III (1888), 239 ff.

12. *Chatham Corr.*, IV, 17–24. See also Walpole, *Memoirs*, IV, 148.

13. Cavendish, *Debates*, II, 89–116; *PH*, XVI, 1127–1211; *Gentleman's Mag.*, XLI (1771), *passim; JHC*, XXXIII, 28.

14. *Chatham Corr.*, IV, 30–34.

15. *Ibid.*, pp. 35–36.

16. Cavendish, *Debates*, II, 121; Walpole, *Memoirs*, IV, 148.

17. Parkes and Merivale, *Francis*, I, 394–97. See also Stephen, "Chatham, Francis, and Junius," *Eng. Hist. Rev.*, III (1888), 243; Herman Merivale, "Junius, Francis, and Lord Mansfield in Dec. 1770," *Fortnightly Review*, III, new ser. (1868), 250–56.

18. *PH*, XVI, 1302–12; Almon, *Pitt Anecdotes*, II, 343; *Chatham Corr.*, IV, 42–44.

19. *PH*, XVI, 1217–1301; Cavendish, *Debates*, II, 121–48; *JHC*, XXXIII, 47; Fortescue, *Correspondence*, II, 179; H. Grattan, *Memoirs of the Life and Times of the Rt. Hon. Henry Grattan* (London, 1839–46), I, 169–70; Walpole, *Memoirs*, IV, 141.

20. *Chatham Corr.*, IV, 46, 48.

21. On this interesting connection between Chatham and the man who may have been Junius see *Chatham Corr.*, IV, 48–51; Merivale, "Junius, Francis, and Lord Mansfield," *Fortnightly Rev.*, III, new ser. (1868), 250–56; Parkes and Merivale, *Francis*, I, 164; Stephen, "Chatham, Francis, and Junius," *Eng. Hist. Rev.*, III (1888), 243–46.

22. *PH*, XVI, 1312–17; Walpole, *Memoirs*, IV, 144.

23. *Rockingham Memoirs*, II, 197–98.

24. *PH*, XVI, 1321–22; Walpole, *Memoirs*, IV, 147–48.

25. Eeles, *Camden*, pp. 114–15; *Annual Reg.*, XIV (1771), 36; Walpole, *Memoirs*, IV, 149.

26. Cavendish, *Debates*, II, 353 n.; *Rockingham Memoirs*, II, 200–203; *Burke*

27. Cavendish, *Debates*, II, 353–55; *Rockingham Memoirs*, II, 200–203; *Burke Corr.* (Copeland), II, 189; Walpole, *Memoirs*, IV, 148.

28. *Burke Corr.* (Copeland), II, 189; *Rockingham Memoirs*, II, 200–204; Cavendish, *Debates*, II, 354–56.

29. *Chatham Corr.*, IV, 98–99, 101–2; *Burke Corr.* (Copeland), II, 193; Cavendish, *Debates*, II, 356 n.

30. *Chatham Corr.*, IV, 100–108; Cavendish, *Debates*, II, 356 n.

31. *JHC*, XXXIII, 237; Cavendish, *Debates*, II, 353–77; *Chatham Corr.*, IV, 109–13; Malmesbury, *Letters*, I, 219–20; *PH*, XVII, 49–58; Fortescue, *Correspondence*, II, 226–27.

32. Fortescue, *Correspondence*, II, 227.

33. *Chatham Corr.*, IV, 112–14.

CHAPTER XII

1. Robert Macfarlane, *The History of the Reign of George the Third* (London, 1770), p. 381.

2. *JHL*, XXXIII, 24; *PH*, XVI, 1317–20; J. E. T. Rogers, *A Complete Collection of the Protests of the Lords* (Oxford, 1875), II, 110–12.

3. Almon, *Memoirs*, p. 119.

4. Cavendish, *Debates*, II, 243–44; *JHC*. XXXIII, 142.

5. Cavendish, *Debates*, II, 257–60; *PH*, XVII, 65–71; *JHC*, XXXIII, 149.

6. Cavendish, *Debates*, II, 311–13; *PH*, XVII, 17–72; *JHC*, XXXIII, 154, 162, 183–84.

7. Cavendish, *Debates*, II, 321–22; *PH*, XVII, 72–73; *JHC*, XXXIII, 194; Fortescue, *Correspondence*, II, 219–20.

8. Cavendish, *Debates*, II, 322–23; *PH*, XVII, 73–74; *JHC*, XXXIII, 208; Fortescue, *Correspondence*, II, 220.

9. Malmesbury, *Letters*, I, 217.

10. B.M. Add. MSS 30871, fols. 69–70.

11. Cavendish, *Debates*, II, 323–24; *PH*, XVII, 74–76; *JHC*, XXXIII, 224, 234.

12. Cavendish, *Debates*, II, 378–92; *PH*, XVII, 75–83; *JHC*, XXXIII, 249–51; Fortescue, *Correspondence*, II, 229; III, 79.

13. Cavendish, *Debates*, II, 393–99; *PH*, XVII, 83–90; *JHC*, XXXIII, 258–59; Adolphus, *History of England*, I, 486.

14. *JHL*, XXXIII, 104, 110, 113–14, 125–26.

15. *JHC*, XXXIII, 258–59.

16. B.M. Add. MSS 30871, fols. 69–70.

17. *Ibid.*, fol. 71.

18. *Ibid.*; *Annual Reg.*, XIV (1771), 92, 121; *Gentleman's Mag.*, XLI (1771), 376;

Cavendish, *Debates*, II, 437; *PH*, XVII, 112–13; Adolphus, *History of England*, I, 486; *Wilkes Corr.*, V, 57.

19. *Annual Reg.*, XIV (1771), 185; *Chatham Corr.*, IV, 116; Haig, *Gazetteer*, pp. 113–14; Almon, *Memoirs*, pp. 119–20; *Wilkes Corr.*, V, 56–60.

20. Cavendish, *Debates*, II, 400–405; *PH*, XVII, 96–102; *Annual Reg.*, XIV (1771), 184–85; B.M. Add. MSS 30871, fol. 72; Stephens, *John Horne Tooke*, I, 337–38.

21. *Chatham Corr.*, IV, 116–18; Fortescue, *Correspondence*, II, 233.

22. Cavendish, *Debates*, II, 406 ff.; *PH*, XVII, 98–103; *JHC*, XXXIII, 264.

23. *Chatham Corr.*, IV, 119–23.

24. *JHC*, XXXIII, 286, 289; H.M.C., *15th Report*, Part V (Foljambe MSS), p. 148.

25. Walpole, *Memoirs*, IV, 201; Cavendish, *Debates*, II, 479–80.

26. *JHC*, XXXIII, 295–96; *PH*, XVII, 103 ff., 221; Malmesbury, *Letters*, I, 224; H.M.C., *15th Report*, Part V, p. 148; *Chatham Corr.*, IV, 123, 141–42; *Grenville Papers*, IV, 533–34.

27. *JHC*, XXXIII, 364; *PH*, XVII, 186–214; *Reports from Committees of the House of Commons* (Reprinted by order of the House, 1803), III, 3–8; *Annual Reg.*, XIV (1771), 70*, 101.

28. *Annual Reg.*, XIV (1771), 88; *Town and Country Mag.*, III (1771), 167.

29. Grattan, *Memoirs*, I, 242–43.

CHAPTER XIII

1. *Annual Reg.*, XIV (1771), 93–94; *London Mag.*, XL (1771), 230–31; *Town and Country Mag.*, III (1771), 221; Stephens, *John Horne Tooke*, I, 168–75; Yarborough, *John Horne Tooke*, pp. 55–71. Bingley's side of the argument may be found in *Case of William Bingley*, p. 129; *Extraordinary Case of William Bingley*, pp. 101–8; and *A Sketch of English Liberty!*

2. B.M. Add. MSS 30871, fols. 74–75.

3. *Ibid.*, fols. 55, 57, 60–63, 90; see also M. D. George, *Catalogue of Political and Personal Satires*, Vol. V, Nos. 4852–5129, *passim*.

4. *Junius* (Everett), pp. 221–22; Stephens, *John Horne Tooke*, I, 361 ff.

5. *Junius* (Everett), pp. 7, 247 ff., 311, 320, 324 ff.

6. *Ibid.*, p. 309.

7. Samuel Johnson, *Thoughts on the Late Transactions Respecting Falkland's Islands* (London, 1771), pp. 56–57.

8. *Burke Corr.* (Copeland), II, 249–50.

9. *Junius* (Everett), pp. 311–15; *The Private Correspondence of David Garrick* (London, 1835), I, 442–45.

10. *Junius* (Everett), pp. 268 ff.; 316–17, 355–57; *Chatham Corr.*, IV, 190–94.

11. "Correspondence between William Strahan and David Hall, 1763–1777," *Penn. Mag. of Hist. and Biog.*, XII (1888), 240.

12. *Junius* (Everett), p. 321.

13. John Taylor, *Records of My Life* (London, 1832), II, 253.

14. *London Mag.*, XL (1771), 516, 518–20.

15. *Gentleman's Mag.*, XLII (1772), 44; *Town and Country Mag.*, IV (1772), 220–21.

16. B.M. Add. MSS 30871, fols. 153, 155–56, 158, 165.

17. *Gentleman's Mag.*, XLIII (1773), 461, 579; *Town and Country Mag.*, V (1773), 614; Treloar, *Wilkes and the City*, p. 144.

18. Parkes and Merivale, *Francis*, I, 254–55; Boswell (Hill-Powell), II, 136–39; Pomfret, "Further Letters of William Strahan," *Penn. Mag. of Hist. and Biog.*, LX (1936), 486.

19. Greig, *Letters of David Hume*, II, 240; Boswell (Hill-Powell), II, 134–36.

20. *Junius* (Everett), pp. 366–73; *Whitefoord Papers*, pp. 153–54; *Cal. H. O. Papers*, IV, 88.

21. Fortescue, *Correspondence*, III, 119–20.

22. *Annual Reg.*, XVI (1773), 100, 178–82; *Gentleman's Mag.*, XLIII (1773), 347 ff.; Almon, *Biographical Anecdotes*, I, 287–321.

23. *Annual Reg.*, XVII (1774), 134–35, 163; Timperley, *Dictionary*, p. 760; Plomer, *Dictionary*, pp. 264–65.

24. *JHC*, XXXIV, 464; *PH*, XVII, 1054–58. See also John Shebbeare, *An Answer to the Queries* (London, 1775).

25. *Annual Reg.*, XVII (1774), 135, 164; *English Reports* (Capel Lofft's report), XCVIII, 914–17.

26. *JHC*, XXXIV, 452; *PH*, XVII, 1003–16; Stephens, *John Horne Tooke*, I, 423–26; Yarborough, *John Horne Tooke*, pp. 74–75.

27. *JHC*, XXXIV, 456; *PH*, XVII, 1016–21; Fortescue, *Correspondence*, III, 64–65.

28. Fortescue, *Correspondence*, III, 65, 68; *JHC*, XXXIV, 465, 469, 472; *PH*, XVII, 1022–47; Stephens, *John Horne Tooke*, I, 426–29.

29. Fortescue, *Correspondence*, III, 68–69.

30. W. B. Donne, *Correspondence of King George the Third with Lord North* (London, 1867), I, 170–71.

31. *JHC*, XXXIV, 492, 526–27; *PH*, XVII, 1047–50; Wade, *Junius*, I, 473–77.

32. Walpole, *Letters* (Toynbee), VIII, 427–28.

33. *Junius* (Everett), pp. 358–59.

34. Macdonagh, *Reporters' Gallery*, pp. 261–62.

35. M. Betham-Edwards (ed.), *The Autobiography of Arthur Young* (London, 1898), p. 63.

36. Almon, *Memoirs*, pp. 120–21. See also Peter D. G. Thomas, "The Beginning of the Parliamentary Reporting in Newspapers, 1768–1774," *Eng. Hist. Rev.*, LXXIV (1959), 630 ff.

37. Morison, *English Newspapers*, pp. 161 ff.; S. Morison, *John Bell* (Cambridge, 1930), p. 2; W. Hindle, *The Morning Post* (London, 1937), pp. 7–13.

CONCLUSION

1. *Town and Country Mag.*, IV (1772), 220–21.

2. Jean Louis de Lolme, *The Constitution of England* (London, 1775), pp. 280–94.

3. Walpole, *Letters* (Toynbee), VIII, 308.

4. *Burke Corr.* (Copeland), II, 352; *Annual Reg.*, XV (1772), 81–82.

BIBLIOGRAPHICAL NOTE

AN EXHAUSTIVE bibliographical treatment of the present subject would repeat much that has already been said, consequently no reference will be made to the many ephemeral pamphlets, magazines, and papers which are mentioned in the text and notes, nor to much of the private correspondence of the late eighteenth century which is tangential to the history of the press in politics. Extensive reference to the literature of journalism may, however, serve as a guide to the historian, and selective reference to the literature of politics may help to direct the student of journalism into the current stream of historiography.

BIBLIOGRAPHIES, AIDS, AND GUIDES*

The standard guides to the period are Stanley Pargellis and D. J. Medley (eds.), *Bibliography of British History: The Eighteenth Century, 1714–1789* (Oxford, 1951), and Frederick W. Bateson (ed.), *The Cambridge Bibliography of English Literature* (New York, 1941), with a *Supplement* (1957), ed. George Watson. *English Literature, 1660–1800* (Princeton, 1950–52), ed. Louis A. Landa *et al.*, is of particular value and is kept up-to-date by annual bibliographies published in the *Philological Quarterly*; similar annual compilations in *Studies in Bibliography* should also be consulted. Other aids include Carl L. Cannon, *Journalism: A Bibliography* (New York, 1924); R. S. Crane and F. B. Kaye, *A Census of British Newspapers and Periodicals 1620–1800* (Chapel Hill, N.C., 1927); Katherine K. Weed and Richmond P. Bond, *Studies of British Newspapers and Periodicals from Their Beginning to 1800* (Chapel Hill, N.C., 1946), the best guide to the field; Joseph B. Williams, *Tercentenary Handlist of English and Welsh Newspapers, Magazines, & Reviews* (1920); Kimball Young and R. D. Lawrence, *Bibliography on Censorship and Propaganda* (Eugene, Ore., 1928); Theodore A. Schroeder, *Free Speech Bibliography* (New York, 1922); William F. Swindler, *A Bibliography of Law on Journalism* (New York, 1947). The professional interests of the *Journalism Quarterly* tend to restrict its utility for historical purposes.

THE POLITICAL SCENE

Two great histories provide the background of eighteenth-century English history; Lord Mahon's *History of England from the Peace of Utrecht to the Peace of Versailles 1713–1783* (1858), and W. E. H.

*Unless otherwise indicated, place of publication is London.

Lecky's *History of England in the Eighteenth Century* (1878–90) are still worthy of mention. More recent guides to the reign of George III include William Hunt, *The History of England from the Accession of George III to the Close of Pitt's First Administration (1760–1801)* (1905); Charles Grant Robertson, *England under the Hanoverians* (16th ed., 1949); and J. Steven Watson, *The Reign of George III 1760–1815* (Oxford, 1960), which represents the most recent orthodoxy. Sharply veering currents of historical interpretation may be noted even in these general works, and the newcomer to the field will do well to consult Herbert Butterfield, *George III and the Historians* (1957), for a review of the arguments and a fair, if hostile, criticism of the contributions of "the Namier school." Modern interest in the period owes its existence in large part to the work of Sir Lewis Namier, whose *The Structure of Politics at the Accession of George III* (1929, 1957), and *England in the Age of the American Revolution* (1930, 1961), effected a reconsideration of the whole political system. Namier's fame has somewhat obscured Denys A. Winstanley's earlier narratives, *Personal and Party Government: A Chapter in the Political History of the Early Years of the Reign of George III, 1760–1766* (Cambridge, 1910), and *Lord Chatham and the Whig Opposition* (Cambridge, 1912), which are still of great value. The fruits of twentieth-century scholarship are best harvested from Richard Pares' *King George III and the Politicians* (Oxford, 1953).

The radical movement should be approached through George S. Veitch, *The Genesis of Parliamentary Reform* (1913), and Simon Maccoby, *English Radicalism 1762–1785* (1955). Keith G. Feiling's *The Second Tory Party 1714–1832* (1938), is rather a general than a party history. Arthur S. Turberville, *The House of Lords in the XVIIIth Century* (Oxford, 1927), provides both political narrative and institutional analysis. The role of the City of London has not been sufficiently studied; Reginald R. Sharpe, *London and the Kingdom* (1894–95), is a fair guide; many possibilities are suggested by Lucy S. Sutherland, *The City of London and the Opposition to Government, 1768–1774* (1959), and George Rudé's *Wilkes and Liberty* (Oxford, 1962).

SOCIAL, CONSTITUTIONAL, AND LEGAL BACKGROUND

The social scene is well portrayed in *Johnson's England,* ed. A. S. Turberville (Oxford, 1933); Mary Dorothy George's *London Life in the Eighteenth Century* (1925); and Dorothy Marshall, *English People* (1956).

Thomas Erskine May's *Constitutional History of England since the Accession of George the Third 1760–1860* (New York, 1880) has been markedly improved upon by Mark A. Thomson, *A Constitutional History of England, 1642 to 1801* (1938), and David L. Keir, *Constitutional History of Modern Britain 1485–1937* (1938). Edward and Annie G. Porritt, *The Unreformed House of Commons* (Cambridge, 1903), has not been entirely outdated by Namier's *Structure of Politics*. Cecil S. Emden's *The People and the Constitution* (Oxford, 1933) is a thoughtful, provocative essay and rather more successful than Betty Kemp's *King and Commons, 1660–1832* (1957). Mark A. Thomson, *The Secretaries of State 1681–1782* (Oxford, 1932), is a model study of the eighteenth-century departmental system.

Nothing surpasses William S. Holdsworth's *History of English Law* (Boston, 1938). Technicalities of legal procedure are dealt with by John Charles Fox in the *Law Quarterly Review:* "The King *v.* Almon," Vol. XXIV (1908), "The Summary Process to Punish Contempt," Vol. XXV (1909), and "The Writ of Attachment," Vol. XL (1924). John Charles Fox, *A Handbook of English Law Reports from the Last Quarter of the Eighteenth Century to 1865* (1913), provides a guide to cases in *The English Reports,* ed. M. A. Robertson and G. Ellis (Edinburgh, 1909), and Thomas B. Howell's *Complete Collection of State Trials* (1816), which reports only the most famous cases. H. M. Lubasz, "Public Opinion Comes of Age: Reform of the Libel Law in the Eighteenth Century," *History Today,* Vol. VIII (1958), is brief but to the point.

THE HISTORY OF THE PRESS

The earliest history of English journalism which is still valuable is Frederick Knight Hunt's *The Fourth Estate* (1850). Most of Hunt's successors have leaned heavily upon him, including Alexander Andrews, *The History of British Journalism* (1859); James Grant, *The Newspaper Press* (1871); and H. R. Fox Bourne, *English Newspapers* (1887). Stanley Morison's *The English Newspaper* (Cambridge, 1932), was the first major attempt to analyze the medium.

Among more specialized studies may be mentioned Arthur Aspinall, "Statistical Accounts of the London Newspapers in the Eighteenth Century," *English Historical Review,* Vol. LXIII (1948); G. F. Barwick, "Some Magazines of the Eighteenth Century," *Transactions of the Bibliographical Society,* Vol. X (1908–9); Edward Hughes, "English Stamp Duties, 1664–1764," *English Historical Review,* Vol. LVI (1941); Fred[rick] S. Siebert, "Taxes on Publications in England in the Eighteenth Century," *Journalism Quarterly,* Vol. XXI (1944).

M. Dorothy George's *English Political Caricature to 1792* (Oxford, 1959), provides an introduction to an area of journalism that is described in the *Catalogue of Prints and Drawings in the British Museum.*

Division I: Political and Personal Satires, ed. F. G. Stephens, Vol. III, Part II—1751 to *c.* 1760, and Vol. IV—1761 to *c.* 1770 (1877, 1883); and in M. D. George, *Catalogue of Political and Personal Satires Preserved in the Department of Prints and Drawings in the British Museum,* Vol. V, 1771–83 (1935).

Henry R. Plomer, *A Dictionary of the Printers and Booksellers . . . 1726–1775* (Oxford, 1932), and Charles H. Timperley, *A Dictionary of Printers and Printing* (1839), are useful guides to the personal history of journalism. John Almon wrote his own *Memoirs* (1790) and left an interesting and frustrating collection of papers, the British Museum Additional MSS 20733. Aspects of Almon's career have been touched on by Robert R. Rea, "John Almon: Bookseller to John Wilkes," *Indiana Quarterly for Bookmen,* Vol. IV (1948); "Bookseller as Historian," *ibid.,* Vol. V (1949); and "Mason, Walpole, and That Rogue Almon," *Huntington Library Quarterly,* Vol. XXIII (1960). Stanley Morison's *John Bell, 1745–1831* (Cambridge, 1930) is concerned with the technical side of publishing. William Bingley is briefly noted by E. S., "A Forgotten Journalist," *Athenaeum* (1899). Ralph Straus's *Robert Dodsley* (1910) contributes little to the period after 1760. James Lackington's *Memoirs* (1794) and *Confessions* (1804) shed little light on his professional career. C. J. Longman and J. E. Chandler, *The House of Longman 1724–1800* (1936), and *The House of Longman, 1724–1924* (New York, 1924), are too impersonal to be very interesting. The same may be said of Samuel Smiles, *A Publisher and His Friends: Memoir and Correspondence of the Late John Murray* (1891). Charles Welsh, *A Bookseller of the Last Century* (1885), and Austin Dobson, "An Old London Bookseller," *Eighteenth Century Vignettes,* 1st ser. (1923), describe the career of John Newbery. Septimus Rivington's *The Publishing House of Rivington* (1894) is chiefly concerned with best-sellers and family feuds. William Strahan's interesting correspondence is published in the *Pennsylvania Magazine of History and Biography,* Vols. X–XII (1886–88), "Correspondence between William Strahan and David Hall, 1763–1777"; and "Some Further Letters of William Strahan, Printer," ed. J. E. Pomfret, *ibid.,* Vol. LX (1936). R. A. Austen-Leigh describes "William Strahan and His Ledgers," *Transactions of the Bibliographical Society,* 2nd ser., Vol. III (1922–23).

Much work needs to be done on the histories of individual newspapers and magazines. Robert L. Haig's *The Gazetteer 1735–1797* (Carbondale, Ill., 1960) is an outstanding example of fine scholarship in this field. Wilfrid Hindle's *The Morning Post, 1772–1937* (1937) is too thin to be of much value, and *The History of The Times, Vol. I, "The Thunderer" in the Making 1785–1841* (New York, 1935), begins too late. Philip B. Gove, "Early Numbers of *The Morning Chronicle and Owen's Weekly Chronicle*," *Transactions of the Bibliographical Society*, 2nd ser., Vol. XX (1940), is very limited. Lucyle Werkmeister's *The London Daily Press, 1772–1792* (Lincoln, Nebr., 1963), appeared after this study was completed.

George Nobbe's excellent book, *The North Briton: A Study in Political Propaganda* (New York, 1939); and Robert R. Rea, "The Impact of Party Journalism in the *Political Register*," *The Historian*, Vol. XVII (1954), may be supplemented by numerous references of widely varying accuracy and importance scattered throughout *Notes and Queries* during the past century.

Both sides of the book trade are dealt with by A. S. Collins, *Authorship in the Days of Johnson* (1927), and Frank A. Mumby, *Publishing and Bookselling* (1949). John Nichols' *Illustrations of the Literary History of the Eighteenth Century* (1817–18) and *Literary Anecdotes of the Eighteenth Century* (1812–15) are mines of antiquarian interest.

The relationship between the press and politics should be approached through Laurence Hanson's *Government and the Press 1695–1763* (1936); it is specifically treated by William T. Laprade, "The Power of the English Press in the Eighteenth Century," *South Atlantic Quarterly*, Vol. XXVII (1928); and Edward Porritt, "The Government and the Newspaper Press in England," *Political Science Quarterly*, Vol. XII (1897). The story is carried on in detail by A. Aspinall's exemplary *Politics and the Press c. 1780–1850* (1949).

The liberty of the press is not easily defined, but Fredrick S. Siebert, *Freedom of the Press in England 1476–1776* (Urbana, Ill., 1952), surpasses all else that has been written on the subject. Among the older works are Collet D. Collet, *History of the Taxes on Knowledge, Their Origin and Repeal* (1899); James Paterson, *The Liberty of the Press, Speech, and Public Worship* (1880); James Routledge, *Chapters in the History of Popular Progress, Chiefly in Relation to the Freedom of the Press and Trial by Jury 1660–1820* (1876); and Douglas M. Ford, "The Growth of the Freedom of the Press," *English Historical Review*, Vol. IV (1889).

The history of parliamentary reporting is set forth by Michael Macdonagh, *The Reporters' Gallery* (1913); and "Strangers in the House," *Blackwood's Edinburgh Magazine*, Vol. CVIII (1870). Peter D. G. Thomas recently published two sound articles: "The Beginning of Parliamentary Reporting in Newspapers, 1768–1774," *English Historical Review*, Vol. LXXIV (1959); and "John Wilkes and the Freedom of the Press (1771)," *Bulletin of the Institute of Historical Research*, Vol. XXXIII (1960).

James A. Farrer, *Books Condemned to Be Burnt* (New York, 1892), and Charles R. Gillett, *Burned Books: Neglected Chapters in British History and Literature* (New York, 1932), treat a unique type of persecution, but neither is particularly valuable.

G. D. H. Cole's *Politics and Literature* (1929) is a delightful essay.

PUBLIC DOCUMENTS

Parliamentary debates may be followed with varying accuracy in William Cobbett (ed.), *The Parliamentary History of England, from the Earliest Period to the Year 1803* (1813), and *Sir Henry Cavendish's Debates,* ed. John Wright (1841–43). The official record is found in the *Journals of the House of Lords,* Vols. XXX–XXXIV, and the *Journals of the House of Commons,* Vols. XXVIII–XXXIV. J. E. T. Rogers' *Complete Collection of the Protests of the Lords* (Oxford, 1875) is also useful.

Some pertinent matter is to be found in "A Report from the Committee Appointed to Examine into the Several Facts and Circumstances Relative to the Late Obstructions to the Execution of the Orders of This House," which was returned April 30, 1771, *Reports from Committees of the House of Commons* (1803). See also *Parliamentary Papers,* No. 608 (1830), "A Return of all Prosecutions During the Reigns of Their Late Majesties Geo. III. and Geo. IV. either by Ex Officio Information or Indictment . . . for Libels . . ."; and *Parliamentary Papers,* Reports, Vol. X, No. 103, "First Report of the Commissioners Appointed . . . to Enquire into the Fees . . . Secretaries of State" (1793).

The *Calendar of Home Office Papers of the Reign of George III. 1760–1775,* ed. J. Redington and R. A. Roberts (1878–99), includes many interesting entries; and the Court of Common Council of the City of London ordered the printing of *Addresses Presented from the Court of Common Council to the King . . . Agreed to between the 23d October, 1760, and the 12th October, 1770* (1778).

MEMOIRS, CORRESPONDENCE, AND BIOGRAPHY

A listing of the more important personal records of this period may begin with Lord John Russell's *Correspondence of John, Fourth Duke of Bedford* (1834). Edmund Burke should be studied through the *Correspondence of the Right Honourable Edmund Burke,* ed. Earl Fitzwilliam and R. Bourke (1844), and *The Correspondence of Edmund Burke,* ed. Thomas W. Copeland (Chicago, 1958——), which should be supplemented by Carl B. Cone's *Burke and the Nature of Politics* (Lexington, Ky., 1957), and Donald C. Bryant, "Burke's *Present Discontents:* The Rhetorical Genesis of a Party Testament," *Quarterly*

Journal of Speech, Vol. XLII (1956). J. A. Lovat-Fraser's *John Stuart, Earl of Bute* (Cambridge, 1912) is very sketchy. Henry S. Eeles, *Lord Chancellor Camden and His Family* (1934) is sound but rather barren. John Almon, *Anecdotes of the Life of the Right Honourable William Pitt, Earl of Chatham* (1796), and W. S. Taylor and J. H. Pringle (eds.), *Correspondence of William Pitt, Earl of Chatham* (1840), gave rise to many biographies, among which Albert von Ruville, *William Pitt, Earl of Chatham*, trans. H. J. Chaytor (1907); Basil Williams, *The Life of William Pitt, Earl of Chatham* (1913); and Brian Tunstall, *William Pitt, Earl of Chatham* (1938), are the best.

The co-editor of the *North Briton* is given his due by Joseph M. Beatty, Jr., "An Essay in Critical Biography—Charles Churchill," *PMLA*, Vol. XXXV (1920), and "The Political Satires of Charles Churchill," *Studies in Philology*, Vol. XVI (1919), and Wallace C. Brown, *Charles Churchill* (Lawrence, Kan., 1953); *The Correspondence of John Wilkes and Charles Churchill*, ed. Edward H. Weatherly (New York, 1954), is of primary importance. *The Diary of the Late George Bubb Dodington, Baron of Melcombe Regis*, ed. H. P. Wyndham (Salisbury, 1784), is enlightening, as is Henry Fox's "Memoirs on the Events Attending the Death of George II. and the Accession of George III. 1760–1763," in Ilchester and Stavordale, *Life and Letters of Lady Sarah Lennox* (1901).

Sir Lewis Namier had more to say about George III than is summed up in the biographical sketch "King George III: A Study of Personality," in *Personalities and Powers* (1955), but the king is still best studied through Sir John Fortescue's *Correspondence of King George the Third from 1760 to December 1783* (1927), with Namier's *Additions and Corrections* (Manchester, 1937), and Romney Sedgwick's *Letters from George III to Lord Bute 1756–1766* (1939). Among the more important political sources are William R. Anson (ed.), *Autobiography and Political Correspondence of Augustus Henry, Third Duke of Grafton* (1898); William James Smith (ed.), *The Grenville Papers* (1852); George Harris, *The Life of Lord Chancellor Hardwicke* (1847); and Philip C. Yorke (ed.), *The Life and Correspondence of Philip Yorke, Earl of Hardwicke, Lord High Chancellor of Great Britain* (Cambridge, 1913). Ninetta S. Jucker (ed.), *The Jenkinson Papers 1760–1766* (1949), is extremely interesting and important.

Above the great mass of Johnsoniana towers George B. Hill's edition of *Boswell's Life of Johnson*, revised by L. F. Powell (Oxford, 1934). Among the pertinent monographs are Edward A. Bloom, *Samuel Johnson in Grub Street* (Providence, R. I., 1957); Arnold D. MacNair, *Dr. Johnson and the Law* (Cambridge, 1948); and Benjamin B. Hoover,

Samuel Johnson's Parliamentary Reporting (Berkeley, Calif., 1953). Junius is best approached through C. W. Everett, *The Letters of Junius* (1927), and Francesco Cordasco's *A Junius Bibliography* (New York, 1949). Cordasco's "Colonel Macleane and the Junius Controversy," *ELH*, Vol. XVI (1949), is the most recent serious attempt at reidentification, but it is not convincing.

Cecil H. S. Fifoot, *Lord Mansfield* (Oxford, 1936), is not satisfactory from the point of view of politics, but it is the best biography available. The *Memoirs of the Marquis of Rockingham and His Contemporaries,* ed. the Earl of Albemarle (1852), is distressingly spotty, and Lord Edmond Fitzmaurice's *Life of William, Earl of Shelburne* (1876) is tantalizingly brief in view of the bulk of Shelburne's papers. The unhappy editor of the *Briton* left little record of the defeat he suffered at Wilkes's hands, but *The Letters of Tobias Smollett, M.D.,* ed. Edward S. Noyes (Cambridge, 1926), and Noyes's "Another Smollett Letter," *MLN,* Vol. XLII (1927), should be consulted. Arnold Whitridge, *Tobias Smollett, A Study of his Miscellaneous Works* (Brooklyn, 1925), is the only significant study of Smollett's political journalism. Alexander Stephens, *Memoirs of John Horne Tooke* (1813), and Minnie C. Yarborough, *John Horne Tooke* (New York, 1926), leave much to be desired. Horace Walpole's *Memoirs of the Reign of King George the Third,* ed. G. F. Russell Barker (1894), are only surpassed by his *Correspondence,* ed. Wilmarth S. Lewis *et al.* (New Haven, 1937——). Until the distant day when it is completed, the Yale Edition must be supplemented by Mrs. Paget Toynbee (ed.), *The Letters of Horace Walpole, Fourth Earl of Orford* (Oxford, 1903–18).

John Almon's *Correspondence of the Late John Wilkes* (1805) fails to suggest the riches of the Wilkes MSS, British Museum Additional MSS 30868–30872. Horace W. Bleackley, *Life of John Wilkes* (1917); William P. Treloar, *Wilkes and the City* (1917); and Raymond W. Postgate, *That Devil Wilkes* (1930), are all valuable.

Also of interest are the following: John Almon, *Biographical, Literary, and Political Anecdotes of Several of the Most Eminent Persons of the Present Age* (1797); Bonamy Dobrée (ed.), *The Letters of Philip Dormer Stanhope, 4th Earl of Chesterfield* (1932); and W. A. S. Hewins (ed.), *The Whitefoord Papers* (Oxford, 1898). The *Reports* of the Royal Commission on Historical Manuscripts also contain much of interest for the diligent searcher.

ACKNOWLEDGMENTS

FOR GRANTING permission to use quoted material in this book, grateful acknowledgment is made to the authors, publishers, and copyright holders of the following works: James Boswell, *Life of Johnson*, ed. G. B. Hill, rev. L. F. Powell (Oxford: The Clarendon Press, 1934). Commission on Freedom of the Press, *A Free and Responsible Press* (Chicago: University of Chicago Press, 1947). Thomas W. Copeland (ed.), *The Correspondence of Edmund Burke* (Chicago: University of Chicago Press, 1958——). Bonamy Dobrée (ed.), *The Letters of King George III* (London: Cassell & Co., 1935). Bonamy Dobrée (ed.), *The Letters of Philip Dormer Stanhope, 4th Earl of Chesterfield* (London: Eyre & Spottiswoode, Ltd., 1932). C. W. Everett (ed.), *The Letters of Junius* (London: Faber & Faber, Ltd., 1927). Sir John Fortescue (ed.), *The Correspondence of King George the Third* (London: Macmillan & Co., Ltd., 1927). J. Y. T. Greig (ed.), *Letters of David Hume* (Oxford: The Clarendon Press, 1932). W. S. Holdsworth, *A History of English Law* (Boston: Little, Brown & Co., 1938). Ninetta S. Jucker (ed.), *The Jenkinson Papers, 1760–1766* (London: Macmillan & Co., Ltd., 1949). Joseph Wood Krutch, *Samuel Johnson* (New York: Holt, Rinehart & Winston, 1945; Harbinger Books ed., 1963). W. S. Lewis (ed.), *The Yale Edition of Horace Walpole's Correspondence* (New Haven: Yale University Press, 1937——). J. A. Lovat-Fraser, *John Stuart, Earl of Bute* (Cambridge: Cambridge University Press, 1912). Stanley Morison, *The English Newspaper* (Cambridge: Cambridge University Press, 1932). [Stanley Morison], *The History of The Times* (London: Macmillan & Co., Ltd., 1935). Sir Lewis Namier, *England in the Age of the American Revolution* (2nd ed.; London: Macmillan & Co., Ltd., 1961). Sir Lewis Namier, *The Structure of Politics at the Accession of George III* (2nd ed.; London: Macmillan & Co., Ltd., 1957). George Nobbe, *The North Briton* (New York: Columbia University Press, 1939). Romney Sedgwick (ed.), *Letters from George III to Lord Bute, 1756–1766* (London: Macmillan & Co., Ltd., 1939). Edward Simpson Noyes (ed.), *The Letters of Tobias Smollett, M.D.* (Cambridge, Mass.: Harvard University Press, 1926). J. E. Pomfret (ed.), "Further Letters of William Strahan, Printer," *Pennsylvania Magazine of History and Biography*, Vol. LX (1936). Albert von Ruville, *William Pitt, Earl of Chatham* (London: William Heinemann, Ltd., 1907). Fredrick S. Siebert, *Freedom of the Press in England, 1476–1776* (Urbana: University of Illinois Press, 1952). Paget Toynbee (ed.), *The Letters of Horace Walpole* (Oxford: The Clarendon Press, 1903–18). Brian Tunstall, *William Pitt,*

Earl of Chatham (London: Hodder & Stoughton, Ltd., 1938). Arnold Whitridge, *Tobias Smollett: A Study of His Miscellaneous Works* (Brooklyn, 1925). Basil Williams, *The Life of William Pitt, Earl of Chatham* (London: Longmans, Green & Co., Ltd., 1938). D. A. Winstanley, *Lord Chatham and the Whig Opposition* (Cambridge: Cambridge University Press, 1912). D. A. Winstanley, *Personal and Party Government* (Cambridge: Cambridge University Press, 1910). Philip C. Yorke (ed.), *The Life and Correspondence of Philip Yorke, Earl of Hardwicke* (Cambridge: Cambridge University Press, 1913).

INDEX

A NOTE ABOUT THE AUTHOR

A native of Wichita, Kansas, Robert R. Rea did his graduate study at Indiana University, receiving the Ph.D. degree in 1950. His present position is Professor in the Department of History and Government at Auburn University, Auburn, Alabama. Throughout his academic career Dr. Rea has been writing about the press and politics. His articles have appeared in several scholarly journals.